CONTEMPORARY ISSUES IN CHILDHOOD

Contemporary Issues in Childhood provides undergraduate students with a comprehensive introduction to the current influences and challenges that surround childhood, families and communities. The text carefully explores the lives of children and young people to make clear the link between this particular demographic and social contexts such as family, community and society. Key theories and concepts are examined in each chapter, using Bronfenbrenner's bio-ecological model to highlight the complex and individual nature of child development.

Written by highly experienced authors who represent a variety of professional disciplines, the book offers a comprehensive introduction to encourage critical reflection on the influences and experiences of children and childhood. A range of rich, practical examples accompany the text, in addition to discussion questions, case studies and further reading designed to support readers in reflecting on their own experiences as learners.

Contemporary Issues in Childhood is essential reading for students on Education Studies courses and Childhood, Family and Community Studies courses, as well as preservice and in-service educators. It will also be of great interest to Early Childhood Studies and Special Needs/ Inclusive Studies students.

Zeta Brown is Lecturer in Childhood, Family and Community Studies at the University of Wolverhampton, UK.

Stephen Ward is Emeritus Professor of Education at Bath Spa University, UK.

THE ROUTLEDGE EDUCATION STUDIES SERIES

Series Editor: Stephen Ward, Bath Spa University, UK

The **Routledge Education Studies Series** aims to support advanced level study on Education Studies and related degrees by offering in-depth introductions from which students can begin to extend their research and writing in years 2 and 3 of their course. Titles in the series cover a range of classic and up-and-coming topics, developing understanding of key issues through detailed discussion and consideration of conflicting ideas and supporting evidence. With an emphasis on developing critical thinking, allowing students to think for themselves and beyond their own experiences, the titles in the series offer historical, global and comparative perspectives on core issues in education.

Inclusive Education
Edited by Zeta Brown

Gender, Education and Work
Christine Eden

International and Comparative Education
Edited by Brendan Bartram

Contemporary Issues in Childhood
Edited by Zeta Brown and Stephen Ward

Psychology and the Study of Education
Edited by Cathal O'Siochru

CONTEMPORARY ISSUES IN CHILDHOOD

A Bio-ecological Approach

Edited by Zeta Brown and Stephen Ward

Routledge
Taylor & Francis Group

LONDON AND NEW YORK

First published 2018
by Routledge
2 Park Square, Milton Park, Abingdon, Oxon OX14 4RN

and by Routledge
711 Third Avenue, New York, NY 10017

Routledge is an imprint of the Taylor & Francis Group, an informa business

British Library Cataloguing in Publication Data
A catalogue record for this book is available from the British Library

Library of Congress Cataloging in Publication Data
A catalog record for this book has been requested

ISBN: 978-1-138-20076-0 (hbk)
ISBN: 978-1-138-20086-9 (pbk)
ISBN: 978-1-315-51385-0 (ebk)

Typeset in News Gothic
by Saxon Graphics Ltd, Derby

Dedications

Zeta Brown:

For Sue and John (Mom and Dad)

Christopher, Mia and Damie

Stephen Ward:

For the young people in my life: Lily, Pearl, Bea and Daisy

Contents

Abbreviations

The following abbreviations are used in the text:

ADHD   attention deficit hyperactivity disorder
ALS   Amyotrophic Lateral Sclerosis
APPG   All-Party Parliamentary Group
ASB   anti-social behaviour
ASBO   anti-social behaviour order
BAME   Black, Asian and minority ethnic (groups)
BAPT   British Association of Play Therapists
BTEC   Business Technology and Education Council
C4EO   Centre for Excellence and Outcomes in Children and Young People's Services
CAMHS   Child and Adolescent Mental Health Services
CIEH   Chartered Institute of Environmental Health
CPD   Continuing Professional Development
CRC   Committee on the Rights of the Child
CSDH   Commission on Social Determinants of Health
CSE   child sexual exploitation
CSJ   Centre for Social Justice
CYP   children and young people
DBS   Disclosure and Barring Service
DCLG   Department for Communities and Local Government
DCSF   Department for Children, Schools and Families
DfE   Department for Education
DfEE   Department for Education and Employment
DfES   Department for Education and Skills
DoH   Department of Health
EPPE   Effective Provision of Pre-school Education
EY   Early Years
EYFS   Early Years Foundation Stage
FE   Further Education
GCSE   General Certificate of Secondary Education
HE   Higher Education

HEFCE	Higher Education Funding Council for England
HMG	Her Majesty's Government
HO	Home Office
ITT	Initial Teacher Training
JAGS	Journal of the American Geriatric Society
JRF	Joseph Rowntree Foundation
KS1	Key Stage 1
LAMDA	London Academy of Music and Dramatic Art
LGA	Local Government Association
MLA	Member of the Legislative Assembly
NCB	National Children's Bureau
NCVO	National Council for Voluntary Organisations
NSPCC	National Society for the Prevention of Cruelty to Children
OBA	outcomes-based accountability
Ofsted	Office for Standards in Education
OSCB	Oxfordshire Safeguarding Children Board
PCS	personal, cultural and structural (levels)
PGCE	Postgraduate Certificate in Education
PPCT	person-process-context-time
PTUK	The UK society for Play and Creative Arts Therapies
RRSA	Rights Respecting School Award
SCR	Serious Case Review
SEN	Special Educational Needs
SENCO	Special Educational Needs Coordinator
SEND	Special Educational Needs and Disability
SENDA	Special Educational Needs and Disability Act
SNP	Scottish National Party
TA	Teaching Assistant
TFP	Troubled Families Programme
TSO	The Stationery Office
UN	United Nations
UNCRC	United Nations Convention on the Rights of the Child
UNESCO	United Nations Educational, Scientific and Cultural Organization
UNICEF	United Nations International Children's Emergency Fund (known as United Nations Children's Fund)
WHO	World Health Organization
ZPD	Zone of Proximal Development

Series editor's preface

Education Studies has become a popular and exciting undergraduate subject in some 50 universities in the UK. It began in the early 2000s mainly in the post-1992 universities which had been centres of teacher training but, gaining academic credibility, the subject is being taken up by post-1992 and Russell Group institutions. In 2004 Routledge published one of the first texts for undergraduates, *Education Studies: A Student's Guide* (Ward, 2004), now in its third edition. It comprises a series of chapters introducing key topics in Education Studies. While teacher education and training are largely determined by government diktat, there is continuing discussion among academics about the aims and curriculum for Education Studies, and the three editions of this book have contributed to the thinking and development of the subject.

Education Studies is concerned with understanding how people develop and learn throughout their lives, the nature of knowledge and critical engagement with ways of knowing. It demands an intellectually rigorous analysis of educational processes and their cultural, social, political and historical contexts. In a time of rapid change across the planet, education is about how we both make and manage such change. So Education Studies includes perspectives on international education, economic relationships, globalisation, ecological issues and human rights. It also deals with beliefs, values and principles in education and the way that they change over time.

It is important to understand that Education Studies is not teacher training or teacher education. Its theoretical framework in psychology, sociology, history and philosophy is derived from teacher education, and undergraduates in the subject may well go on to become teachers after a PGCE or school-based training. However, Education Studies should be regarded as a subject with a variety of career outcomes, or indeed, none: it can be taken as the academic and critical study of education in itself. At the same time, while the theoretical elements of teacher training are continually reduced in PGCE courses and school-based training, undergraduate Education Studies provides a critical analysis for future teachers who, in a rapidly changing world, need so much more than training to deliver a government-defined curriculum.

Intended for second- and third-year undergraduates, this book is the third in a series of Routledge publications which builds on the introductory guide and looks in depth at a current priority in education. While derived from the theory for teaching in schools, Education Studies in recent years has broadened its scope beyond teaching and schools to the analysis of childhood and the family in society. Child development has long been a part of teacher education, but in a somewhat under-theorised way. For the serious Education Studies student this book explores competing theories of the concept of childhood in its social context, with examples of and recommendations for good practice in the relationship between education professionals and communities.

Probably the strongest and most distinctive feature of Education Studies is its potential to apply critique to policy and practice: we should not take the status quo or government policy for granted. Each chapter in the book applies a critique to the area discussed, raising questions about the claims made for inclusion and presenting alternative possibilities. Activities interspersed through the book raise such questions and enable us to reflect on our own understanding and assumptions.

Note: The academic network for tutors and students in Education Studies is the British Education Studies Association (BESA). It has an annual conference that shares academic practice and research in Education Studies and to which students are welcome. There are two e-journals, one designated for students and early researchers: see www.educationstudies.org.uk.

Stephen Ward, Bath Spa University, UK

Reference

Ward, S. (2004) *Education Studies: A student's guide.* London: Routledge.

Foreword

Michael Reed and Rosie Walker

We were very pleased to be asked to write the foreword for this book. As experienced writers and university tutors we were interested in the subject area and as we started to read the book it quickly became clear how the editors have drawn together a range of highly experienced authors representing a variety of professional disciplines to produce a body of work which is informative, thought provoking and professionally relevant.

Each of the chapters carefully explores and makes visible the lives of children and young people. This is done through the central theme of the book which sees those lives as intrinsically connected to social contexts that include the family, education, community and society – in particular observing the influence of the environment *on* human development and the interaction of those beings *with* their environment. This positioning is made clear at the start of the book underscoring a bio-ecological systems theory framework which is seen in terms of micro-systems (family), meso-systems (educational settings) and macro-systems (economic and social policies) and how these affect children's and young people's development. This allows the reader to understand how values, beliefs, needs and agendas are interconnected, and additionally, how their influence becomes relative one to another in order to reveal societal, political and philosophical perspectives on the lives of children and families.

The topics and themes of each chapter make for essential reading for both preservice and in-service educators while promoting the analysis necessary for critical reflection. The scope and range are impressive, taking the reader on a journey from the importance of researching children's lives through a bio-ecological model as well as atypical development and social determinants of health. They explore play and learning, identity, the impact of families and community and the way the community has a responsibility to protect children and young adults. Power, security, inclusion and debates about assessment are also examined alongside policy and professional systems and ways of seeing the future in terms of policy and practice.

The use of case studies and examples from practice offers a wide-ranging representation of the world of children and young people. The interactive tone of each chapter should inspire readers and ask appreciative questions about the construction of effective practice and thus guides them to acquire knowledge as well as provoking their thinking skills. This is of particular importance given the recent review and recommendations regarding higher education and the emphasis these place on textbooks which support effective teaching and learning. Indeed, the instructional design of chapters allows the reader to engage with ideas and think about the complexities of professional support and intervention at many levels: in particular, the barriers and opportunities which foster productive learning and development of children and young people and how each offers an effective view on professional practice as an evolving contextual and cultural experience. This provides an explanation and a theorisation on how a systems approach can be examined as a joint function of the characteristics of the person and of the world they inhabit. Therefore, the chapters provide a careful consideration of the way reciprocal interactions between a person and his or her environment occur and are modified.

The result is a book which underlines and respectfully interrogates the systems approach but also conveys another central theme – which is a recognition of the way quality education and care improves the life chances of children. It recognises how this is influenced by a whole variety of factors such as the availability of government finance, the training of professional services, policy formation and the requirements of regulatory and inspection services. It also touches upon less visible features such as the need for policies which see quality education as enhancing employment opportunities and a means to lessen disadvantage.

In terms of an aid to study, the book has particular features which we welcome as experienced university tutors. For example, the chapters each have what can be termed 'learning provocations' and 'dialogue prompts'. Put simply, these are how a chapter author focuses the attention of the reader to particular points in the chapter and offers them an opportunity to engage with the content with others or as part of self-directed study. This involves responding to critical questions about personal experience and how it relates to the content of a chapter. This strategy highlights features which encompass quite complex issues such as protecting the welfare of children and young people, the impact of family and community and the importance of maintaining positive relationships with other professionals. Importantly, the book enhances professional thinking, challenges assumptions and prompts a deeper consideration of the subject.

When seen together the chapters therefore help those most closely involved in the study of social policy, education and learning to look beyond prescribed policies and regulatory frameworks and consider questions about how best to refine and shape the world of children and young people. It is therefore wise to see the chapters as expounding an interrelationship between the influence of national policies, the environment and community education and how these interconnect and impact upon day-to-day practice. This may well form the basis for new understandings and a consideration of the actions which illustrate innovative approaches.

We think this is a book which informs the reader and provokes questions. Not just any questions but the right questions that act as a companion to study and learning. We hope you enjoy reading it as much as we did and our congratulations go to everyone who was involved in its production.

Section one

Bronfenbrenner and his bio-ecological model

1 Bronfenbrenner's 'bio-ecological' model and its application to understanding children's development

Tunde Rozsahegyi

Introduction

Societies which aspire to develop all-embracing childhood services appreciate the multiplicity of backgrounds, lives and needs of children and their families. As part of an ambition to become increasingly inclusive in such services, it is imperative that stakeholders – educators, para-professionals, managers, national and local policy-makers, as well as researchers themselves – understand the impacts of such diversity, so that every child's growth and progression can be supported without stereotyping or categorising (Swick and Williams, 2006). Subsequent chapters in this book explore aspects of this intricacy through discussion of identities of the developing child; social and professional environments that seek to promote their well-being; interfaces of children and others within and between these settings and the aspirations which underpin upbringing and professional support for development and learning.

As an essential opening, this chapter introduces a major theoretical perspective which helps the reader to comprehend and value this complexity and work with it in practice and research. This perspective, the 'bio-ecological model', is the mature conceptualisation of Urie Bronfenbrenner, a Russian-born American psychologist. The evolution of the framework and its comprising elements are introduced, followed by discussion of the benefits and challenges associated with its application to our better understanding of children's development.

Bronfenbrenner and theories of child development

Starting in the 1970s, Bronfenbrenner established a complex system of ideas about child development with which he sought to influence social policy and childcare practice in the USA. He termed his early ideas as 'ecological', 'ecology' being the branch of biology that deals with the relationships between living organisms and their environment. He argued that child development was dependent on contextual elements. Later, with recognition of a broader and more extended range of factors influencing growth and progression (Bronfenbrenner, 1995; Bronfenbrenner and Evans, 2000), his model became termed as 'bio-ecological'.

These evolving propositions challenged the nature and relevance of the kind of knowledge which stemmed from traditional scientific research studies. Bronfenbrenner (1994:37–38) himself described his work as a 'reaction to the restricted scope of most research then being conducted by developmental psychology' and addressed what he saw as limitations of two conventional research approaches: the first a 'rock' to symbolise studies conducted in unnatural, scientific environments, the second a 'soft place', signalling excessive naturalistic observations (1977:513).

Individual/group task

List a range of theoretical perspectives on children's development, such as those associated with behaviourism, constructivism or social learning theories. Include both long-standing and more contemporary perspectives. Choose one or more of these. Then, using Bronfenbrenner's categorisation of conventional research about child development as either a 'rock' or a 'soft place', find out what kind of research informed theorists in their attempts to construct ideas about children's development when using this perspective.

In his own writings, Bronfenbrenner drew in particular from developmental and behavioural psychological theories which reflected Russian traditions. He used the words of the Russian psychologist, Aleksei Leontiev, to contrast perceptions in Western and Soviet psychological research:

> It seems to me that American researchers are constantly seeking to explain how the child came to be what he is; we in the USSR are striving to discover not how the child came to be what he is, but how he can become what he not yet is.
>
> *(Leontiev, 1964, quoted in Bronfenbrenner, 1979:40)*

Bronfenbrenner's perspectives indeed incorporated a forward momentum, seeking to elucidate not only the complex ways in which children's development and progression could be perceived, but also how such development might be enhanced in the practice of parenting, childcare and early education. These ideas drew in particular from the concepts of two developmental psychologists. The first was Kurt Lewin, a passionate follower of Gestalt psychology, which viewed human behaviour as a holistic entity (Thomas, 1996), whereby our minds predominantly perceive objects as a whole, rather than focusing on every small component. The second was the Soviet psychologist, Lev Vygotsky, whose perspectives prioritised social and cultural factors in human development.

Two of Lewin's notions are particularly evident in Bronfenbrenner's writings. The first is the idea that child development takes place in 'life spaces' or 'psychological fields' (Bronfenbrenner, 1979:23). These are real-life social contexts which are prominent in shaping a child's growth. The notion is evident in Bronfenbrenner's central concern for the role of social environments, such as the family and the nursery school. The second is Lewin's idea of the young developing person as a whole integrated organism whose growth brings about rearrangements in his or her social relations and interactions (Thomas, 1996). Bronfenbrenner extended this concept to a more complex synergy of a wide range of influences: biological, environmental, interpersonal.

Individual/group task

List environments in which developing children may have social contact with others. Consider and discuss what sort of relationships children may have within these environments. Discuss also how these relationships may change over time as a result of growing physical, social, emotional, cognitive, linguistic, cultural and spiritual competence.

Bronfenbrenner gained even greater inspiration from his understanding of the ideas of Lev Vygotsky. In particular, his viewpoints reflect Vygotsky's thoughts on the child as both a biological and social entity, the importance of the surroundings in which she or he grows up, and the interactions that connect these two elements. For Vygotsky, child development was a multifaceted phenomenon and in Sutton's (1980) interpretation of his ideas, there were two main aspects. Firstly, there were the processes of growth, sensory maturation and neurological changes, all linked to and enhanced by individual experiences. Observation of these could lead to generalised understanding about biological aspects of child development, for instance patterns or sequences of physiological changes or acquisition of motor skills. Secondly, and even more decisively, there were other processes linked to the child's dispositions and character. These were not universal and could not be quantified. Such changes, also explained by Sutton (1980), could only be mapped and comprehended as a series of qualitative alterations in a child's personal attributes. Hence, in the view of Vygotsky (1993), when children's development is interrogated, the focus should be on social, emotional and cognitive qualitative characteristics, rather than on the transformations that derive from quantifiable biological and neurological maturation.

Bronfenbrenner also took up Vygotsky's idea of development as the outcome of socially influenced interpersonal relationships, termed by Vygotsky as 'dialogues' (Moore, 2000) and by Bronfenbrenner (1977, 1979) as 'interactions'. According to this idea, the way in which a child's developmental characteristics are understood and projected is subject to socially and culturally determined outlooks which are significant in the child's life, and these are influenced by norms, expectations and demands embedded in these contexts. In Vygotsky's interpretation, understanding of the attributes and characteristics of children only emerges if the features of relevant social and cultural milieux are properly understood and if the nature of interactions between the developing child and his or her social environments is interrogated. Both Vygotsky and Bronfenbrenner believed that the child was an 'active agent' in these interpersonal connections – initiating, forming, navigating, changing interfaces – resulting in the child's increased social competence to meet the expectations and demands set by changing environments. Vygotsky's strong emphasis on the social and interactive nature of development and learning directly steered Bronfenbrenner to focus on the contextual circumstances of children's development, ideas which led both theorists to recognise its historically, culturally and socially embedded nature.

Discussion

Focusing on the notion of the 'historically, culturally and socially embedded nature of child development' in relation to children of different ages (for instance 2-, 4-, 6- and 10-year-olds), consider from your own experiences:

- What are the particular demands and expectations for children of these age ranges in your current society?
- Have these demands and expectations been constant historically? In what ways have they changed over time?
- To what extent are they similar or different in other cultures and societies?

Over time, Bronfenbrenner developed a substantial model which incorporated the intricate nature of complex influences affecting children's lives and development. He explained these as 'extending far beyond the immediate situation directly affecting the developing person' (Bronfenbrenner, 1979:7). Furthermore, he proposed his conceptualisation not only as a model for understanding child development itself, but also as an operational framework for research into such development. Both propositions are examined here.

A model for understanding child development

As we have seen, Bronfenbrenner explicated the 'phenomenological' nature of child development. In other words he believed that children over time mature in their capacity to perceive, interpret, respond to and subsequently assimilate developmental stimuli from the environment. From this perspective the extent to which a child makes sense of the environment underpins the ways in which she or he shows growth or decline in capabilities. Furthermore, Bronfenbrenner argued that this process was time-bound and progressive, with the child drawing from both personal and environmental resources to respond to the social settings of which she or he is a part (Bronfenbrenner and Evans, 2000).

Bronfenbrenner's conceptualisation was not, therefore, about incremental stages or changes in capacity, nor about age-related levels, stages or expectations for performance and achievement, as in other developmental theories such as those of Piaget (1936). Instead, acknowledging again Vygotsky's findings, he stressed the developing child's increasing and changing social awareness and ability to make sense of social situations, either positively instigating and enhancing progression, or hindering and negating it. As Bronfenbrenner (1979:8) argued, the ecology of child development is a 'theory of environmental interconnections and their impact on the forces directly affecting psychological growth', forces that are always intertwined with particular social and physical environments – in his words: 'development-in-context' (7).

A framework for research

Bronfenbrenner regarded his conceptualisation also as a research framework by which children's development could be studied. He dismissed scientific enquiries predominantly focused on the attributes of the developing child. Instead, he constructed an investigative framework which highlighted not just the link between the child and his or her environment, but also (and more significantly) the nature of reciprocal interactions between the two.

This idea drew attention to the child's interpersonal relationships with others in social environments such as the immediate and extended family, childcare and educational settings and the local community. It also incorporated the influence of social contexts more distanced from the child and with which the child did not necessarily have personal contact at all. These included community, health and social arrangements, local outlooks on child-rearing and even national policies such as those on parenting, childcare and education. For Bronfenbrenner, understanding children's lives and their development could only be accomplished if features of all these multiple-level settings were interrogated in research.

From ecological to bio-ecological orientation

Bronfenbrenner's original 'ecological' model argued for the importance of both environmental and social factors in children's development. They were incorporated within his model under the dual notions of 'context' and interpersonal 'process'. Later, these were complemented with a growing concern for and recognition of the child's own 'biological' attributes as significant contributors to her or his development, this notion being summarised as 'person'. Bronfenbrenner (1993:38) described this conceptualisation as the 'person-process-context' model, an 'integrated system' in which human beings functioned and 'where various psychological domains interact with each other' (1995:636).

Finally came the addition of a further notion, incorporating 'change or consistency over time, not only within the person but also of the environment in which the person lives' (Bronfenbrenner, 1994:1647). Ultimately, therefore, the model was termed as PPCT – 'person-process-context-time' (Bronfenbrenner, 1995) – and referred to by Bronfenbrenner and Ceci (1994) as a 'bio-ecological' model. It is worth now discussing each of these four bio-ecological elements in this order: context, person, process and time.

Context

Bronfenbrenner explained how influential contexts were located at a range of distances from the child's personal day-to-day experiences. The first and most proximate were termed as 'microsystems', defined as the 'complex relations between the developing person and environment in an immediate setting containing the person' (Bronfenbrenner, 1977:514). The most crucial of these is the family, then childcare and educational settings – all, he argued, are social places where relations between the child and 'significant others' are underpinned by regular shared times and some form of attachment.

The next layer was termed as 'mesosystems' (Bronfenbrenner, 1977). These contexts do not involve the child, but instead incorporate connections between other people, for instance between parents, the broader family, childcare practitioners and educators or other professionals with whom the child is regularly engaged. Connective elements within these environments derive from a shared interest in the child's well-being and upbringing.

The third and most distanced level in Bronfenbrenner's model referred to contexts in which the child has no explicit or active involvement, but which indirectly influence processes within the child's microsystems. These 'exosystems' include parents' work and a family's social network, more formal agencies representing health, welfare and education, and even relevant national policies. These contexts impinge upon the more immediate systems and therefore affect what happens within them.

Finally, 'macrosystems', perhaps the least explicit element of the overall model, encompassed the broadest social arrangements, related to but most distanced from the developing child. These included society's outlooks and value systems about childhood and child-rearing, and the ways in which these are manifested in social, legal, economic, health and educational arrangements. He saw these macrosystems as being informal and implicit, 'made manifest through custom and practice in everyday life' (Bronfenbrenner, 1977:515). Their impact was filtered down, influencing perceptions of policy-makers, professionals and parents. Subsequently he included social priorities, expectations and resources at this level too, clearly seen when changing historical or cultural conditions alter the ways in which parenting, education, community support and resources advance or hinder the overall functioning of the microsystems.

Within these four levels, Bronfenbrenner stressed interconnectivity as a prominent feature. This was encapsulated in Bronfenbrenner's (1979:3) frequently cited description of 'concentric, nested structures, each inside the next', wrapped around the child, with each systemic level contributing to a complex overall scheme of influences. This understanding had implications for research also – if the aim is to delineate contextual influences on child development, then an ecologically or bio-ecologically influenced investigation should encompass more than a single setting or systemic level and take into account their interactional, combined effects.

Individual/group task

As part of his model, Bronfenbrenner did not see contextual influences simply as being 'top-down', i.e. directly or indirectly determining the nature and extent of a child's development. He argued that there were also 'bottom-up' influences whereby the child, through her or his individual needs, characteristics and course of development, instigates changes in contexts. An example can be seen when a child's growing independence causes parents to ask their child to eat or dress alone, or when in the nursery adaptations are made to accommodate the needs of a child using mobility aids.

What is your stance on this proposition? Can you find other examples of how change (growth or decline, or even a simple lack of change) in a child's developmental capabilities might have an impact on, or influence change in, systems at various levels?

Process

Within this model of a range of contextual influences, Bronfenbrenner devoted most scrutiny to the first and most immediate level: the microsystem. Crucial at this level were interpersonal relations, the most important of these being 'dyads', the young developing child's interactions with others, usually a parent or caregiver. He identified different types of dyads: observational, joint-activity and primary, signalling different kinds of involvement by the child in shared pursuits with another person. When more people were involved, for instance both parents or others in a childcare or educational setting, he symbolised this (as he often tended to do) as a mathematical formula, 'N + 2' (Bronfenbrenner, 1979:58).

For Bronfenbrenner (1979) these dyadic and multi-person interactions were the 'basic building block of the microsystem' (56), as well as the 'most powerful environmental forces that instigate and influence … development' (45). Most imperative amongst them were primary dyads, those which continued to influence a child's behaviour and learning when the other person was not present. When these occurred, they formed the highest level of interpersonal relationship: the 'developmental dyad' (1979:60).

Bronfenbrenner examined extensively the developmental influences derived from dyadic interactions, again mirroring Vygotsky's theories. Amongst many propositions, he emphasised the pertinence of 'reciprocity': 'What A does influences B and *vice versa*' (Bronfenbrenner, 1979:57). For a very young child this involved an uneven power distribution, with the child in a less influential position. There was, however, a 'gradual transfer of power' (1979:57) from an adult to a child, as the child learnt and grew up. Bronfenbrenner (1994:39) eventually concluded that these reciprocal processes were 'more powerful than those of the environmental contexts in which they occur'. He postulated that where interfaces between the child and adult, or indeed amongst children themselves, were under-applied, the child was left with untapped potential for development.

Discussion

Bronfenbrenner also related the idea of 'process' to interactions at a mesosystemic level, i.e. between parents, educators, other professionals, members of the community etc., representing the interest of the child. Identify and discuss from your experience some ways in which interactions between such stakeholders might positively or negatively affect a child's development.

Person

Bronfenbrenner's bio-ecological model also encompassed the personal factors which the child brings, often congenitally, to her or his dyadic or multi-person activities. His growing concern for and recognition of such attributes as unique and significant contributors to development were summarised in the notion of 'person'. Bronfenbrenner (1993) distinguished three different kinds of traits that determine the child's interactions. Firstly, there were 'demand' characteristics, such as age, gender or physical assets that are recognisable during motions. Then there were 'resource' characteristics, for instance intelligence or cognitive qualities that emerge from the child's previous experience of interactions with others and from accessing resources in broader contexts, such as within the education or health systems. Bronfenbrenner depicted the third type as 'force' characteristics, referring to children's motivation, persistence and temperament, which are observable for instance in the child's determination in interactions with others.

Bronfenbrenner stressed that such 'personal stimulus characteristics' (1993:11) were exposed during interactions, producing unique development for children. With this proposition he therefore stressed the interface between the biological and environmental influences in children's development and provided explanation for the varied developmental outcomes for individual children who grow up in comparable surroundings and have access to the same social, professional and material resources but show varied developmental outcomes despite these similarities in circumstances.

Group task

When a developmental difficulty is present (for instance, physical, cognitive, language, social or emotional – or a combination of these), the child's unique characteristics are likely to relate in part at least to that developmental difficulty or that combination. In this situation, parents and practitioners may find it hard to choose between focusing on the child's 'strengths' on the one hand and providing opportunities for the child to develop areas in which he or she is developmentally challenged on the other. Can you identify examples of this dilemma from your own experiences? What are your thoughts on this issue?

Time

The final piece in Bronfenbrenner's jigsaw of ideas draws attention to the features of the environment and their influence on children's development. He termed his latest, and perhaps least explained, component as 'time', recognising that 'the individual's own development life course is seen as embedded in and powerfully shaped by conditions and events occurring during the historical period throughout which the person lives' (Bronfenbrenner, 1995:641). In his explanation the most important influence derived from 'change and consistency' (1994:1647) within different contexts which play significant roles in the child's life. Again, drawing on and extending Vygotsky's ideas about development being the product of a child's growing independence in social capabilities, Bronfenbrenner stressed the importance of examining expectations and opportunities set by various developmentally pertinent contexts. In other terms he argued that in different historical periods expectations that are set by society, education and health systems, nurseries and schools, the community and family itself will have historically rooted outlooks that change little over time. But inevitably there will also be demands which alter from one historical period to another. Contexts may develop opportunities to meet these expectations, but also may remain unchanged over time. When applied to research the time element may include exploring these changes and consistencies across generations or even within the childhood period of a person, termed by Bronfenbrenner (1995:641) as a 'life-course perspective'.

Reflection

Taking Bronfenbrenner's idea of 'change and consistency' in relation to expectations and opportunities to a practical level, return to the social norms that you identified earlier for particular ages. In your view, how have children's opportunities to meet these demands changed since you were a child or even since your parents'/grandparents' childhood?

Application

In order to consider practical application of this bio-ecological model, it is useful to look into the different ways in which its ideas have influenced practitioners, policy-makers, academics and researchers. In scholarly work the model has indeed enjoyed a healthy degree of popularity over the years, predominantly in literature published in the USA, but also to a certain degree in wider international studies. For instance, Lee *et al.* (2010) used Bronfenbrenner's concepts as a framework for research in South Korea; Thurston and Vissandjée (2005) in Canada; Kulik (2007) in Israel; and Tyson (2011) and Rozsahegyi (2014) in the UK. Reference to Bronfenbrenner's propositions is clearly evident in literature and research about social science and education, in particular in areas related to special education and inclusion.

A common feature of many empirical studies is their focus on one or more elements of a bio-ecological system, rather than subscription to the whole integrated model. For instance, Schweiger and O'Brien (2005) examined the role of various social environments and adoption of children with special educational needs, but paid no regard to person-related characteristics. Similarly, Lee *et al.* (2010) evaluated a range of empirical studies into suicide amongst young people by interrogating micro- to macrosystems, but did not examine person-related attributes or their interactions within these environments. Others focused more on 'person' and personal characteristics. For instance, Stolzer's (2005) reconceptualisation of ADHD was concerned with perceptions of children's person-related difficulties; research by Algood *et al.* (2011) about the maltreatment of children with developmental disabilities emphasised the socio-demographic characteristics of those involved. Tissington (2008) scrutinised the attributes of trainee teachers in social contexts, involving peers, mentors and instructors in a range of school sites, but how these trainees interacted with such social environments was not part of the research.

In their systematic review of twenty-five research studies, all published between 2001 and 2008 and claiming to use the bio-ecological model, Tudge *et al.* (2009) were specifically interested in how Bronfenbrenner's system of ideas was reconceptualised for use in research. Their review found that only four of the examined papers applied three or all four elements of Bronfenbrenner's later theoretical framework: Campbell *et al.* (2002), Riggins-Caspers *et al.* (2003), Tudge *et al.* (2003) and Adamson *et al.* (2007).

Wider scrutiny of Bronfenbrenner-inspired work can, however, show more comprehensive utilisation of the model. An important example is a systematic review by Odom *et al.* (2004) which used all four elements of Bronfenbrenner's bio-ecological model to evaluate research publications about classroom inclusion published in the USA between 1990 and 2002. In relation to person, the authors noted how children's impairments, and the impact of these on learning, were examined in the reviewed publications. In relation to context, the researchers sought connections between children's impairments on the one hand and forms of inclusion on the other, while stakeholders' attitudes were investigated within micro to macro environments. Scrutiny of process encompassed instructional approaches, curriculum strategies and social interactions between disabled and non-disabled children. Finally, Odom *et al.* used the time element to interrogate how various social systems changed to accommodate disabled children's needs.

Challenges with application

Application of the bio-ecological model to research is therefore not without its challenges. A critique by Tudge *et al.* (2009) on application gave several possible reasons for partial application, or for 'misinterpretation' of his theories as a whole. One was that researchers may have been unaware of changes in Bronfenbrenner's constantly developing model; another 'that it is viewed as simply too difficult to translate effectively into research' (207). A third possible reason was that the model was simply too extensive. Researchers have needed to focus on particular elements, making choices about which to incorporate and interrogate and which to leave to other researchers: 'If one considers designing a study that includes each and every aspect of the theory, the research would indeed be a large and complex study' (207). On the other hand, Thomas (1996) considered the multiple elements and dimensions of the framework as a dynamic feature, rather than as a drawback.

It is important to bear in mind, as Tudge *et al.* (2009) pointed out, that 'Bronfenbrenner never implied (let alone stated outright) that every aspect of the model had to be included within any study' (207). It is reasonable to expect that for many or most enquiries, consideration has to be made about how limited studies can be usefully and reliably carried out and how particular parts of Bronfenbrenner's model can be used. In the longer term, researchers need to consider how investigations can be conducted which accumulatively reflect the key elements of the most mature form of the bio-ecological model, including multilevel social environments, their interrelations and the activities which take place between their members and the child to instigate development and learning. If and when such choices are made, they need to be articulated transparently and explained explicitly, avoiding 'conceptual incoherence' (Tudge *et al.*, 2009:199); the researcher must be honest about what was intended and what was carried out.

An attempt to meet these challenges has been made by Rozsahegyi (2014). The research drew directly on the whole of Bronfenbrenner's most mature form of bio-ecological perspective, the PPCT model, to examine outlooks on early development and learning of young children with cerebral palsy, but set boundaries on the extent to which each element was examined. Scrutiny of the first element of Bronfenbrenner's framework focused on how the child was perceived as a developing 'person' with the disability of cerebral palsy. Analysis of 'context' recognised the multiplicity of environments playing a role in children's nurturing, while limiting its focus to particular social and educational niches. In relation to 'process', the research principally interrogated interfaces between child and EY educator, while 'time' was interpreted not as a whole longitudinal element of the investigation, but as a specific aspect of the thinking of stakeholders relating to each child's developmental and educational future. The attractiveness of the model as a framework for the study reflected the match between the wide-ranging nature of the investigation's topic and the all-encompassing interpretive nature of the framework itself. Its use enabled the researcher to reach a more comprehensive and sophisticated understanding of the experience of disability through the lenses of a range of stakeholders and of children themselves, rather than that derived from approaches framed solely around singularly medical or social perspectives (Rozsahegyi, 2014). Ultimately, the approach allowed the researcher to make use of the model in its entirety, retaining its connectivity between all four elements.

Individual/group task

The influence of Bronfenbrenner's ideas on research is relatively straightforward to analyse. However, it is perhaps less easy to identify the influence of his ideas, or of research investigations based on them, on social and educational policy and practice, and this possibility is dealt with in the literature hardly at all.

Try and do this yourself. First, find and examine a current national policy document concerned with improving opportunities for children. To what extent can you relate ideas in the document to the four constituent elements of Bronfenbrenner's model: 'context', 'process', 'person' and 'time'?

Collate and examine also your own experiences of social and educational practice. In what ways can you relate these experiences to Bronfenbrenner's four elements?

Finally, consider to what extent it is possible to say that the influence of Bronfenbrenner's ideas on actual practice might be direct or indirect.

Summary points

This chapter has demonstrated that:

- Bronfenbrenner's ideas grew from an early 'ecological' perspective which was relatively limited in scope.
- In its final form, his 'bio-ecological' model incorporated interconnected notions of 'person', 'process', 'context' and 'time'.
- This bio-ecological model provides an all-encompassing, systematic framework for understanding and investigating child development, and for suggesting how this development might be nurtured within the family, in childcare and in education.
- However, the model is generally seen as highly intricate. Students, researchers, policy-makers and practitioners who draw on it should therefore consider the extent of its use and justify their own stance in relation to its application to research, policy and practice.

References

Adamson, K., O'Brien, M. and Pasley, K. (2007) An Ecological Approach to Further Involvement in Biological and Stepfather Families. *Fathering*, **5**(2), pp.129–147.

Algood, C.L., Hong, J.S., Gourdine, R.M. and Williams, A.B. (2011) Maltreatment of Children with Developmental Disabilities: An ecological system analysis. *Children and Youth Services Review*, **33**(7), pp.1142–1148.

Bronfenbrenner, U. (1977) Toward an Experimental Ecology of Human Development. *American Psychologist*, **32**(7), pp.513–531.

Bronfenbrenner, U. (1979) *The Ecology of Human Development*. London: Harvard University Press.

Bronfenbrenner, U. (1993) The Ecology of Cognitive Development: Research models and fugitive findings. In R. Wonziak and K. Fischer (Eds.), *Development in Context: Acting and thinking in specific environments*. Hillsdale, NJ: Erlbaum.

Bronfenbrenner, U. (1994) Ecological Models of Human Development. In T. Husén and T. N. Postlethwaite (Eds.), *International Encyclopedia of Education*, vol. 3, 2nd edition. Oxford: Elsevier. Reprinted in M. Gauvain and M. Cole (Eds.), *Readings on the Development of Children*, 2nd edition. New York: Freeman.

Bronfenbrenner, U. (1995) Developmental Ecology through Space and Time: A future perspective. In P. Moen, G.H. Elder Jr. and K. Lüsher (Eds.), *Examining Lives in Context*. Washington, DC: American Psychological Association.

Bronfenbrenner, U. and Ceci, S.J. (1994) Nature-Nurture Reconceptualised in Developmental Perspective: A bioecological model. *Psychological Review*, **101**(4), pp.568–586.

Bronfenbrenner, U. and Evans, G. (2000) Developmental Science in the 21st Century: Emerging questions, theoretical models, research designs and empirical findings. *Social Development*, **9**(1), pp.115–125.

Campbell, F.A., Pungello, E.P. and Miller-Johnson, S. (2002) The Development of Perceived Scholastic Competence and Global Self-worth in African-American Adolescents from Low-income Families: The roles of family factors, early educational intervention and academic experience. *Journal of Adolescent Research*, **17**(3), pp.277–302.

Kulik, L. (2007) Explaining Responses to Volunteering: an ecological model. *Nonprofit and Voluntary Sector Quarterly*, **36**(2), pp.239–255.

Lee, S., Hong, J.S. and Espelage, D.L. (2010) An Ecological Understanding of Youth Suicide in South Korea. *School Psychology International*, **31**(5), pp.531–546.

Moore, A. (2000) *Teaching and Learning: Pedagogy, curriculum and culture*. London: RoutledgeFalmer.

Odom, S.L., Vitztum, J., Wolery, R., Lieber, J., Sandall, S., Hanson, M.J., Beckman, P., Schwartz, I. and Horn, E. (2004) Pre-school Inclusion in the United States: a review of research from an ecological system perspective. *Journal of Researching Special Educational Needs*, **4**(1), pp.17–49.

Piaget, J. (1936) *Origins of Intelligence in the Child*. London: Routledge and Kegan Paul.

Riggins-Caspers, K.M., Cadoret, R.J., Knutson, J.F. and Langbehn, D. (2003) Biology-Environment Interaction and Evocative Biology-Environment Correlation: Contribution of harsh discipline and parental psychopathology to problem adolescent behaviors. *Behavior Genetics*, **33**(3), pp.205–220.

Rozsahegyi, T. (2014) *A Bio-ecological Case-study Investigation into Outlooks on the Development and Learning of Young Children with Cerebral Palsy*. Doctoral thesis. University of Warwick: Centre for Education Studies.

Schweiger, W.K. and O'Brien, M. (2005) Special Needs Adoption: An ecological system approach. *Family Education*, **54**(4), pp.512–522.

Stolzer, J. (2005) ADHD in America: Biological analysis. *Ethical Human Psychology and Psychiatry*, **7**(1), pp.65–75.

Sutton, A. (1980) Cultural Disadvantage and Vygotskii's Stages of Development. *Educational Studies*, **6**(3), pp.199–209.

Swick, K.J. and Williams, R.D. (2006) An Analysis of Bronfenbrenner's Bio-ecological Perspective for Early Childhood Educators: Implications for working with families experiencing stress. *Early Childhood Education Journal*, **33**(5), pp.371–378.

Thomas, R.M. (1996) *Comparing Theories of Child Development*. London: Brooks/Cole.

Thurston, W.E. and Vissandjée, B. (2005) An Ecological Model for Understanding Culture as a Determinant of Women's Health. *Critical Public Health*, **15**(3), pp.229–242.

Tissington, L.D. (2008) Bronfenbrenner's Ecological Perspective on the Transition to Teaching for Alternative Certification. *Journal of Instructional Psychology*, **35**(1), pp.106–110.

Tudge, J.R., Mocrova, I., Hatfield, B.E. and Karnik, R.B. (2009) Uses and Misuses of Bronfenbrenner's Bioecological Theory of Development. *Journal of Family Theory and Review*, **1**(4), pp.198–210.

Tudge, J.R.H., Odero, D.A., Hogan, D.M. and Etz, K.E. (2003) Relations between the Everyday Activities of Preschoolers and their Teachers' Perceptions of their Competence in the First Years of School. *Early Childhood Research Quarterly*, **18**(1), pp.42–64.

Tyson, H. (2011) *An Exploration of the Transition Planning Experiences of Young People with Additional Educational Needs in a Mainstream Context, as they Consider their Post-16 Plan*. Doctoral thesis. University of Birmingham: School of Education.

Vygotsky, L.S. (1993) *The Collected Works of L.S. Vygotsky. Vol. 2: The Fundamentals of Defectology*. New York: Plenum Press.

Section two

Social, development and learning identities

2 Child and young person development

Biological, environmental and interpersonal influences

Kay Bennett, Zeta Brown and Tracey Edwards

Introduction

If you type 'child development' into an academic search engine such as 'Google Scholar' you will find many publications on aspects of a child and young person's (CYP) development, including relevant theorists who have influenced our thinking over time. The study of child development is actually relatively new, beginning only around 150 years ago.

There has been a recent rapid surge of research that has informed our practice as professionals, carers and parents. Doherty and Hughes (2014) suggest that increase in interest is because of changes in how society now views 'childhood'. The field of CYP development is now a broad subject area, with many societal and theoretical perspectives that have influenced policy-makers and practice. It is, therefore, important to state the focus of this chapter.

The focus of the book is Bronfenbrenner's ecological and bio-ecological models of childhood outlined in Chapter 1, and the content and structure of the chapter reflect his theory. Bronfenbrenner regarded child development as a complex synergy between biological, environmental and interpersonal influences. He also saw the child was an 'active agent' in interpersonal connections, 'resulting in the child's increased social competence to meet the expectations and demands set by changing environments' (Rozsahegyi: Chapter 1).

The chapter is in three sections: societal perspectives on CYP and their influence on education; CYP and their environment; and CYP and the involvement of practitioners/teachers, parents and carers. Each section includes four dimensions: cognitive, social, emotional and health. We discuss relevant societal outlooks and value systems that have influenced the current perceptions of policy-makers, professionals, carers and parents as well as the influence of societal factors and real-life contexts, inclusive of race, class and gender. These factors are compared and contrasted in relation to differing ways CYP live and learn, considering local, national and at times global contexts. Interpersonal relationships are explored in relation to CYPs' development and will include their relationships with immediate and extended family and settings including childcare, schools and activities in the local community.

Societal perspectives on CYP and their influence on education

Cognitive development

Various disciplines carry out research in the area of cognitive development from different perspectives, including neuroscience, developmental psychology and behavioural genetic research. Neaum (2013:54) states 'cognitive development is concerned with the construction of thought processes. It is concerned with how we acquire, organise and use what we learn. It involves the development of conceptual and conscious thought, memory, problem-solving, imagination and creativity.' Information from these disciplines then influences policy, especially in education. For example, the white paper *Educational Excellence Everywhere* (DfE, 2016:89) states:

> Cognitive science has shed light on long-running debates about whether a school curriculum should focus more on 'knowledge' or 'skills'. It shows that knowledge and skills are partners, and that attempts to teach skills without knowledge fail because they run counter to the way our brains work.

Cognitive skills, including perception, memory and concept-formation, underpin the ability to learn, reason and problem-solve (Dowling, 2013). However, they are not in isolation from other areas such as health, emotional and social development. Teaching and supporting these areas of development in isolation would not support CYPs' overall development. As Dowling (2013:7) suggests: 'we can of course teach an isolated skill such as categorising, but it's not much use if a child is not inclined to categorize things or people…'

Cognitive theorists have also influenced our understanding of developmental approaches to the curriculum. They originated with Piaget's theory of stages of development and provide us with an understanding of development in relation to a CYP's peers and their subsequent development. In the UK we use a national curriculum and assessment processes (e.g. statutory assessment tests – SATs – and GCSEs), and the curriculum anticipates the development of CYP at each of four key stages. However, our understanding of what CYP are capable of doing has advanced significantly since it was found that Piaget had underestimated the capabilities of children. Influenced by post-Piagetians we now expect more of CYP at each stage of development (Donaldson, 1987). For instance, by 5 years old children should be able to count reliably from one to twenty, place numbers in order and say whether they are more or less than another (DfE, 2014). Since Piaget we have also enhanced our understanding of CYPs' individualised development. We now understand that 'children develop and learn in different ways and at different rates' (DfE, 2014:6). That being said, our national system has been critiqued by scholars and teachers for not fully considering this complexity by requiring all CYP to meet the same developmental milestones, and by narrowly measuring CYPs' achievement in assessments such as SATs.

Individual/group task

Consider a cognitive skill, such as perception, attention, memory or processing. Remember that these skills are dependent on the age range of CYP. Pick an age range, reflect on the relevant curriculum and list the differing areas of development that may be used, supported or developed while CYP learn the chosen cognitive skill.

Social and emotional development

Theorists such as Howard Gardner (1993) and Daniel Goleman (1998) have influenced our understanding of emotional well-being as the intelligence of interpersonal and intrapersonal skills. For Goleman and Gardner there is acknowledgement that personal goals, targets and intentions as well as empathy and understanding of others are vital steps towards the development of relationships and ultimately academic success. It can be said that in England and Wales attention has been paid to CYPs' social and emotional development for many years, as evidenced in the implementation of the National Curriculum and Early Years Foundation Stage (EYFS). However, in recent years, greater emphasis has been placed on developing CYPs' social and emotional development, especially in young children, to ensure that they're able to take every opportunity to learn and express their feelings (Dowling, 2013). In 2012, the All-Party Parliamentary Group (APPG) published a report on social mobility and found that 'personal resilience and emotional well-being are the missing link...' to support children to succeed, regardless of the circumstances of their birth (Paterson *et al.*, 2014:10). They state that social and emotional skills (known as 'soft skills') should underpin academic skills ('hard skills') and that skills such as resilience can be taught in school. This is further supported in the white paper *Educational Excellence Everywhere* (DfE, 2016) that has objectives specifically set to build CYPs' character and resilience (see Chapter 4). Moreover, in the *What Works* report by Clarke *et al.* (2015) an optimistic view is taken of evidence-based programmes, particularly in schools and after-school clubs such as *the Leadership Programme, Girls on the Move* and *Outdoor Education Centres* that have had a positive impact worldwide on social and emotional development in CYP.

However, it can be surmised that our understanding of CYPs' social and emotional development is linked to our concept of their capabilities and competencies. Psychologist Susan Isaacs considers that adults underestimate the developing abilities of CYP, noting that they have similar thought processes and intellect to adults. She states 'they know less than adults and have less developed minds than adults; but they do not understand the world in fundamentally different ways from adults' (Wooldridge, 1995:121). James and Prout (1997) suggest that childhood in the twenty-first century is evolving into a new model of thinking: a paradigm fraught with negotiated and complex individual and unique influences and relationships. In education, policies and initiatives are often put in place in the best interests of CYP. However, it can be said that social and emotional development requires CYP to have more *agency* in their development. This is supported by theorists such as Bandura, who argues that children's self-efficacy is fundamentally important, considering their belief about themselves and their successes (Bandura, 1977). The concept of CYP having agency is supported by the United Nations Convention on the Rights of the Child (UNCRC) (1991) and specifically Article 12 that states that CYP have the right to have a say. It can be debated how much CYP get to exercise this right in their education. Richards (in Chapter 10) suggests that CYP could exercise this right further if they were given more opportunities to express their own thoughts, for instance in school councils.

Individual/group task

Reflect on your own schooling experiences. How were you supported to develop your social and emotional skills?

Consider also your time in practice: how are CYP supported to develop socially and emotionally in these particular settings?

Health development

Health and development are intrinsically linked. As such many studies have produced findings that indicate poor health as a risk factor that may compromise the CYP's development. The Marmot Review (Marmot, 2010:22) was premised on this concept and made clear the link between the early years of a child's life and the 'lifelong effects on many aspects of health and well-being'. Physical health problems have been found to have an impact on cognitive functioning, resulting in poor academic achievement (Needham *et al.*, 2004). Crosnoe (2006) examined this concept further and found that, whilst health may not be the strongest predictor of academic achievement in children, it is certainly a significant enough factor which can be used to predict lower achievement growth year after year.

Poor health impacts too on the CYP's emotional and social development, affecting their self-esteem and self-efficacy. Health conditions may lead to instances of bullying and the development of emotional disorders such as anxiety or depression (DfE, 2015), impacting on the CYP's self-confidence and motivation. And whilst there is widespread acceptance that early relationships impact on social and emotional development, less is said about the relationship between these interactions and the physical and mental health and well-being of the child and, later, the adult. Draper *et al.* (2007) emphasise the link between early dysfunctional relationships, childhood trauma and subsequent physical and mental illnesses such as depression, cardiovascular diseases, cancers and emphysema.

However, it is widely known that there are inequalities in health, described by the World Health Organization (WHO, 2008:1) as 'the unequal distribution of health-damaging experiences … not … a "natural" phenomenon but the result of a toxic combination of poor social policies and programmes, unfair economic arrangements, and bad politics'. Where a child is born in the world, as well as the family they are born into, can determine their health and development outcomes. In general, those individuals in society who occupy higher socio-economic positions tend to be less affected by ill health, whilst those who occupy a lower economic position experience a greater impact (Marmot and Bell, 2012). Unhealthy weight gain, socio-emotional difficulties which impact upon children's readiness to learn and, therefore, the likelihood of academic success as well as intellectual delays are widely documented in the UK and elsewhere as markers of socio-economic inequalities in child health and development (APPG, 2015). There is some correlation between low birth-weight (LBW) babies, described as those weighing less than 2.5kg at birth, and impaired development (Hack *et al.*, 1995) and poorer academic achievement (Corman and Chaikind, 1993). Socio-economic position is a factor as LBW babies are more likely to be born to mothers at the lower end of the socio-economic spectrum (Wave Trust, 2013). In addition to this are the higher rates of accidents, suicide and mental health issues associated with CYP from disadvantaged families (Rehkopf and Buka, 2006).

The World Health Organization in 1948 acknowledged that health is about much more than the absence of disease or any clinical diagnosis. Contemporary measures of health encompass the well-being of the individual, their feelings about themselves and their lives. In essence health and well-being, if looked at holistically, should include all key aspects that may impact on the lives of individuals such as their physical environment, their social and economic environment, their lifestyle and their behaviour. Therefore, the health and well-being of an individual cannot be viewed or discussed in isolation.

Individual/group task

Under the four categories in Figure 2.1, state what factors may impact on health and development.

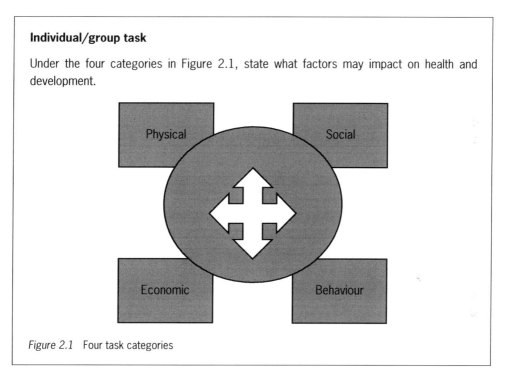

Figure 2.1   Four task categories

CYP and their environment

Cognitive development

There has been a debate in cognitive research for many years as to whether cognitive development is biological or environmental. Disagreement about whether children are born with cognitive skills or are influenced by the environment is one of the fundamental variations in perspective across disciplines. Developmentalists have concluded for some time that cognitive development is dependent on the child's environment and their social interactions.

We can see the significance placed on the education environment in any setting across the UK, from the early years to secondary schools. Theorists such as Piaget, Donaldson and Carr and educational pioneers such as Montessori, Malaguzzi, who developed the Reggio Emilia approach, Steiner and Froebel have provided us with evidence that suggests we must provide CYP with an 'enabling environment' (Smith *et al.*, 2011). The environment should be thoughtfully created to be developmentally appropriate for CYP and their learning. For instance, you will find home corners and possibly mud kitchens in the early years (EY), lessons on natural and local environments and classrooms full of artwork and displays in primary schools. Moreover, in secondary education, young people require specific environments, such as science laboratories.

Individual/group activity

Consider an environment you're interested in (EY, primary, secondary). Think about a particular age range/year group and list the things that may be present in the environment. How many of these environmental influences would support the CYPs' cognitive development?

Tucker-Drob and Harden (2011) discuss the results from behavioral genetic research that has challenged the significance of the environment. They state that if we focus on the importance of the CYP's environment then we would expect to see a variance in cognitive outcomes based on environmental differences, which also include the CYP's socio-economic experiences, their relationships with significant caregivers and the involvement of professionals. In contrast, the opposite has been found: hereditability and academic achievement increase while environment differences decrease over the lifespan. In citing relevant research the authors state that by late adolescence genetic differences account for more than 50 per cent of the variance. In practice, Neaum (2013:54) considers there to be a complex interplay of influential factors in CYPs' overall development: 'Children's learning and development occur as a result of who they are and what they experience. The pace and progress is determined by both genetic imperative and social experiences.' This perspective has been influenced by theorists such as Bronfenbrenner and Vygotsky (1980:88), who says:

> development is subject to the influence of the same two main factors which take part in the organic development of the child, namely the biological and the social ... human learning presupposes a specific social nature and a process by which children grow into the intellectual life of those around them.

Social and emotional development

Social and emotional well-being has been found to be significantly influenced by the environment in which CYP grow and learn. Bandura's (1977) *Social Learning Theory* investigated the impact that both negative and positive actions can have on the individual. This was particularly evident in his 'Bobo Doll' experiment in 1961 when a woman was filmed by Bandura violently hitting a large inflated (Bobo) doll. The footage was played back to a group of children who then went on to hit the Bobo doll in the same manner they had observed in the video. Bandura's theory was that children do not need reinforcement to carry out a set behaviour. Instead he finds that children can observe practice or behaviour and then imitate it. In current family, community and educational practice we place emphasis on the need for positive role models. These may be parents, carers or professionals such as practitioners and teachers. They may also be athletes, entertainers or fictional characters from CYPs' favourite stories or television programmes.

Individual/group task

Think about a specific age range of children and consider the differing positive role models they may have. Consider books, films and TV programmes that include positive role models and are targeted at this age range.

In recent reports there has been an increased emphasis on the development of emotional and social skills as a vital means of ensuring best outcomes for CYP in later life (Allen, 2011). This has supported the development of programmes and initiatives that have been offered in the educational environment. In September 2013 the National Institute for Health and Care Excellence (NICE) issued a Government Briefing on 'Social and Emotional Wellbeing for Children and Young People'. Key factors such as targeted family intervention groups and EY home visits were identified as ways to ensure the development of healthy attitudes and support the prevention of bad behaviours, as well as laying the foundations for higher attainment within education.

The emphasis on EY has strengthened the argument that the earlier the state intervenes, the more likely we are to avoid social problems in later adulthood (Sutton, 2016). Allen (2011) states the importance of intervention programmes in all stages of childhood, youth into adulthood, in CYP becoming 'the good parents of tomorrow'. Some of the most recent interventions were implemented through the Inclusion Development Programme (DCSF, 2010b) in EY. This was through 'Social and Emotional Aspects of Development' (SEAD) and via whole school programmes in Primary and Secondary as 'Social and Emotional Aspects of Learning' (SEAL). It is important to note here, however, that intervention programmes such as anger management and how to be a good citizen, when delivered alongside the curriculum, are only effective when CYP school attendance is regular and when parental involvement and support are available (Jackson *et al.*, 2012).

Health development

Health and its overall influence on development are not limited to the individual alone but are affected by the wider environment and the health and behaviours of those in it. As such the CYP may be more susceptible to particular types of ill health on account of their closest interactions and relationships – the lifestyle and behaviours of those around them. For example, second-hand smoke inhalation is associated with children developing certain respiratory infections such as asthma and also recurrent incidents of middle-ear disease (Royal College of Physicians, 2010). Children who have been exposed to domestic violence are prone to serious anxiety and other stress disorders (UNICEF, 2006). Severe obesity in young people and adults has been linked to distressing early childhood experiences (Hemmingsson *et al.*, 2014), whilst it is suggested that certain high-risk behaviours adopted by young people, such as smoking or alcohol abuse, may be coping mechanisms used to deal with the aftermath of trauma experienced earlier in life (Draper *et al.*, 2007). Both smoking and excess alcohol consumption have been linked to the development of some cancers (Parkin, 2011).

According to Ecological Systems Theory (Bronfenbrenner, 1979), the home forms part of the individual's microsystem. As the microsystem is the most influential aspect in determining outcomes, the home and the home environment are crucial factors having a bearing on the individual's development and also their health. Tickell (2011:8) states:

> Children's experiences in their early years provide the essential foundations for both healthy development and their achievement through school … the most important influences on children's early development are those that come from home…

There are links to depression in CYP associated with their home environment and their experiences such as parenting styles that are low in warmth or include harsh forms of discipline (Ge *et al.*, 1994; Blatt and Homann, 1992). However, there is some debate about the extent to which parenting behaviours are reciprocal and therefore dictated, in some part, by the behaviours or temperament of the child (Dunn and Plomin, 1986).

As discussed earlier in this chapter, the economic environment has proved to be a key determinant of health. Children from poorer families have higher rates of morbidity, are more likely to experience poor physical and mental health, have higher incidents of tooth decay and comparatively lower academic test scores which measure academic ability and readiness to learn at age five (APPG, 2015) (see also Chapter 8).

The physical environment is one of many factors that can have an influence on the health of the CYP. The Chartered Institute of Environmental Health (CIEH) (2013) highlight a core set of environmental indicators impacting on health such as unfit dwellings, overcrowding and homelessness. Poor housing conditions are known to negatively affect health, contributing to conditions such as eczema, hypothermia, heart disease and respiratory tract conditions (Barnes *et al.*, 2013). The Institute of Health Equity (2011) identified cold homes as a key determinant of health, having both direct and indirect health impacts. An obvious consequence of physical illness in CYP is chronic absenteeism affecting education and/or work. This can impact on peer relationships and educational attainment, having a bearing on the CYP's general well-being and emotional health (DfE, 2015). As there are also associations with unfit dwellings and increased stress levels affecting mental health (Barnes *et al.*, 2013), the chronically ill CYP at the centre of the home is greatly disadvantaged. Evidence presented by the DfES (2007) found that children from families with multiple problems had very poor life chances that are manifested in the teenage years.

Individual/group task

Reflect on your own childhood. Are there behaviours, healthy or unhealthy, or conditions that you have today that can be attributed to your childhood environment? To what extent do you feel they are reversible?

CYP and the involvement of practitioners/teachers, parents and carers

Cognitive development

The involvement of significant caregivers in children's cognitive development is broader than simply discussing how parents or carers support this area of development. The socio-economic status and socio-cultural experiences of CYP have also been seen as influences. There is growing evidence across disciplines and policy that the CYP's environment, including such features as poverty and low income, is significantly influential for their development and educational attainment (Field, 2010).

Equally, a CYP's socio-cultural background is seen as an influential factor in their overall development, including their community and family experiences. Bruce (2011:73) cites the work of Rogoff *et al.* (2003) and states 'children do not leave the socio-cultural aspects of their lives behind when attending a group or school. Their culture and the people they live with are part of them.' The quality and level of support of CYPs' relationships with parents or carers are seen as a significant influential factor. Parents' interactions, such as engagement and cognitive stimulation, have been said to 'mediate' between socioeconomic environments, academic achievement and cognitive ability (Tucker-Drob and Harden, 2011).

Practitioners and teachers are important in CYPs' development. However, the amount they should be involved in children's learning is fiercely debated. Theorists who have a socio-cultural perspective, such as Vygotsky and Bruner, emphasise the importance of self-expression and the co-construction of meaning to support children's cognitive development. Neaum (2013:47) stresses the importance of the child as an agent in their own development: 'a child is part of the context in which they are conceived, born and develop, and because social processes are dynamic two-way processes the child will necessarily have an impact on the context in which they grow and learn.' These perspectives emphasise an important role for practitioners and teachers, but also for CYP in cognitive development. That being said, opportunities for the co-construction of meaning can be seen to reduce as CYP progress from the EYFS to the national curriculum. This is because of the constraints and formality of the latter primary and secondary years. It can be concluded that children actually have more agency in their cognitive development during their early years.

Individual/group task

Reflect on your own education. Who supported your cognitive development? Did you feel that you had agency in developing cognitive skills?

Social and emotional development

Our understanding of the social and emotional development of CYP has been influenced by many theorists such as Erikson, a renowned psychoanalyst who marked eight stages of man (Erikson, 1993). His theory was developed on the premise that each stage enables development through the resolution of crisis in order for emotional and psychological development to occur. The first five of the eight stages are pertinent to this chapter and cover the struggle with the, at times unresolved, feelings which CYP have to navigate as they move towards adulthood. Erikson's psychosocial theory suggests that moving steadily through the eight stages – hope, will, purpose, competency, fidelity, love, care and wisdom – can result in a successful and healthy development of personality. Research by John Bowlby (1979) and Mary Ainsworth (Ainsworth *et al.*, 1978) also contributed significantly to the understanding of the role of the primary caregiver and the emotional development that secure attachments can offer CYP throughout their lives. Experts on social constructionism such as Bronfenbrenner (1979) (see Chapter 1) and Vygotsky (1980) highlight the importance of relationships and significant interactions with peers to support learning. Vygotsky's 'zone of proximal development' (ZPD) acknowledged not only the importance of collaborative peer interactions but the social relationships that could support and bridge the gap to new knowledge. We now recognise that Vygotsky has had significant influence on policy and practice within the UK's educational system, evident particularly in the *National Strategies Early Years Document* through the social context in which learning is to take place (DCSF, 2010a).

Recommendations from the analysis by Gibb *et al.* (2016) suggest that CYP should be supported in developing positive relationships through the curriculum and school-based activities, but that this support also needs to extend to parents, carers and families. They also cite the Joseph Rowntree Foundation (JRF) report on links between poverty and CYPs' relationships with their parents, peers and siblings. Poverty was highlighted as having the most negative impact on the interactions of CYP with peers outside of education, including fighting and bullying. Gibb *et al.* found that poverty has an overall negative impact on family relationships too, particularly when linked with parents' educational achievement, working hours and personal relationship conflicts. That is unless they can be positively influenced by parents and/or carers. It is significantly important that we do not generalise the experiences of all CYP living in poverty. (See Chapter 4 on resilience.) In response to such reports and research, couples counselling has been developed to help overcome issues such as inter-parental conflict, and to promote positive parenting practices. This recognised that the wider family context is an important early intervention point.

Individual/group task

Research one local authority and list the parent and family programmes that are offered to support development, including social and emotional development. How many programmes are there? Do these programmes differ between local authorities in your regional area?

Health development

Of course, the home is the most influential of all the environments that the CYP may be exposed to in early life. Whilst it is acknowledged that these early life experiences are crucial in predicting health and development outcomes, the effects are by no means avoidable or irreversible. Therefore, when seeking to alleviate the many variables which contribute to inequalities, recent UK government policy has sought to integrate delivery between the key services: health, education, EY and/or social care. Of this transformation Coombs (2011:112) states:

The underlying emergent ontological assumption is that inter-related problems such as health, social housing, finance and education can be dealt with best by adopting inter-related or multi-agency approaches to service delivery…

A recent early intervention cross-party manifesto, *The 1001 Critical Days* (Leadsom *et al.*, 2015), is evidence of this change in action. It acknowledges the prenatal period combined with the first two years of life as being the most crucial in terms of averting or reversing any negative impacts that may otherwise affect the CYP's outcomes. Importantly it puts forward a vision of tiered, holistic support whereby services work together, pooling their budgets and other resources, to 'encourage innovative commissioning and induce a culture of joined-up working' (7). Therefore, there is an expectation that practitioners will engage in inter-agency collaboration, as endorsed by the Children Act (2004; see DfES, 2004), to influence CYP outcomes.

In younger children, this collaboration can be seen through the implementation of 'The Integrated Review at Age Two', an amalgamation of two assessments: The Healthy Child Programme (HCP), traditionally carried out by staff from the health domain; and the EYFS Progress Check, an EY statutory responsibility used to assess children's development, identify risks and offer opportunities for early intervention. These seek to intervene early in the life of a problem, or indeed early in the life of an individual, in order to reduce the negative outcomes associated with prolonged trauma in the lives of children and/or their families. Allen (2011:4) states:

> the right type of Early Intervention programmes, those that build social and emotional capabilities, have resulted in significant and sustainable improvements in health, behaviour and social and economic outcomes.

The Wave Trust (2013:4) also makes links to early intervention and the promotion of infant mental health, reducing 'the risk of children's development being hampered by abuse, neglect or other early parent-child relationship difficulties'. Therefore, any negative effects of the CYP's environment can be offset by the support given by professionals, not only to the families but also to each other.

Inter-agency working is also evident in the fields of education and health with the introduction of the National Healthy Schools Programme, which aims to promote the link between good health, behaviour and achievement (*The Lancet* UK Policy Matters, 2011).

Individual/group task

Health promotion is the name given to various approaches that seek to promote health through education about healthy lifestyles: foods, choices, behaviours, habits.

What approach might you take if working with parents and the CYP to promote health?

Conclusion

This chapter has utilised Bronfenbrenner's ecological and bio-ecological model as a backdrop in exploring the CYP's development through a biological, environmental and interpersonal lens. Who and what we become happens as a direct, or indirect, result of our individual lived experiences.

Each of these experiences is made up of a unique, complex network of contributing factors that influence every aspect of our being. Therefore, intellect, health and social and emotional maturity can be either stimulated or constrained by the dynamics of the CYP's existence. The CYP is not merely a passive agent but is active in shaping her/his own development. By using day-to-day interactions as building blocks in order to construct their worlds, the CYP is literally learning through, as Kolb (1984:41) puts it, a 'combination of grasping and transforming experience'.

However, whilst childhood experiences may shape the individual, the effects are by no means irreversible. Clarke and Clarke (1998) question the extent to which these experiences are preserved and state they 'represent no more than an initial step in an ongoing life path' (435). Sylva *et al.* (2012) concur that, whilst a child's background can be an indicator of possible poorer outcomes, it is not an exact and reliable determinant. Therefore, some contributory factors *may* increase the likelihood of certain behaviours or outcomes; there is recognition that early life experiences are not definitive in determining the life-course of individuals. Much social policy over recent years has been aimed at introducing early intervention measures that aim to maximise the opportunities for all CYP; thus the role of the practitioner is to work with other professionals, parents or carers and the young people themselves, to challenge the 'subtle lowered expectancies' identified by Clarke and Clarke (1998:436) that can become a by-product of disadvantage and an obstacle when working with children, young people and their families.

Summary points

- CYP areas of development are intrinsically linked.
- Societal perspectives are influential in our understanding of CYP development and our practice.
- CYPs' environment at home and in the community, such as schools, is significantly important to CYP development.
- Relationships including those with parents, carers, practitioners and teachers are also influential and can counter adverse circumstances such as poverty.
- CYP are active agents and need to be given agency to be involved in their own learning and development.

Recommended reading

Allen, G. (2011) *Early Intervention: the next steps. An Independent Report to Her Majesty's Government.* London: HM Government.

CSDH (2008) *Closing the Gap in a Generation: Health equity through action on the social determinants of health.* Final Report of the Commission on Social Determinants of Health. Geneva: World Health Organization. [Online]. http://apps.who.int/iris/bitstream/10665/43943/1/9789241563703_eng.pdf (accessed 14 August 2016).

DfE (2016) *Educational Excellence Everywhere.* London: DfE. [Online]. https://www.gov.uk/government/uploads/system/uploads/attachment_data/file/508447/Educational_Excellence_Everywhere.pdf (accessed 15 August 2016).

References

Ainsworth, M.D., Bleha, M., Waters, S. and Wall, S. (1978) *Patterns of Attachment: a psychological study of the strange situation*. Hillsdale, NJ: Lawrence Erlbaum.

Allen, G. (2011) *Early Intervention: the next steps. An Independent Report to Her Majesty's Government*. London: HM Government.

APPG (2015) *The Early Years*. London: APPG. [Online]. www.toomuchtoosoon.org/uploads/2/0/3/8/20381265/appg_report_early_yearsfinal.pdf (accessed 11 August 2016).

Bandura, A. (1977) *Social Learning Theory*. New York: General Learning Press.

Barnes, M., Cullinane, C., Scott, S. and Silvester, H. (2013) *People living in Bad Housing – Numbers and health impacts*. London: NatCen Social Research.

Blatt, S. and Homann, E. (1992) Parent-Child Interaction in the Etiology of Dependent and Self-critical Depression. *Clinical Psychology Review*, **12**(1), pp.47–91.

Bowlby, J. (1979) *The Making and Breaking of Affectional Bonds*. London: Tavistock.

Bronfenbrenner, U. (1979) *The Ecology of Human Development: Experiments in human design*. Cambridge, MA: Harvard University Press.

Bruce, T. (2011) *Early Childhood Education*, 4th edition. London: Hodder Education.

CIEH (2013) *Effective Strategies and Interventions: Environmental health and the private housing sector*. London: CIEH.

Clarke, A. and Clarke, A. (1998) Early Experience and the Life Path. *The Psychologist*, **11**(9), pp.433–436.

Clarke, A.M., Morreale, S., Field, C.A., Hussein, Y. and Barry, M.M. (2015) *What Works in Enhancing Social and Emotional Skills Development during Childhood and Adolescence? A Review of the Evidence on the Effectiveness of School-based and Out-of-school Programmes in the UK*. A report produced by the World Health Organization Collaborating Centre for Health Promotion Research. Galway: National University of Ireland.

Coombs, S. (2011) Designing Accredited Continuing Professional Development for the Children's Workforce: Challenges and opportunities facing higher education in England. *Professional Development in Education*, **37**(1), pp.111–129.

Corman, H. and Chaikind, C. (1993) The Effect of Low Birth Weight on the School Performance and Behaviour of School-aged Children. *Economics of Education Review*, **17**(2/3), pp.307–316.

Crosnoe, R. (2006) Health and the Education of Children from Racial/Ethnic Minority and Immigrant Families. *Journal of Health and Social Behavior*, **47**(1), pp.77–93.

DCSF (2010a) *The National Strategies Early Years Document*. Annesley, Nottingham: UK Data Archive.

DCSF (2010b) *The National Strategies Early Years: Inclusion development programme*. Annesley, Nottingham: UK Data Archive.

DfE (2014) *Statutory Framework for the Early Years Foundation Stage. Setting the Standards for Learning, Development and Care for Children from Birth to Five*. London: DfE.

DfE (2015) *Supporting Pupils at School with Medical Conditions*. London: DfE.

DfE (2016) *Educational Excellence Everywhere*. London: DfE. [Online]. https://www.gov.uk/government/uploads/system/uploads/attachment_data/file/508447/Educational_Excellence_Everywhere.pdf (accessed 15 August 2016).

DfES (2004) *Summary of the Children Act (2004)*. London: DfES.

DfES (2007) *Aiming High for Children: Supporting families*. London: DfES.

Doherty, J. and Hughes, M. (2014) *Child Development: Theory and practice 0–11*, 2nd edition. Harlow: Pearson.

Donaldson, M. (1987) *Children's Minds*. London: Fontana.

Dowling, M. (2013) *Young Children's Thinking*. Los Angeles, CA: Sage.

Draper, B., Pfaff, J., Pirkis, J., Snowdon, J., Lautenschlager, N. and Wilson, I. (2007) Long-term Effects of Childhood Abuse on the Quality of Life and Health of Older People: Results from the Depression and Early Prevention of Suicide in General Practice Project. *Journal of the American Geriatrics Society*, **56**(2), pp.262–271.

Dunn, J. and Plomin, R. (1986) Determinants of Maternal Behaviour towards 3-year-old Siblings. *British Journal of Developmental Psychology*, **4**(2), pp.127–137.

Erikson, E.H. (1993) *Childhood and Society*. New York: W.W. Norton and Company.

Field, F. (2010) *The Foundation Years: Preventing poor children from becoming poor adults*. London: HM Government.

Gardner, H. (1993) *Multiple Intelligences*. New York: Basic Books.

Ge, X., Lorenz, F., Conger, R., Elder, G. and Simmons, R. (1994) Trajectories of Stressful Life Events and Depressive Symptoms during Adolescence. *Developmental Psychology*, **30**(4), pp.467–483.

Gibb, G., Rix, K., Wallace, E., Fitzsimons, E. and Mostafa, T. (2016) *Poverty and Children's Personal and Social Relationships: Secondary analysis of Millennium Cohort Study data*. York: Joseph Rowntree Foundation. [Online]. https://www.ncb.org.uk/sites/default/files/uploads/documents/Research_reports/poverty_and_children_s_personal_and_social_relationships_-_final_report_-_march_2016.pdf (accessed 19 August 2016).

Goleman, D. (1998) *Working with Emotional Intelligence*. London: Bloomsbury.

Hack, M., Klein, N.K. and Taylor, H.G. (1995) Long-term Developmental Outcomes of Low Birth Weight Infants. *Future Child*, **5**(1), pp.176–196.

Hemmingsson, E., Johansson, K. and Reynisdottir, S. (2014) Effects of Childhood Abuse on Adult Obesity: A systematic review and meta-analysis. *Obesity Reviews*, **15**(11), pp.882–893.

Institute of Health Equity (2011) *The Health Impact of Cold Homes and Fuel Poverty*. London: IHE.

Jackson, C., Henderson, M., Frank, J. and Haw, S. (2012) An Overview of Prevention of Multiple Risk Behaviour in Adolescence and Young Adulthood. *Journal of Public Health*, **34**(S1), pp.i30–i40.

James, A. and Prout, A. (1997) *Constructing and Reconstructing Childhood: Contemporary issues in the sociological study of childhood*. London: Routledge.

Kolb, D.A. (1984) *Experiential Learning: Experience as the source of learning and development*. Englewood Cliffs, NJ: Prentice Hall.

Leadsom, A., Field, F., Burstow, P. and Lucas, C. (2015) *The 1001 Critical Days. The Importance of the Conception to Age Two Period. A Cross-party Manifesto*. London: 1001 Critical Days Campaign. [Online]. www.wavetrust.org/sites/default/files/reports/1001%20Critical%20Days%20-%20The%20Importance%20of%20the%20Conception%20to%20Age%20Two%20Period%20Refreshed_0.pdf (accessed 26 August 2016).

Marmot, M. (2010) *Fair Society, Healthy Lives. The Marmot Review. Strategic Review of Health Inequalities in England Post-2010*. London: The Marmot Review. [Online]. www.instituteofhealthequity.org/Content/FileManager/pdf/fairsocietyhealthylives.pdf (accessed 20 August 2016).

Marmot, M. and Bell, R. (2012) Fair Society Healthy Lives. *Public Health*, **126**(1), pp.4–10.

National Institute for Health and Care Excellence (NICE) Local Government Briefing (2013) *Social and Emotional Wellbeing for Children and Young People*. London: NICE. [Online]. https://www.nice.org.uk/advice/lgb12/chapter/introduction (accessed 18 August 2016).

Neaum, S. (2013) *Child Development for Early Years Students and Practitioners*, 2nd edition. London: Sage.

Needham, B.L., Crosnoe, R. and Muller, C. (2004) Academic Failure in Secondary School: The inter-related role of physical health problems and educational context. *Social Problems*, **51**(4), pp.569–586.

Parkin, D. (2011) The Fraction of Cancer Attributable to Lifestyle and Environmental Factors in the UK in 2010. *British Journal of Cancer*, **105**(S2), pp.S77–S81.

Paterson, C., Tyler, C. and Lexmond, J. (2014) *Character and Resilience Manifesto. The All Parliamentary Group on Social Mobility*. [Online]. www.educationengland.org.uk/documents/pdfs/2014-appg-social-mobility.pdf (accessed 11 August 2016).

Rehkopf, D. and Buka, S. (2006) The Association between Suicide and the Socio-economic Characteristics of Geographical Areas. *Psychological Medicine*, **36**(2), pp.145–157.

Royal College of Physicians (2010) *Passive Smoking and Children: A report of the Tobacco Advisory Group of the Royal College of Physicians*. London: RCP.

Smith, P., Cowie, H. and Blades, M. (2011) *Understanding Children's Development*, 6th edition. Chichester: John Wiley and Sons.

Sutton, C. (2016) *Promoting Child and Parent Wellbeing: How to use evidence and strengths-based strategies in practice*. London: Jessica Kingsley.

Sylva, K., Melhuish, E., Sammons, P., Siraj-Blatchford, I. and Taggart, B. (2012) *Effective Pre-school, Primary and Secondary Education 3-14 Project (EPPSE 3-14). Final Report from the Key Stage 3 Phase: Influences on students' development from age 11-14*. London: DfE.

The Lancet UK Policy Matters (2011) *National Healthy Schools Programme*. London: UKPM. [Online]. http://ukpolicymatters.thelancet.com/policy-summary-national-healthy-schools-programme/ (accessed 20 August 2016).

Tickell, C. (2011) *The Early Years: Foundations for life, health and learning. An Independent Report on the Early Years Foundation Stage to Her Majesty's Government*. London: DfE.

Tucker-Drob, E.M. and Harden, K.P. (2011) Early Childhood Cognitive Development and Parental Cognitive Stimulation: Evidence for reciprocal gene–environment transactions. *Developmental Science*, **15**(2), pp.250–259.

UNICEF (2006) *Behind Closed Doors: The impact of domestic violence on children.* New York: UNICEF.

Vygotsky, L.S. (1980) *Mind in Society: The development of higher psychological processes,* 2nd edition. Cambridge, MA: Harvard University Press.

Wave Trust (2013) *Conception to Age 2.* Croydon, UK: Wave Trust.

WHO (2008) *Closing the Gap in a Generation: Health equity through action on the social determinants of health.* Geneva: WHO. [Online]. www.who.int/social_determinants/final_report/media/csdh_report_wrs_en.pdf (accessed 6 September 2016).

Wooldridge, A. (1995) *Measuring the Mind.* Cambridge: Cambridge University Press.

3 The role of play in childhood

Graham Jones and Helen Lyndon

Introduction

'The view that play is important, if not essential for children is something that is often assumed rather than demonstrated' (Maynard and Powell, 2014:115). Whilst in a general sense it is near-universally agreed that play is a vital part of children's well-being and development and the United Nations Convention on the Rights of the Child (UNCRC) recognises the right to play as a fundamental aspect of childhood, play is often overlooked in academic study.

All aspects of Bronfenbrenner's ecological and bio-ecological models (Chapter 1) can be applied to children's play. In terms of the context of children's play, much research has focussed on the microsystem and how a child's immediate environment, and the dyadic and multi-person interactions within it, influence their play. Interactions in the other systems also have an impact on the child: for example the connections between parents and teachers in the mesosystem, education policy and developments of technology in the exosystem and general societal attitudes towards play in the macrosystem (Bronfenbrenner and Ceci, 1994).

This chapter covers several issues regarding play. We investigate the difficulty in defining play and the different types of play. We then go on to explore theories of why children play and how play can be incorporated into school curricula. The changing nature of play and the rise of technological play are examined. The chapter ends with a discussion of the effects of play deprivation and of how play can be used as a therapeutic tool.

Definition of play

Case study of a conversation one of the authors had with a five-year-old child:

Me: What is play?
Jamie: Play is when you're playing and stuff.
Me: Can you tell me any more about what play is?
Jamie: It's when you're having nice time.
Me: Why do you like to play?
Jamie: Because it makes me feel happy.
Me: Do you get to play much at school?
Jamie: Sometimes we're allowed to play when we finish our activities.

Like many commonly used words, 'play' turns out to be rather difficult to define. As Wainwright *et al.* (2016:514) state, 'what is meant by play is far from straightforward, with numerous definitions and interpretations of the concept across the world.' In studying play it can seem as though there are as many definitions as there are play researchers, with some definitions too brief and some overly elaborate. Moyles (2015:16) likens trying to define the concept of play as, 'trying to seize bubbles, for every time there appears to be something to hold on to, its ephemeral nature disallows it being grasped'. Reed and Brown (2000) suggest that play is something 'felt'; we intuitively know when we are playing and can recognise play in others, but it is difficult to articulate this feeling. Indeed, the child in the earlier conversation clearly knows what play is but is somewhat puzzled by being asked to define it.

In looking at several definitions from a range of sources, a consensus appears that echoes what was said by Jamie: that play is fun to do and freely chosen by the child. Play England (2016) put this nicely, with play being 'what children and young people do when they are not being told what to do by adults'.

It is also difficult to differentiate what counts as play and what does not. Youell (2008) notes that in Western culture there is a clear distinction made between work and play. She points out that at school being allowed to play is often used as a reward for doing good work, and that restricting play is a common punishment for bad behaviour. This idea has clearly been internalised by Jamie and is an example of how societal values in the macrosystem influence individual attitudes. However, 'play' and 'work' are not opposites, nor are they mutually exclusive: some tasks can be set by others but be highly enjoyable. For instance, we can have a playful attitude to our work. Pellegrini (1991) argues that we should not distinguish between categories of 'play' and 'not play' but rather see a continuum from 'pure play' to 'non play' where different elements of play can be present or absent.

Types of play

The difficulties in defining the concept of play are also present when trying to categorise different types of play. Developmental categorisation was suggested by Parten in 1932 where she observed that children's play was initially solitary and became more socially based and cooperative as they developed. She offered five distinctive and socially based stages of play: solitary, spectator, parallel, associative and cooperative. But she also recognised that most of the children demonstrated several of the stages in any one observation, highlighting the complexity of play activity.

Hughes (2002) outlined sixteen different types of play which have assisted in giving practitioners a common language through which play can be described. These sixteen types range from role play and rough and tumble play, which have been readily explored in the literature, to more obscure play types such as 'recapitulative play' which allows children to explore ancestry, rituals and history. Bronfenbrenner's PPCT model can be applied here (see Chapter 1). The types of play children engage in are determined by the interaction of a number of factors: the type of 'person' the child is; the 'context' the child is located within; and the 'processes' that occur within this context.

Individual/group task

Consider a variety of play types (e.g. mastery play, deep play or rough and tumble play) and when you may have observed children engaging in such activity. Consider how many different types there may be and how these might be defined.

What quickly becomes apparent when exploring play types is the potential for overlap; much of children's play could in fact be categorised in many ways, not forgetting that we may never fully understand the motivation behind the play. The child that is running around the outdoor area as their favourite superhero may be engaging in *fantasy, locomotor* and *rough and tumble play* simultaneously. *Role play* and *socio-dramatic play* could also be *symbolic* as children would take on roles or characters in order to participate in the play. Once the play becomes social it can also offer differing play types for different participants depending upon the child's role within the play.

Theories of play

Individual/group task

In any search engine, look for videos of kittens or puppies playing. You can spend a pleasant half-hour watching lots of cute animals chasing toys and pouncing on each other:

- From the animals' point of view, why are they doing this?
- What are they gaining from this?
- Can the answers given to these two questions be applied in a general sense to humans?

Play theories attempt to answer such questions as: Why do children play? What do children gain from playing? How important is play for healthy development? The vast majority of theories agree that play is valuable for children's physical, emotional and cognitive development. However, there is still, in some quarters, a trivialisation of the benefits of play. Whilst play might be seen as a useful way of allowing children to 'let off steam', it is often seen as being of low intellectual challenge (Hall and Abbott, 1991). This dismissive attitude towards play was typified by Michael Gove (2013) who, as Education Secretary, was dismissive of 'child-initiated play' as a means of learning, instead arguing that direct instruction of a knowledge-rich curriculum was the key to educational success.

Discussion of play theories relates to the nature–nurture debate. The fact that all young mammals play and that play is found in all human cultures suggests that play is a natural activity for children. The fact that children in different cultures engage in different play activities suggests play is socially constructed. The debate over the relative influences of genes vs environment is as contested in the area of play as in other areas of development.

Wood and Attfield (2005) highlight the different attitudes towards play of the early pioneers in childhood education. Friedrich Froebel (1782–1852) and Rudolf Steiner (1861–1925) placed an emphasis on the child's natural tendencies for free play, exploration and fantasy, with the role of the adult being to encourage and respond sensitively to the child's play. Others, such as Maria

Montessori (1869–1952), placed more emphasis on a planned environment and more adult direction of play activities.

This difference in approach underlies the difference between the theories of Jean Piaget and Lev Vygotsky. Piaget (1962) linked play to biological and cognitive development. His was a child-centred theory where the drive to play came from within the child. Through play, the child constructs their understanding of the world, continually testing, changing and retesting this understanding against their changing environment. In this way play is a very individual and self-directed activity. According to Piaget, the type of play engaged in depends on the stage of development the child is in. The sensorimotor stage is characterised by play based on physical activity, the pre-operational stage by symbolic, pretend play and the operational stages increasingly by rule-based, logical games. The implication from Piaget is that the role of the adult or teacher is to provide a stimulating environment for the child, but then to take a step back and allow the child to play in that environment by themselves or with peers. Although he focussed more on the environmental context in which play occurs, Bronfenbrenner was not dismissive of Piaget's ideas. Bronfenbrenner's concept of the child as an 'active agent' resonates with Piaget's ideas and through his concept of 'person' (see Chapter 1), he acknowledges the importance of personal characteristics in influencing play.

In contrast to Piaget, other theorists emphasise the learnt, socio-cultural, aspects of play, with play enabling children to learn the social norms and values of their community. Even in hunter-gatherer times, Gray (2009) suggests that play was used as a means of educating children and enabling bonding. Vygotsky (1978:86) suggested a more direct, participatory role for adults in children's play than did Piaget. Vygotsky saw the role of the adult as to engage with children in their Zone of Proximal Development (ZPD), the 'distance between the actual development level … and the level of potential development'. He believed that, in play, children operate to the top of their potential, at the limit of their ZPD. Vygotsky (1987) showed how this can be done in two ways: firstly, children experience cultural situations and practices and they reflect these in spontaneous pretend play. Secondly, children engage in play that involves more direct instruction from adults or older children. In both of these ways, play enables children to learn the skills necessary to live in their community. From Chapter 1 we can see how Bronfenbrenner's focus on interpersonal relations within the microsystem was influenced by Vygotsky's work and that the 'dyads' of Bronfenbrenner's theory build upon Vygotsky's ideas of how people interact.

Individual/group task

According to Vygotsky and Bronfenbrenner, through play we are socialised to become members of our community. From a critical standpoint, play can be seen to perpetuate class and power differentials in society. Although they never wrote directly about play, we can speculate on the attitudes of different sociological theorists. Research to elaborate on the following.

Karl Marx: Through play, working-class children achieve a false consciousness where they see their needs as being fulfilled by ever-more-expensive toys and games.

Pierre Bourdieu: Through play children acquire their cultural and social capital. For example, from a young age children from richer backgrounds make valuable connections with others at the rugby club and on skiing holidays.

Play in the curriculum

The extent to which play is utilised varies between different models of education and can be linked back to the theorists and pioneers discussed earlier. Educational philosophers such as Steiner, Montessori and Froebel place an emphasis on play in children's development, and this is evident internationally in the settings which follow these approaches. Bronfenbrenner's emphasis on the child as an 'active agent' has implications for who might lead play and with what outcomes in mind, if any. The Early Years Foundation Stage (EYFS) and national curriculum in England would also be seen as providing part of the 'exosystem' influenced by a broader 'macrosystem' in which we value attainment and economic success (see also Chapter 1). To what extent can children remain 'active agents' within such a system?

The EYFS, which provides statutory guidelines for all EY providers in England (DfE, 2014), states that 'Play is essential for children's development … Children learn by leading their own play' (DfE, 2014:9). The importance of play in early childhood is evident and practitioners are encouraged to allow both the environment and their own intervention to facilitate learning through play. Play is recognised as one of three characteristics of effective learning and practitioners are encouraged to plan, observe and assess this element of provision (DfE, 2014).

This planned and assessed element of play brings about a tension. If we return to the definitions of play which were explored at the start of the chapter we are reminded that children's own perception of play is very different and often is removed from adult intervention; children *play* when *work* is complete.

This difference between *work* and *play* increases with age and children experience class-based lessons with breaks in between which are usually defined as playtime. Once following the national curriculum guidelines at a primary age in England, play becomes less apparent and is only discussed in terms of role-play in the English curriculum materials, playing musical instruments and team sports (DfE, 2013).

Individual/group task

Reflect upon your own experiences of play and work at school:

- When did you engage in play?
- Can you remember examples of playful learning?
- How did your play at school change with age?

The Effective Provision of Pre-school Education (EPPE) study informed the EYFS and highlighted the importance of the role of the adult in developing instructive environments and routines as well as in teacher-initiated group work (Sylva *et al.*, 2004). The most effective settings were considered to be those that could provide a balance of child-initiated and adult-led opportunities. This is reflective of the tension that exists within education as to the value of play and its impact on pedagogical approaches; what practitioners may define as learning through play might be defined by the children as work.

For some the need for a curriculum model removes the playful element and introduces an outcome-based or directive approach to education (Wood, 2010). A current goal of the EYFS is to improve children's progression and achievement against the early learning goals (DfE, 2014), which are a predetermined list of outcomes. This encourages practitioners to focus on these outcomes rather than to follow individual interest and this would appear to be at odds with a play-based approach. The contrasting emergent or responsive approach (Wood, 2010) would enable children to engage in spontaneous play without a set of predetermined outcomes. It would respond to the interests of the individual child and develop from their play, rather than being directed by curriculum guidance. The EYFS does encourage child-initiated play and requires practitioners to follow the interests of the child; here lies a tension for practitioners as they struggle to follow children's interests whilst addressing a set curriculum. The most effective practitioners are those who are able to work within this tension; those who do not seek a difference between play and teaching but adopt an individualised playful approach to learning (Ofsted, 2015).

Play and technology

With the developments in information and communication technology (ICT) and digital technologies one might argue that technological play should have been included in the previous section on types of play, or should we alternatively see technology as a means to enhance play in those areas previously discussed? There is currently the option for children to utilise technology to facilitate many aspects of play, including social and locomotor play. Interactive technologies are added to toys aimed at children from birth onwards. Regardless of the possibilities now found in technological play, the research in this field struggles to keep up with the technology itself.

Children are considered to be *digital natives* (Prensky, 2001) who grow up able to confidently utilise digital technology as opposed to a *digital immigrant* who might turn to technology after using a more traditional method, e.g. looking something up online only when it cannot be found elsewhere. Prensky, writing in 2001, described a tension between the *native* and *immigrant* generations which saw children's capabilities with technology progressing in advance of their teachers' and parents'.

With technology children are potentially offered a wider environmental and social influence and the chance to advance beyond the social sphere of their parents; this interconnected technological environment will impact upon children's psychological development, a direct link to Bronfenbrenner's view on the importance of the intertwined social and physical environment, as discussed in Chapter 1.

As technology develops further, and the first generation of digital natives have children of their own, technology is being utilised at an earlier age. Palaiologou (2016) reported that 60 per cent of children under 3 years of age are experiencing digital technology and that their parents believe that such devices are the same as any other toys.

Individual/group task

Take a few moments to explore and consider the range of technologically aided toys which are available to children from birth onwards and the benefits that such technologies are said to afford.

Can you find ways in which technology is used for the different types of play discussed earlier?

How does this differ from the technological play that you experienced?

How does this differ from the technological play experienced by your parents?

Parents do believe that early exposure to technological play will be advantageous to their children (McPake and Plowman, 2010), but the extent to which they provide access to such technology is very much influenced by their own beliefs and experiences. The role of educational settings in supporting parents with technological play will become of greater importance as schools develop learning platforms for children to access at home and as technology is more readily integrated into the mainstream curriculum. The development of educational *apps* and the availability of touchscreen technology have opened up greater play and learning opportunities, particularly for EY. Such advances have been found to have beneficial effects: touchscreen tablets have been found to have beneficial effects on emerging literacy (Neumann and Neumann, 2014) and they have reduced barriers to learning for those with special educational needs (Ryan, 2016).

The increasing popularity of technological play has not been without its critics and there has been concern (expressed primarily in the media) regarding children's safety as well as rising obesity levels which have been linked to a more sedentary lifestyle. We are currently experiencing technologies which aim to combat such issues as companies develop games which encourage users to be outdoors and develop child-friendly search engines such as *KidRex* by Google.

The rise in technology and its breadth of applications forms part of the argument by those such as Postman (1994) and Palmer (2007) for the disappearance of childhood and the increase of toxic influences which impact upon our children. The speed at which we can interact with a broader community continues to develop, as does the speed with which we might take delivery of our Internet purchases! This developing technology, Palmer (2007) would argue, reduces the frequency with which we communicate and play with our children and is having an increasingly negative impact.

Individual/group task

Consider the following:

- Has technology shifted the wider macrosystem through our values and the very socialisation of our children?
- Do all children within society have equal access to this technology and what might the influence of this technological environment be?

Play deprivation

Individual/group task

Do you agree with the following statements?

'The opposite of play … is not work, it is depression' (Sutton-Smith, 1999, in Brock *et al.*, 2009:217).

Several psychologists have added the *capacity to play* to Freud's *to love* and *to work* as the key ingredients to being a well-adjusted individual (Youell, 2008:121).

What other forms of play deprivation can you add to the following list? Which of Bronfenbrenner's 'systems' would you place each one into?

- Detention during playtime;
- The local playground being closed due to lack of funds;
- Parents being too busy to play with their children;
- An education policy that favours didactic over play-based learning.

Hughes (2003) believes that children need to experience a range of different types of play during their childhood to attain and maintain a state of well-being. Problems can arise from both play deprivation, a lack of play in childhood, and play bias, when some types of play are engaged in more than others. Hughes suggests that deprivation and bias in children's play are far more widespread than society acknowledges, and far more damaging.

Play deprivation has been linked to a range of problems including physical and emotional illnesses, especially obesity and depression, diminished impulse control, addictive predilections, low school achievement and a lack of social skills. Causes of play deprivation include: changing attitudes to playing outdoors, with perceived risks ranging from traffic to strangers; the focus on curriculum and standards in schools; parents working long hours; and an increase in technological play leading to reduction in other types of play (Play Wales, 2003, 2013). These risks and causes of play deprivation have been supported by a number of studies.

A UNICEF (2007) report on the well-being of children around the world ranked the UK at the bottom of the world's twenty-one richest countries. Following this, a comparative study (UNICEF, 2011) compared the lives of children in the UK with those in Sweden and Spain, to uncover why the UK was ranked so poorly in relation to children's well-being. The research indicated that children in the UK had fewer opportunities for playful outdoor activities compared to the other two countries, and that this was a significant contributor towards reduced well-being in the UK. Decisions made in the child's exosystem to cut funding for local play spaces, they argue, are detrimental for children's well-being, particularly for children from low socio-economic groups, whose parents struggle to find affordable play provision in their area. The study also found that UK parents had less free time to spend with their children, due to work and other commitments. This shows how work pressures in the exosystem affect children's interactions with their parents in the microsystem. They called for policy-makers to consider how UK policies impinge on family time.

The use of drugs prescribed to children under the age of 16 in order to control the symptoms of ADHD increased by 56.6 per cent from 2006–2012 (Bachmann *et al.*, 2017). However, there is evidence to suggest that spending time in green spaces can be an effective means of reducing symptoms of ADHD. In fact Panksepp (2008) suggests that poor play opportunities may be responsible for the growth in ADHD, and that creating exciting play opportunities for children may be the best way to tackle this problem.

Brown (2012) reported on the discovery of neglected children in Romania after the overthrow of Ceausescu in 1989. It was found that over 100,000 children had been living in orphanages, many suffering from severe neglect and institutional abuse. Children were found who had lived their lives tied into a cot, poorly fed, with their nappies rarely changed. When discovered, the children stared vacantly into space, rocked backwards and forwards, had very poor motor skills, were incapable of meaningful social interaction and had poor cognitive functioning. A therapeutic playwork project began in 1999. Recovery was greater than expected. The main factor in the recovery was the fact that these children now had playmates.

These studies, although extreme examples of play deprivation, do alert us to its dangers and show again how vital play is to the mental, physical and emotional health of children. They also suggest the value of play as therapy.

Play therapy

The therapeutic benefits of play could be expressed through some of the theorists and pioneers detailed previously, through Vygotsky, for example, and the role the adult can play in the developing child, through Bronfenbrenner with the support of the interpersonal influences within the shifting microsystem, or, for Piaget, in the assimilation of new knowledge. There is also a body of research and study in the field of psychotherapy which advocates the value of play as a healing tool for children. This work is based largely on the work of Virginia Axline (1990) who detailed the recovery of 'Dibs' in her 1964 case study. Axline proposed eight principles of play therapy which are utilised in therapy today (PTUK, 2016). These involve building trusting relationships with the child and allowing them to lead the direction and pace of their recovery, during which the therapist recognises the child's feelings and reflects these back, allowing the child to gain insight.

Play therapy is available to children through health, education and social care for a range of issues such as for those who have suffered difficult life circumstances such as victims of abuse or to assist with psychological difficulties such as anxiety or depression. The British Association of Play Therapists was founded in 1992 to support clinical practice in this area (BAPT, 2016).

Conclusion

Play clearly remains central to childhood, though exactly what we mean by play could vary depending upon our age, experiences or culture. There is little doubt that play of any and every type can be utilised effectively to enhance learning and development and this is often the case in early childhood settings. Indeed, play deprivation provides a stark reminder of the importance of play for our children. However, this playful approach tends to diminish as children age and often a more didactic approach to education is experienced.

Although the importance of play has long been acknowledged, its importance is often downplayed. From the authors' experience, children would benefit if play was given more consideration by policy-makers and employers in terms of the development of curricula, implementing family-friendly working conditions, giving greater emphasis to children's play when planning outdoor spaces and considering how we want our children to interact with technology.

In relation to Bronfenbrenner's bio-ecological model, there can be seen to be a tension in the importance of play at the different levels. In the microsystem those who directly interact with children can see the importance of play through their own observations of and interactions with children. However, in the exosystem parental work patterns and local and national policies that affect children might mean play opportunities are reduced. Also in the macrosystem the importance of play will continue to be downplayed as long as there is a greater cultural emphasis placed on children's academic achievements than on their emotional and physical well-being.

Summary points

- There is no one agreed definition of play. Our own experiences, age and culture will influence what we consider play to be.
- Perhaps one of the difficulties in defining play is that it is a very broad concept. It is beneficial to examine the different types of play.
- Explanations of why we play focus on child-led theories and socially constructed theories.
- The idea that children learn through play has been incorporated into different school curricula.
- Technological play, and its possible benefits and problems, are of increasing interest to parents, educators and researchers.
- There is an increasing realisation that lack of play causes physical and psychological problems and that play therapy can help children with such problems.

Recommended reading

Brock, A., Jarvis, P. and Olusoga, Y. (Eds.) (2013) *Perspectives on Play: Learning for life,* 2nd edition. Abingdon: Routledge.

Moyles, J. (Ed.) (2015) *The Excellence of Play,* 4th edition. Maidenhead: McGraw-Hill Education.

Wood, E. (2013) *Play, Learning and the Early Childhood Curriculum,* 3rd edition. London: Sage.

References

Axline, V. (1990) *Dibs: In search of self.* Harmondsworth: Penguin.

Bachmann, C.J., Wijlaars, L.P., Kalverdijk, L.J., Burcu, M., Glaeske, G., Schuiling-Veninga, C.C., Hoffmann, F., Aagaard, L. and Zito, J.M. (2017) Trends in ADHD Medication Use in Children and Adolescents in Five Western Countries, 2005–2012. *European Neuropsychopharmacology,* **26**(3), pp.411–419.

BAPT (2016) About BAPT. [Online]. www.bapt.info/bapt/ (Accessed 11 July 2016).

Brock, A., Dodds, S., Jarvis, P. and Olusoga, Y. (2009) *Perspectives on Play: Learning for life,* 1st edition. Harlow: Pearson Education.

Bronfenbrenner, U. and Ceci, S.J. (1994) Nature-nurture Reconceptualised in Developmental Perspective: A bio-ecological model. *Psychological Review,* **101**(4), pp.568–586.

Brown, F. (2012) The Play Behaviours of Roma Children in Transylvania. *International Journal of Play,* **1**(1), pp.64–74.

DfE (2013) The National Curriculum in England: Key stages 1 and 2 framework document. [Online]. https://www.gov.uk/government/uploads/system/uploads/attachment_data/file/425601/PRIMARY_national_curriculum.pdf (accessed 3 July 2016).

DfE (2014) Statutory Framework for the Early Years Foundation Stage. [Online]. www.foundationyears.org.uk/files/2014/07/EYFS_framework_from_1_September_2014__with_clarification_note.pdf (accessed 3 July 2016).

Gove, M. (2013) Michael Gove Speaks about the Importance of Teaching. [Online]. https://www.gov.uk/government/speeches/michael-gove-speaks-about-the-importance-of-teaching (accessed 27 July 2016).

Gray, P. (2009) Play as a Foundation for Hunter-Gatherer Social Existence. *American Journal of Play,* **1**(4), pp.476–522.

Hall, N. and Abbott, L. (1991) *Play in the Primary Curriculum.* London: Hodder and Stoughton.

Hughes, B. (2002) *A Playworker's Taxonomy of Play Types,* 2nd edition. Ely: PlayEducation.

Hughes, B. (2003) Play Deprivation, Play Bias and Playwork Practice. In F. Brown (Ed.), *Playwork: Theory and practice.* Buckingham: Open University Press.

McPake, J. and Plowman, L. (2010) At Home with the Future: Influences on young children's early experiences with digital technology. In N. Yelland (Ed.), *Contemporary Perspectives on Early Childhood Education.* Maidenhead: McGraw-Hill Education.

Maynard, T. and Powell, S. (2014). *An Introduction to Early Childhood Studies,* 3rd edition. London: Sage.

Moyles, J. (ed.) (2015) *The Excellence of Play,* 4th edition. Maidenhead: McGraw-Hill Education.

Neumann, M. and Neumann, D. (2014) Touch Screen Tablets and Emerging Literacy. *Early Childhood Education Journal,* **42**(4), pp.231–239.

Ofsted (2015) Teaching and Play in the Early Years: A balancing act? [Online]. https://www.gov.uk/government/publications/teaching-and-play-in-the-early-years-a-balancing-act (accessed 10 July 2016).

Palaiologou, I. (2016) Children under Five and Digital Technologies: Implications for early years pedagogy. *European Early Childhood Education Research Journal,* **24**(1), pp.5–24.

Palmer, S. (2007) *Toxic Childhood: How the modern world is damaging our children and what we can do about it.* London: Orion Books.

Panksepp, J. (2008) Play, ADHD, and the Construction of the Social Brain: Should the first class each day be recess? *American Journal of Play,* **1**(1), pp.55–79.

Parten, M.B. (1932) Social Participation among Pre-school Children. *Journal of Abnormal and Social Psychology,* **27**(3), pp.243–269.

Pellegrini, A.D. (1991) *Applied Child Study.* Hillsdale, NJ: Lawrence Erlbaum.

Piaget, J. (1962) *Play, Dreams and Imitation in Childhood.* New York: Norton.

Play England (2016) Why Play is Important. [Online]. www.playengland.org.uk/about-us/why-play-is-important/ (accessed 28 July 2016).

Play Wales (2003) Play Deprivation. [Online]. www.playwales.org.uk/login/uploaded/documents/INFORMATION%20SHEETS/play%20deprivation.pdf (accessed 8 July 2016).

Play Wales (2013) Play Deprivation: Impact, consequences and the potential of playwork. [Online]. www.playwales.org.uk/login/uploaded/documents/INFORMATION%20SHEETS/play%20deprivation%20impact%20consequences%20and%20potential%20of%20playwork.pdf (accessed 8 July 2016).

Postman, N. (1994) *The Disappearance of Childhood.* New York: Random House.

Prensky, M. (2001) Digital Natives, Digital Immigrants. [Online]. www.marcprensky.com/writing/Prensky%20-%20Digital%20Natives,%20Digital%20Immigrants%20-%20Part1.pdf (accessed 11 August 2016).

PTUK (2016) [Online]. www.playtherapy.org.uk (accessed 11 August 2016).

Reed, T. and Brown, M. (2000) The Expression of Care in Rough and Tumble Play of Boys. *Journal of Research in Child Education,* **15**(1), pp.104–116.

Ryan, D. (2016) Using Tablet Technology for Personalised Learning. *Journal of Research in Special Educational Needs,* **16**(S1), pp.1071–1077.

Sylva, K., Melhuish, E., Sammons, P., Siraj-Blachford, I. and Taggart, B. (2004) The Effective Provision of Preschool Education (EPPE) Project: Final report. [Online]. http://eprints.ioe.ac.uk/5309/1/sylva2004EPPEfinal.pdf (accessed 5 July 2016).

UNICEF (2007) Child Poverty in Perspective: An overview of child well-being in rich countries. [Online]. https://www.unicef-irc.org/publications/pdf/rc7_eng.pdf (accessed 14 July 2016).

UNICEF (2011) Child Well-being in the UK, Spain and Sweden: The role of inequality and materialism. [Online]. https://www.unicef.org.uk/publications/ipsos-mori-child-well-being/ (accessed 14 July 2016).

Vygotsky, L.S. (1978) *Mind in Society: The development of higher psychological processes.* Cambridge, MA: Harvard University Press.

Vygotsky, L.S. (1987) *The Collected Works of L.S. Vygotsky.* Vol. 1: *Problems of General Psychology.* New York: Plenum Press.

Wainwright, N., Goodway, J., Whitehed, M., Williams, A. and Kirk, D. (2016) The Foundation Phase in Wales: a play-based curriculum that supports the development of physical literacy. *Education 3-13,* **44**(5), pp.513–524.

Wood, E. (2010) Developing Integrated Pedagogical Approaches to Play and Learning. In P. Broadhead, J. Howard and E. Wood (Eds.), *Play and Learning in the Early Years.* London: Sage.

Wood, E. and Attfield, J. (2005) *Play, Learning and the Early Childhood Curriculum,* 2nd edition. London: Paul Chapman.

Youell, B. (2008) The Importance of Play and Playfulness. *European Journal of Psychotherapy and Counselling,* **10**(2), pp.121–129.

4 The complexities of childhood resilience

Zeta Brown and Jayne Daly

Introduction

Have you ever asked yourself why some individuals continue to fight on through life in the face of adversity? Why they continue to develop and succeed no matter what life throws at them? What are their hidden inner strengths? Why are they so *resilient?*

In 2006 Palmer first revealed in detail how children are exposed to the world of 'toxins' from environmental influences on a day-to-day basis in the modern world. More recently, Field (2010) reported that we must do something about preventing children living in poverty from becoming adults in poverty. Each author develops a robust argument about the deficit model of childhood. However, we suggest that there are children, young people and adults who, no matter what life throws at them, have some kind of 'superpower' in overcoming the challenges of life. These might be financial burdens on families, lack of access to quality education, disability, family illness, addiction, prejudice or bereavement. For some individuals these disadvantages only seem to develop their resilience and encourage them to seek to change the course of life for themselves.

More than three decades before Palmer's and Field's work there were examples of children living in post-war Britain who had other challenges to deal with. Healthcare and the National Health Service (NHS) was in its infancy and family support was not prevalent; there was no joined-up thinking in terms of care, education, social policy, equality and culture. Children were falling through the gaps in the system; there was not the child-centred model we have today (Siraj-Blatchford, 2007). Yet despite this 'doom and gloom' many children went on to avoid the negative environmental influences of their past and develop into successful and happy young people and adults with limited intervention from the state. In current family, community and educational practice there is a lot of emphasis rightly placed on supporting children and their families. However, this chapter critically questions whether we recognise children's resilience and their capacity to overcome adversity and disadvantage.

We ask: What does human resilience mean? Does it exist in childhood, adolescence and adulthood in terms of an inbuilt mechanism that supports the individual independently to overcome adversity? Can resilience be taught through education and schooling?

Defining resilience

Individual/group task

Reflective question: before you read on, consider your definition of resilience. What does resilience mean to you?

The term 'resilience' is complex and multifaceted. Masten (2014) notes that a simple definition of resilience is not possible and maintains there is not one all-encompassing definition. According to Luthar *et al.* (2000:543), whilst it is complex, resilience refers to:

> a dynamic process encompassing positive adaptations within the context of significant adversity. Implicit within this notion are two critical conditions: (1) exposure to significant threat or severe adversity; and (2) the achievement of positive adaptation despite major assaults on the developmental process.

Similarly, Southwick *et al.* (2014:2) define resilience in the main as 'the ability to bend, but not break, bounce back and perhaps even grow in the face of adverse life experience'. In citing Luthar and colleagues' work, Cefai (2008) states the common thread in most definitions are competence and success in conditions of adversity and disadvantage. In reviewing these definitions it would appear that there is consistency in defining resilience. However, to add to the complexity there are also no clear measures to determine what is meant by adversity and disadvantage in this context, or how well an individual needs to achieve to be considered resilient.

In the literature many question why some people are able to cope against adversity (Southwick *et al.*, 2014). Personality factors of those who are deemed resilient include a proactive approach to problem-solving, positive social relationships including positive attention from family members, persistence and concentration, autonomy, independence and positive self-esteem and self-concept (Mayr and Ulich, 2009). There are links here to characteristics that could be perceived as inherited and/or influenced by individuals' families, communities and societies. Southwick *et al.* (2014:2) state that there is 'a host of biological, psychological, social and cultural factors that interact with one another to determine how one responds to stressful experiences'. In considering these links, we are able to reflect on Bronfenbrenner's bio-ecological model and relate his theory to the development of resilience. In Chapter 1 Rozsahegyi details the developments from Bronfenbrenner's ecological model to his bio-ecological model. She notes that Bronfenbrenner's theory focuses on the synergy of a range of influences, including biological, environmental and interpersonal. From the bio-ecological perspective the development of resilience is related (positively or negatively) to social connections that include the family, education, community and society.

Resilience: hereditary versus environmental

In the 1980s and 1990s both Rutter (1985) and Masten *et al.* (1990) searched for answers to why some youngsters develop into well-balanced, healthy adults despite harsh conditions or misfortune in their lives.

Rutter (1981) was one of the first researchers to note the phrase 'resilience' in his work, asking the question 'Why do children not succumb to deprivation or disadvantage?' He asked other questions too: for example, 'What is it about the children who rise above the tide of disadvantage? What are the protective factors? What are the ameliorating circumstances?' (208).

At that time these questions seemed a mystery that would not go away. Rutter tried to answer some of them in his early research, particularly in relation to family discord. He noted that children in families where parents are not present can be successfully and emotionally supported by an extended family who are prepared to foster a resilient, well-structured, disciplined home life and prevent the child from 'delinquency'. Rutter (1981) recognised that these were not clear answers to the questions he posed. As he pointed out, these were 'no more than a few scattered pointers' (214). He recognised the stability and balance that these children were experiencing in their extended families, but could not predict how they would fare later on in life.

In 2014 Masten recognised from her research that early, close, supportive relationships with others can help a child overcome challenges, and that close cultural encouragement and guidance are beneficial to support resilience. The change from extended family to others in this resource is important as we are now experiencing the era of the postmodern family. This means that there is no longer an ideal nuclear family and instead differing family structures, including lone parents, gay couples as parents and adoptive families, are accepted in society. There is also an acceptance that supportive relationships can extend beyond the immediate family to relationships in other aspects of a child's life, including school. According to Southwick *et al.* (2014) supportive relationships give the child a 'sense of hope' (6) in the face of adversity, therefore supporting the child to overcome difficult situations.

Rogoff (2003) determined the commonalities we share as human beings and our biological and cultural heritage. She argues that, whilst we share some similar traits, there are variations in our make-up because of the differences in our biological and cultural positions. This can have an impact on our strengths and perceptions as an individual. She suggests that as babies we are born with 'patterns of action, preferences and biases in learning based on individual and species-wide genes and prenatal experience' (2003:65). The kind of community we are born into will determine how we develop as human beings. Rogoff also interestingly posits that caregivers have an important role to play as they adjust the child's social world which welcomes them into a carefully constructed cultural intervention and evolution of their own, based on their own experiences. Whilst this seems an idealised view, more recently Furedi (2008) expressed concerns about the distrust of extended family and community and the destruction of adult cohesion when it came to supporting child progress. There is a worry here, as Palmer (2006) had also recognised, that society may be 'physically containing the next generation of children' (Wright, 2015:155).

Individual/group reflective task

Consider Rogoff's point about supporting the next generation to be strong and resilient. If families no longer work together as a community as Furedi points out, what may be the impact on the strength of character and resilience of the next generation?

Do you think children can be resilient? Can they accomplish resilience on their own, or do they need the support of parents or carers, extended family, communities and society?

Can children be resilient?

Given the links identified between the child, family and society, societal perceptions of childhood are likely to influence the perceptions of parents, carers, communities and the experiences of children. Our perception of childhood is also linked to our own experiences of childhood, with our families, communities and society. However, as James and Prout (2015) suggest, childhood can be seen as a social construction that changes over time. This social construction is likely to also influence our current perception of what terms such as 'childhood' mean, what children are capable of doing and what they should be experiencing. France (2007:23) argues that 'politics has always had a major influence in shaping and reflecting core values and assumptions about the social landscape around us'. The current social construction of childhood defines children as vulnerable, with the concomitant need for adults to protect and make decisions for them (Alderson, 2008). Lancaster and Lansdown (2001:40) state 'this welfare model of adult/child relationships constructs the child as a passive recipient of adult protection and good will, lacking the competence to exercise responsibility for his or her own life'. The social construction of youth differs from childhood and can be associated with danger and threat, linking young people to anti-social behaviour and promoting fear and anxiety (France, 2007).

James and Prout (2015) explain that often it is more correct to consider 'childhoods' rather than generalising all children's experiences into the category 'childhood'. This is because social constructions can vary cross-culturally and differ depending on individual perception. James and Prout cite Frones (1993:xiv) who states 'there is not one childhood, but many, formed at the intersection of different cultural, social and economic systems, natural and man-made physical environments. Different positions in society produce different experiences'. For instance, some children will experience adults who believe that they are social agents in their own lives. Mayall *et al.* (1996:207) argue that 'children are regarded as social actors, who aim to order their own lives in interaction with adults. But they are a minority group who lack power to influence the quality of their lives'. This perspective of children links to the rights-based model, focusing on children having the competency to be social actors. This perception of childhood differs from children being seen as vulnerable, innocent and in need of protection. Individuals who perceive children as social actors are likely to provide them with opportunities to make decisions and are likely to believe that children are capable of resilience.

Examples of childhood resilience

Individual/group task

Reflect on your concept of childhood. Do you believe children are social actors? Where do you believe your perceptions originate from?

This section of the chapter reviews the literature and research showing the complex ways children can be resilient by acknowledging the diversity of experiences in childhood. Mayr and Ulich (2009) provide a list of longitudinal studies that have found that children who have experienced high-risk adversity can show resilience and develop positively and successfully into adulthood. If you search for articles on resilience in childhood, there are examples of resilience that portray a wide variety of experiences. They include individualised case-specific experiences: for instance, children who have experienced abuse and neglect, illness, bereavement and trauma. It is important to note that the adversity children experience may not be apparent to all and may only be known by the child's immediate family, friends and possibly local community members, such as a teacher. Examples of such adverse circumstances may include the educational experiences of children. The following case study provides a detailed example of a real-life scenario. For confidentiality purposes it has been anonymised.

Case study 1: Joseph's story

Joseph is an only child, a happy teenager and he enjoys school. His teachers notice he has a tight network of friends and a particularly close relationship with his mother and father. Joseph's mother has been recently diagnosed with multiple sclerosis and his father is her full-time carer. Joseph's extended family is limited, but his mother's sister (his aunt) helps out where she can.

It won't be long now before Joseph needs to sit his GCSE exams. Suddenly his teachers notice there is a marked change in his behaviour. He is much quieter than normal and seems to distance himself from his friends. One of the teachers asks Joseph to stay behind after school to discuss this. She learns that his father has just been diagnosed with terminal cancer and has only months to live. Joseph has been helping his mother whilst his father has been attending hospital for treatment, but now his father has discharged himself to support Joseph as best he can. He tells Joseph he is the 'man of the house' now and prepares him for the worst.

Individual/group task

This is a really traumatic time for Joseph. Given his circumstances, what would you expect to happen to Joseph? How might his education suffer?

Whom might Joseph turn to for support in helping him to build resilience in this time of adversity?

Joseph's story (continued)

So what did happen to Joseph?

Joseph's father unfortunately passed away, but the request that his father left him with was that he needed to be strong as he was the 'man of the house'. With this in mind Joseph went on to complete his exams (all A grades). His mother was now cared for by his aunt when Joseph was at school, but Joseph took on his 'fatherly role' within the household at all other times. Joseph left school and went on to study business at college and then university. He and his mother remained close until her death when Joseph was in his 20s.

Today Joseph is a happy, extremely well-educated and successful self-employed businessman with a family.

Individual/group reflection

Do you think that Joseph's parents (particularly his father) had an influence on his ability to be resilient? It would be easy to say 'yes' here but reflect upon who would support Joseph in adulthood (once his mother and father had both died) to go on to be so successful in his education and his career.

Examples of resilience often place importance on the child's supportive relationships, which mirror the experiences Joseph had with his mother and father. Bronfenbrenner (see Chapter 1) concluded that these types of interpersonal relationships were more important than environmental contexts (Bronfenbrenner and Evans, 2000). He concluded that if these interfaces were under-applied then children are unable to fulfil their full potential. For example, Orbuch et al. (2005:171) discuss the importance of parent–child links for childhood cancer survivors and focus on the resilience of families. In citing relevant research, they state:

> We argue that when children report having supportive and open relationships with their parents, they also report positive coping and recovery even under distressing circumstances. This argument is consistent with scholars ... who proposed that parent-child relationships that are warm and supportive allow children to develop positive self-esteem and increased social competence and life satisfaction. The quality of parent-child relationships might be especially important for children when they are experiencing a stressful life event, such as a serious and chronic illness.

There are some adverse circumstances, such as serious and chronic illness, that are experienced by many children. It can be surmised that some children are likely to be developing and demonstrating resilience in a diverse range of adverse experiences. For instance, the experiences of looked-after children, children with special educational needs (SEN), children living in poverty and children who are asylum seekers. Given the current war-torn circumstances in countries such as Syria we have included next a case study on refugee children and childhood resilience for you to consider.

Case study 2: Amira's story

Amira is a 10-year-old girl who, until two years ago, was living happily with her family in a small Syrian village. The family were well-liked in the community and there were many close contacts. Amira's family were farmers and she loves animals, but now this is all gone. War has meant that Amira witnessed her father's and her grandfather's murder at the farm as they protected their livestock and home. The farm and animals were destroyed.

   The rest of the family, which included Amira's mother, grandmother and her six-year-old brother, set up home in a derelict former school. Food was scarce and the family lived mainly on whatever they could forage or beg. Bellies were no longer full as they had been in the old days.

Amira's mother decided that things were now becoming too dangerous, so Amira and her brother were sent on the long and arduous journey to reach the safety of Europe. Her mother, however, would not be going as she needed to stay behind to care for Amira's ailing grandmother.

Amira's and her brother's journey was long and traumatic. During their journey they had seen people they had been travelling with die of disease, malnutrition, dehydration, drown and even be shot.

Amira steadfastly protected her brother and together they arrived in Europe. She knew nothing of the new culture and could not speak the language. Amira has lost contact with her mother and grandmother and does not know if they are still alive.

Individual/group task

Consider Amira's and her brother's situation and the many traumas that they have faced in their short lives. How could their host country offer them support in overcoming these terrible experiences? How do you think it is possible for Amira and her brother to demonstrate such resilience?

Individual/group task

The case study examples do not present an exhaustive list. Can you think of other individualised and collective experiences where children may demonstrate resilience?

Resilience in education

Southwick *et al.* (2014) comment that resilience is a process in 'harnessing resources in order to sustain well-being' in the form of structural resilience 'to support fullest human potential' (7). This, they suggest, may include good-quality education, healthcare and financial security. In this chapter we have discussed the social construction of childhood and its present association with vulnerability and the need for adults to protect and make decisions for children. Mainstream education can be said to be an example of such decision-making by adults, where the focus is on safeguarding and providing a good-quality education to all. However, it can also be surmised that children can experience adversity during their education and that they may need resilience to effectively progress through the system. In the UK we have a standards-driven system that includes a national curriculum taught to all mainstream educated children, with national assessment such as Statutory Assessment Tests (SATs) and GCSEs. At present, we cannot say that all children achieve in our nationalised system and that all children are ready, willing and able to achieve in its national assessment (Brown and Manktelow, 2016). This may lead to children experiencing adversity.

Wang *et al.* (2015:368) concluded within their study that 'assets and resources' are needed in order to support resilience if the notion is true that resilience can be truly curriculum-based and taught as a positive and preventative educational tool. It is important to note that the need to develop resilience in children has been considered in education for some time. The *Every Child Matters* agenda introduced by the New Labour government of 2001 stressed to schools their duty to promote and support pupils' well-being and there was increased concern about children's health, behaviour and academic attainment. In 2007, three local authorities, South Tyneside, Manchester and Hertfordshire, responded to this and piloted the UK Resilience Programme (UKRP) – and more schools taught the programme after 2007. The programme used the Penn Resiliency Program (PRP) curriculum developed by psychologists at the University of Pennsylvania. The original aim of this programme was to reduce adolescent depression. However, it was broadened to include 'building resilience and promoting realistic thinking, adoptive coping skills and social problem-solving in children' (Challen *et al.*, 2011:8). The programme was used to support year 7 pupils and originally twenty-two secondary schools across the UK carried out the staff facilitator-led workshops. Professionals including teachers, teaching assistants (TAs) and learning mentors were trained to be facilitators. The programme included encouraging participants to challenge (unrealistic) negative beliefs, to use effective coping mechanisms in adversity, and taught techniques including positive social behaviour, assertiveness and decision-making.

The study concluded that pupils reported a greater understanding of what resilience was and their responses to questions about the study were linked to how they had encountered day-to-day problems and conflict, and dealt with them. By 2009/10 some schools were continuing to deliver UKRP whilst others had to abandon the project for various reasons. This was widely due to staffing levels and staff stress as children divulged the real-life problems they were facing. The evaluation of the project also noted that the impact of the programme on pupils' depression scores, school attendance and grades was short-lived and it was recommended that the programme would need to be longer for more lasting results. Whilst overall this project showed success in terms of an increase in pupil well-being, particularly in relation to mental health, there was also the issue that the project had a negative impact on staff and children alike due to its sensitive nature (Challen *et al.*, 2011).

Nevertheless, Cefai (2008:21) noted the benefits of an increased recognition of resilience in education. She said:

> [the resilience perspective] shifted the focus from deficit and disadvantage to growth and strength development. It asks 'what makes children in difficulty achieve and be successful?' rather than 'what prevents children in difficulty from succeeding?' Through the study of children and young people who managed to strive and be successful at school despite negative circumstances in their lives, the resilience perspective has led to a reconsideration of the ways in which schools can foster success in children and young people. It suggested that we may be more effective in supporting children's and young people's development and well-being by focusing on their strengths rather than their weaknesses.

In 2012, the All-Party Parliamentary Group (APPG) published a report on social mobility and sought to investigate why some children achieve while others never reach their full potential. They wanted to find out what could be done to help children succeed in life, regardless of the circumstances of their birth. The report concluded that 'personal resilience and emotional well-being are the missing link to the chain' (Paterson *et al.*, 2014:10). They state in this report that social and emotional skills (known as 'soft skills') should underpin academic skills ('hard skills') and state that skills such as resilience can be taught. In the report Baroness Claire Tyler states that character and resilience are 'about having the fundamental drive, tenacity and perseverance needed to make the most of opportunities and to succeed whatever obstacles life puts in your way' (6). The report linked the development of these 'soft skills' to success in the workplace. In doing so, its recommendations focused on the development of character and resilience from the early years to the transition into the workplace. These recommendations included:

- The development of the Early Years Pupils Premium
- Developing a robust school readiness measure at reception that includes character and resilience
- Incorporating character resilience into Initial Teacher Training (ITT) and Continuing Professional Development (CPD) programmes
- Extra-curricular activities should be a formal part of teachers' employment contracts
- Supporting the development of a best practice toolkit for interventions that aid character and resilience in conjunction with the Pupil Premium
- Encouraging the growth of the National Citizenship Service and establishing a recognised National Volunteering Award Scheme
- Seizing the opportunity of the rise in the education participation age to re-engage the most disengaged 16- and 17-year-olds by providing character and resilience programmes. (8–9)

In 2015 the Department for Education set up a new monetary award scheme for schools to bid for funding to develop excellent character education programmes. This was in response to criticisms from business leaders that school leavers were not prepared with 'soft skills' for work. Secretary of State Nicky Morgan said, 'the new character awards will help give schools and organisations the tools and support they need to ensure they develop well-rounded pupils ready to go on to an apprenticeship, university or the world of work' (Gurney-Read, 2015:1). Moreover, in 2016, the white paper *Educational Excellence Everywhere* set out plans for the next five years in education. Links to resilience are explicit, including a section specifically on building character and resilience in every child. The paper states:

> A 21st century education should prepare children for adult life by instilling the character traits and fundamental British values that will help them succeed: being resilient and knowing how to persevere, how to bounce back if faced with failure, and how to collaborate with others at work and in their private lives … These traits not only open doors to employment and social opportunities but underpin academic success, happiness and well-being. (DfE, 2016:94–95)

The paper notes resilience activities that can be seen in many state schools, including activities in sport, art and the Duke of Edinburgh Award, and advocates increased partnerships between local and national businesses and voluntary and sports organisations. Importantly, it proposes an increase in funding to £1bn over the next four years, so that by 2021 60 per cent of all 16-year-olds can access the National Citizenship Service programme, making it the largest programme in Europe. The paper refers to this programme as 'life-changing' and explains that it includes adventure challenges and staying away in university-style accommodation. The paper also details the new Educate Against Hate website that provides practical advice to parents, teachers and school leaders to protect children against extremism, radicalisation and to support building their resilience.

Individual/group task: discussion point

Consider the Joseph case study (no. 1) and reflect on your experiences in education. Do you believe you developed resilience during your early years, primary and/or secondary experiences?

Do you know of any examples of friends or family members who developed resilience during their experiences in education?

Conclusion: making links between the child, family and society

It is apparent in this chapter that resilience is a complex term that is used to refer to the ability some individuals have to bounce back in the face of multiple adversities. It is, therefore, understandable that there are many questions around what resilience means and how we can develop and support childhood resilience. Children can experience many forms of adversity, including abuse and neglect, childhood illness and bereavement and trauma. They may have adverse circumstances such as SEN, they may be looked-after, living in poverty or they may have experienced adversity generally in aspects of their life such as their education. What is certain is that children can be resilient, and for some children they have developed this skill without any support from their families, communities or society.

There has been an important shift in education and society (including the perspectives of business leaders) in acknowledging that resilience is an essential skill that can be taught to children. This has prompted more focus and funding in education on developing these 'soft skills' in order to effectively prepare all children for the world of work. Time will tell whether the provision and funding provided will support 'closing the gap' and successfully support children in succeeding in life, regardless of the circumstances of their birth. It therefore appears that here our findings will lead us back full circle to the yet-unsolved mysteries of resilience that Rutter and others had pondered.

Summary points

- Resilience is a complex and multifaceted term.
- Environmental factors are significant to the development of resilience.
- Children are capable of resilience and, given the opportunity, can be social agents in their own lives.
- Some children, in a diverse range of adverse experiences, are likely to develop and demonstrate resilience.
- There has been an important shift in education and society in acknowledging that resilience is an essential skill that should be taught to children. This skill is now linked to increased employment opportunities and academic success.

Recommended reading

Cefai, C. (2008) *Promoting Resilience in the Classroom. A guide to developing pupils' emotional and cognitive skills.* London: Jessica Kingsley.

DfE (2016) *Educational Excellence Everywhere.* London: DfE. [Online]. https://www.gov.uk/government/uploads/system/uploads/attachment_data/file/508447/Educational_Excellence_Everywhere.pdf (accessed 11 August 2016).

Luthar, S., Cicchetti, D. and Becker, B. (2000) The Construct of Resilience: a critical evaluation and guidelines for future work. *Child Development,* **71**(3), pp.543–562.

References

Alderson, P. (2008) *Young Children's Rights.* London: Jessica Kingsley.

Bronfenbrenner, U. and Evans, G. (2000) Developmental Science in the 21st Century: Emerging questions, theoretical models, research designs and empirical findings. *Social Development,* **9**(1), pp.115–125.

Brown, Z. and Manktelow, K. (2016) Perspectives on the Standards Agenda: Exploring the agenda's impact on primary teachers' professional identities. *Education 3-13,* **44**(1), pp.68–80.

Cefai, C. (2008) *Promoting Resilience in the Classroom. A guide to developing pupils' emotional and cognitive skills.* London: Jessica Kingsley.

Challen, A., Noden, P., West, A. and Machin, S. (2011) *UK Resilience Programme Evaluation: Final report.* London: DfE. [Online]. https://www.gov.uk/government/uploads/system/uploads/attachment_data/file/182419/DFE-RR097.pdf (accessed 11 August 2016).

DfE (2016) *Educational Excellence Everywhere.* London: DfE. [Online]. https://www.gov.uk/government/uploads/system/uploads/attachment_data/file/508447/Educational_Excellence_Everywhere.pdf (accessed 11 August 2016).

Field, F. (2010) *The Foundation Years: Preventing poor children becoming poor adults. The Report of the Independent Review on Poverty and Life Chances.* London: Crown HMSO.

France, A. (2007) *Understanding Youth in Late Modernity.* Maidenhead: Open University Press.

Furedi, F. (2008) *Paranoid Parenting,* 2nd edition. London: Continuum.

Gurney-Read, J. (2015) Lessons in 'Grit and Resilience' Recognised by New Award. *The Telegraph.* [Online]. www.telegraph.co.uk/education/educationnews/11330877/Lessons-in-grit-and-resilience-recognised-by-new-award.html (accessed 11 August 2016).

James, A. and Prout, A. (2015) *Constructing and Reconstructing Childhood: Contemporary issues in the sociological study of childhood.* Abingdon: Routledge.

Lancaster, P. and Lansdown, G. (2001) Promoting Children's Welfare by Respecting their Rights. In G. Pugh and B. Duffy (Eds.), *Contemporary Issues in the Early Years,* 3rd edition. London: Paul Chapman.

Luthar, S., Cicchetti, D. and Becker, B. (2000) The Construct of Resilience: a critical evaluation and guidelines for future work. *Child Development,* **71**(3), pp.543–562.

Masten, A.S., Best, K.M. and Garmezy, N. (1990) Resilience and Development: Contributions from the study of children who overcame adversity. *Development and Psychopathology,* **2**(4), pp.425–444.

Masten, A.S. (2014) *Ordinary Magic: Resilience in development.* New York: Guilford Press.

Mayall, B., Bendelow, G., Barker, S., Storey, P. and Veltman, M. (1996) *Children's Health in Primary Schools.* London: The Falmer Press.

Mayr, T. and Ulich, M. (2009) Social-emotional Well-being and Resilience of Children in Early Childhood Settings – PERIK: an empirically based observation scale for practitioners. **29**(1), pp.45–57.

Orbuch, T., Parry, C., Chester, M., Fritz, J. and Repetto, P. (2005) Parent-Child Relationships and Quality of Life: Resilience among childhood cancer survivors. *Family Relationships,* **54**(2), pp.171–183.

Palmer, S. (2006) *Toxic Childhood: How the modern world is damaging our children and what we can do about it.* London: Orion Books.

Paterson, C., Tyler, C. and Lexmond, J. (2014) Character and Resilience Manifesto. The All-Party Parliamentary Group on Social Mobility. [Online]. www.educationengland.org.uk/documents/pdfs/2014-appg-social-mobility.pdf (accessed 11 August 2016).

Rogoff, B. (2003) *The Cultural Nature of Human Development.* New York: Oxford University Press.

Rutter, M. (1981) *Maternal Deprivation Reassessed.* London: Penguin.

Rutter, M. (1985) Resilience in the Face of Adversity: Protective factors and resistance to psychiatric disorder. *British Journal of Psychiatry,* **147**(6), pp.598–611.

Siraj-Blatchford, I. (2007) The Case for Integrating Education with Care in the Early Years. In I. Siraj-Blatchford, K. Clarke and M. Needham (Eds.), *The Team around the Child*. Stoke on Trent: Trentham Books.

Southwick, S.M., Bonanno, G.A., Masten, A.S., Panter Brick, C. and Yehuda, R. (2014) Resilience Definitions, Theory, and Challenges: Interdisciplinary perspectives. *European Journal of Psychotraumatology*, **5**(1), pp.1–19.

Wang, J.L., Zhang, D.J. and Zimmerman, M.A. (2015) Resilience Theory and its Implications for Chinese Adolescence. *Psychological Reports*, **117**(2), pp.354–375.

Wright, H.R. (2015) *The Child in Society*. London: Sage.

5 Being mentally healthy

Children and young people navigating their mental well-being

John Thain and Dean-David Holyoake

Introduction

In this chapter we consider the wider aspects of children and young people's (CYP) mental health and well-being within the UK. Year on year there are increases in the incidence and prevalence of mental ill health amongst young people within the UK, reflecting many other countries (Belfer, 2008; McGorry *et al.*, 2013). Whilst this may in part be due to individual pathology, it has also been attributed to several factors including family dysfunction, poverty, abuse and neglect, parental substance misuse, school and study-related factors, bullying (particularly cyber-mediated) and peer pressure exacerbated by the young person's specific circumstance such as being in the Looked-After System. Young people increasingly report these factors; yet it is suggested that mental ill health in this group is under-reported, lacks wider recognition and lacks approaches which are joined up and reflect their lives. Responsive behaviours to mental stressors can be ignored, misinterpreted as 'naughty' or 'bad' or considered a reflection of inappropriate or poor parenting. Other behaviours such as self-harming or overdosing, clear responses to specific stressors, may similarly be considered as attention-seeking behaviours. These are clearly embedded within an ecological network which more broadly influences their development whilst at the same time impacting on their well-being, sometimes in deleterious ways. Whilst these impacts may be construed as resulting in passive responses, children's active agency in managing their lives is clearly of importance in their decisions to undertake specific behaviours. Ultimately CYP navigate their mental well-being through a range of insults/assaults, in relation to others and the professionals around them who have differing expectations and responses. Referring to Bronfenbrenner's work this chapter follows a discussion of the ways in which they navigate their responses and lives in order to cope and, for some, to survive. We consider how CYP are active agents in their unfolding lives as well as those disempowered in their attempts to be responded to. The chapter closes by considering responses of professionals and the wider community in recognising and responding to mental well-being in an ever-evolving society.

> **Individual/group task**
>
> Before you read this chapter, consider: What do young people's mental health and well-being mean to you?
>
> Referring to the discussion on Bronfenbrenner's ecological 'layers' in Chapter 1, identify the factors that might influence young people's mental health and well-being.
>
> After you have identified these factors draw some links between them, noting the ways in which being mentally well might be influenced by individual issues and equally impact on others.
>
> Referring to specific age groups, consider how their mental well-being is influenced by wider experiences (such as school), communities and perhaps time (that is, how society changes)?
>
> You might find this develops into quite a complex map of interactions and processes (similarly to Bronfenbrenner's bio-ecological model).

I'm sound, bro!

Your reading and completion of the preceding activities should have alerted you to a range of influences on mental well-being, and in particular those that might be considered crucial to the overall development of the young person. Your ideas probably included family, school, friends and relationships; yet as Rozsahegyi in Chapter 1 outlines, the network of connections are multiple, complex and crucial to the young person's development. Implicit within this is that the development and state of the young person's mental well-being are not just an individual issue but are greatly influenced through all those connections Bronfenbrenner alludes to. The complexity of society, rising populations and the ever-increasing pressures on young people certainly highlight the importance of context and connections for their mental well-being. Given these factors, some definitions of mental health and well-being are useful, not only in order to clarify what is meant, but also for effectively focusing service provision.

A broad definition of mental health from the World Health Organization (2004:10) proffers 'A state of wellbeing in which the individual realises his or her own abilities, can cope with the normal stresses of life, can work productively and fruitfully, and is able to make a contribution to his or her community'. In this chapter we also refer to mental well-being, a more recent term encompassing a range of issues including development, emotional health, mental health and links to wider states of mental ill health. Mental well-being can be defined as 'a dynamic state, in which the individual is able to develop their potential, work productively and creatively, build strong and positive relationships with others, and contribute to their community', whereby 'it is enhanced when an individual is able to fulfil their personal and social goals and achieve a sense of purpose in society' (Foresight Mental Capital and Well-being Project, 2008:10).

Added to the mix is a range of terms including 'emotional health', 'emotional well-being', 'psychological well-being' and 'subjective well-being' amongst many, all designed to focus on aspects of young people's lives. Many definitions are broad in order to encompass the scope of mental health and well-being for the wider population and in particular adults. Yet young people's lives are multifaceted, complex, emerging from and through their age, stage of development, status and places, calling into question the applicability of such definitions. Ongoing work by the Children's Society (2015) evidenced in the *Good Childhood Reports* provides more of a focused approach to understanding young people's subjective well-being. Similarly the development of KIDSCREEN (Ravens-Sieberer *et al.*, 2014) to measure a wide range of Quality of Life indicators based around young people's lives reflects a more ecological approach. We need though to be wary of those that, as Kendall-Taylor and Mikulak (2009:6) note, 'are quick to fall back on a more implicit understanding in which child mental health, practically speaking, is the absence of psychological disorders and pathology'. On the one side there is the focus on well-being; conversely the medical/ psychiatric model is still powerful in determining how we view mental health and how it is responded to.

Individual/group task

The National Institute for Health and Care Excellence (NICE, 2013) guideline on *Social and Emotional Wellbeing for Children and Young People* utilises three definitions:

1. Emotional well-being – this includes being happy and confident and not anxious or depressed.
2. Psychological well-being – this includes the ability to be autonomous, problem-solve, manage emotions, experience empathy, be resilient and attentive.
3. Social well-being – has good relationships with others and does not have behavioural problems, that is, they are not disruptive, violent or a bully.

How do these definitions relate to children's everyday lives? Do you think they reflect the systems in Bronfenbrenner's ecological model?

So what you going to do for me?

As we said earlier, the mental well-being of young people is an expanding sphere of interest; nonetheless, the way in which this has been both situated and addressed has been contested by policy-makers and professionals working in this arena. Whilst we are concerned here with a more contemporary take on well-being, and particularly so given recent policy changes (DoH, 2011; DoH/NHS England, 2015; PHE, 2015), it is apposite to consider where the issue of young people's mental health has 'fitted' and how this has been responded to historically.

   During the last century three broad processes occurred which are of relevance here. Firstly an increasing focus on the scientific study of childhood, in particular that of developmental psychology (Woodhead, 2013). Secondly the increasing medicalisation of many aspects of life (Conrad, 1992), and by this we refer to the ways in which non-medical issues are reconfigured as medical problems. Lastly, and linked into the latter point, is the influence of psychiatry and the similar categorisation and labelling of differing behaviours and conditions under an umbrella of mental illness. These processes have impacted on all ages, but none more so than for young people, exacerbated by the ways in which they were often deemed to be vulnerable, in need of support and protection. The dominant discourse of vulnerability related to childhood has influenced the way society views young people such that their capabilities were often underestimated and policy development has been concerned with protection and their best interests (from the adult perspective) – points raised in Chapter 2.

These changes and the accumulation of young people with mental health issues led in 1995 to the development of Child and Adolescent Mental Health Services (CAMHS), a tiered approach to service provision (Holyoake, 2015). The four tiers were conceived to ensure that professionals, young people and families could access services seamlessly and facilitate intervention for those with increasingly serious mental health issues. This led to an expansion of reactive services across the broad field of mental health dominated by healthcare and then in more of a piecemeal fashion provided by the education, private and voluntary sectors. Whilst several of these developments were welcome, it is evident the system is not meeting the needs of young people (McGorry *et al.*, 2013; Ashton, 2017), with the Health Select Committee finding 'serious and deeply ingrained problems' (House of Commons Health Committee, 2014) which are in turn exacerbated by recent funding changes (Docherty and Thornicroft, 2015) and the impact of austerity measures (Callaghan *et al.*, 2017). Some of these approaches are beneficial, though when taken across the board they represent specific interventions at specific points rather than being embedded in a life-course trajectory reflecting the multidimensional nature of children's lives, their local communities and wider society. On the whole we are better at identifying mental illness than the wider parameters of what constitutes mental health in CYP of all ages (Kvalsvig *et al.*, 2014). Relatedly we are better at treating individual and specific mental illnesses than responding to the wider context of where young people's actions and behaviours are situated, despite early models suggesting approaches which more reflect ecological and developmental perspectives (Hoagwood *et al.*, 1996).

Recent changes through the Health and Social Care Act (2012) in England (and similar legislation in the other three countries of the UK) have moved the responsibility for promoting well-being to local authorities, who in turn are undertaking joint strategic needs assessment (NHS England, 2015) of their local communities, leading to the development of systematic public health approaches based on the needs of young people rather than those of professionals. For a range of practitioners this potentially fits better with an ecological model that reflects developing lives, the context and mental well-being, whilst concurrently accommodating those young people in need of specialist services. This is in line with the UNCRC as a framework for developing policies to support health and well-being (UNICEF UK, 2015) as well as the *Five Year Forward View for Mental Health* (Mental Health Taskforce, 2016). Crucially it is an opportunity to fully involve young people who can in turn provide unique insights into policy and service provision (Bone *et al.*, 2015).

Individual/group task

You might need a large sheet of paper for this activity. Make a list of all the mental health issues you think young people might experience. The age range here is from newborn through to 18 years.

Highlight what services or support might be available for the issues you have identified.

Are there issues or groups which don't appear to have support or access to services?

Duh … I'm not mad you know!

Many hours by many professionals have been spent pondering on the mental health issues of young people; of these issues the most interesting and perhaps poignant are those shared from the young person's perspective. It was not too long ago when the professional expert was sought by young people and their parents to put things right, but many CAMHS have been quick to take up what could be considered in its own right a Bronfenbrenner perspective: that is, a systemic, joined-up and seamless ordering of mental health provision. To this end, the views of young service users are considered critical in the enhancement of improving specialist services. This section considers the ethos of collaboration and joint working to explore how, from a Bronfenbrenner standpoint, the range of CAMHS emerge young people's journeys through mental health.

To be blunt, the ideas of Bronfenbrenner could not be further from the thoughts of many current-day teenagers. In fact, the fancy-sounding words of macrosystem and mesosystem seem more akin to online gaming fraternities rather than to ongoing health needs or service provision. But, having said this, it is also possible to see how the feelings of individuality, identity, personhood and the associated 'growing up' feelings of confusion, self-loathing, guilt, anger, isolation, alienation, rejection and so on allow themselves to be easily positioned in the immediate as well as the extended systems impacting on modern living. Most of us would be shocked if Jim aged 14 were to suddenly start recognising that his ability to socialise at the macro or microsystems level was being seriously hindered by a lack of CAMHS provision, an out-of-touch GP or unforgiving parental attitude. Yet, these spheres are recognisable to most young people who make sense of their world through an increasingly chaotic, fluid, hectic and demanding sphere of the individual, with its immediate connections to mesosystems and the functional and fluctuating macrosystems.

Therefore, on examination, the site of mental health is a well-known one for most young people and their families. It is the site where good and bad things happen. The site where physical development both scares and excites, where social awareness takes root, where bullies land the threats and first punches, where Internet and cyber networking worm their way in, get filtered and made sense of. The site of the individual is to Bronfenbrenner the same as the sun is to the universe. It radiates the intrinsic sense of self that young people use to determine their appreciation of who they are and confirms a transient determination to become something, and become it quick. In developmental terms and as signified by all models of the Bronfenbrenner ilk, the purpose and outcome is a sense of personal identity – connected to others in the immediate geography, whilst all the time aware that beyond the boundary of the safe concentric rings there is a bigger, more macro world into which they will eventually have to forge.

The mental health provision of young people in the UK is, therefore, unreservedly based upon the ethical inspirations adopted from these types of developmental models, yet responsive symbolically at least to the fast-changing demands made of teenagers today. This in itself is to recognise the functioning and organic elasticity of Bronfenbrenner's ideals. Yet young people rarely appear to think rationally, and if they do their parents are likely to quickly put a stop to it. This is an age where life is taken day by day under constant pressures of being compared, achieving exam results, hearing the immediate as well as constant uncensored stream of opinion. We as professionals are now realising that the old order and sanctity of the self and its brother self-identity are under a constant barrage of imagined and seemingly fragmented illness diagnoses which have gravity-defying effects. To this end, we read more and more about the pressure of growing up in cyberspace, but this is a tad misleading because young people's perspective on mental health is dominated by notions of fitting in, avoiding bullying, being accepted and feeling at least a little bit attractive. These are no less concerns of every generation, but never before have issues of identity and the outcomes of self-harm, isolation, depression, drug use, eating disorders and issues of personality development been so strongly exemplified. The space between the public and the private as perfectly symbolised between the individual and the macro has never been so blurred as in today's climate. The Internet pipes the opinion of friends and others right into the bedroom of every child, a 'habitus' unknown to previous generations.

Age 5 to 12: the lightning speed of the macro, loss of the private and fragmenting selves

So what is the experience of mental health for the young preteen? More than ever this age group is exposed to changing expectations of what childhood is supposed to be and what it actually is. The young are imagined to enjoy a well-defined sense of childhood whilst bumping and grazing against the pixelated sharps of an increasingly sophisticated healthcare system. To put this idea into perspective we only need to ask ourselves how, even with more knowledge than ever, we find ourselves unable to keep pace with the increasing needs of many out-of-control toddlers, with educationally situated psychiatric diagnoses such as Asperger's syndrome, ADHD and Semantic Pragmatic Language Disorders. How come there is a growing acceptance that preteens are susceptible to a range of eating disorders, anxiety and suicidal thoughts at which our grandparents would baulk? Where has this increase in psychiatric classification come from and what are the implications for the needs of this age group?

The idea of systemic connectivity within models such as that of Bronfenbrenner is useful for considering how this age group changes at both the individual and societal levels. The shift from the individual to something more akin to the systemic represents an acknowledgement that not only is the knowledge base of parents, teachers and professionals expanding at a digital pace, but the ramifications for the experience of this age group are unknown. The recent work of Burton (2014) on CYPs' mental health notes that the initiation of initiatives such as Sure Start in 1998 was based on Bronfenbrenner's (1979, 1992) theories that development is a joint function of both the person and the environment. Her work suggests that Bronfenbrenner's bio-ecological model seeks to demonstrate how individuals relate to the environment and how cultural values and norms become played out in relationships. The role of the young individual changes depending on the layer of the model. As such, in this information age, the private experiences of young people and teenagers are far more public than ever before.

It could be said that information is the currency which defines this age. As such the specific healthcare issues to do with individual, micro and macro levels are informed quite readily. Rather than having to wait for professional validation and confirmation, families are now able to surmise and research everything for themselves. This information age has led to the expectation that 'to be' a parent requires training on things which, in the past, would have simply been considered natural. Parents are expected to act as involved confidants, consultants, carers, enforcers and so on by an ever growing pallet of professional groups. Not only is the individual becoming more porous, the macro is also expanding. Beyond the perfect child-rearing technique there is the suspicion that these ideas are still informed by foundational psychotherapeutic truths. So when a parent is instilled with shame over an unruly overstimulated child in an ever increasingly stimulating world and macro space they should be able to set limits, but do it firmly, with warmth, whilst believing the reasoning. These levels of insight are not the sole reserve of the parent or professional.

They are also at the forefront of, or at least somewhere in, the knowing of the child who responds to the stresses of parents from an early age. These ideas of didactic trauma point up that there is a belief that early emotional experiences remain the bedrock of what most consider to be the cause of later mental health issues in most adolescents. Thus the quality of care and attachment remains a primary consideration when exploring the perceptions of young people with regard to how they experience their preteen mental health. The role of the extended family brings to mind the role of social isolation, financial burden and the changed nature of the nuclear family of generations gone by. Add to this an increased level of academic expectation, more rigorous assessment and operant conditioning of socialisation in the digital age and we can see that CAMHS have inevitably changed beyond the complex needs defined by Marchant (2003) as 'complicated and compound'. The following represents the range of psychological interventions which transverse the individual into the realms of the macrosystem of young people's mental well-being:

- art therapy
- play therapy
- interpersonal counselling
- cognitive behavioural therapy
- mentoring.

Parenting interventions, and perhaps more tactical ones, as noted by Pavord and Burton (2014) are:

- animal-assisted therapy
- narrative therapy
- adventure-based therapy
- wilderness therapy.

The work of Geldard and Geldard (2008) offers a number of interpersonal interventions that all professional groups could utilise at the site of the individual. The key is about 'joining the child' and 'inviting and enabling them to tell their story'. Resolution is seen to come about through a mixture of trust, opportunities for learning and play, empowerment of the child or young person, enabling a space for change to occur and a working towards closure. At the macro level the family approach is about identifying processes and interactive patterns, giving feedback, raising awareness, modelling, advocating and referral advice.

Age 13 to 18: managing a porous contextual self against the backdrop of the macro

If the 5–12 age group is one of the individual, then the teenage years are those of the macrosystem. The deluge of the macro into the sanctity of the individual has for more and more signalled alarm for many professionals and parents and a warning for an era in which physical and material boundaries and explanations to mental health issues have blurred. The site of the individual has collapsed the old foundations of what constitutes psychiatry in CAMHS. The traditional illness models easily encapsulated broad diagnosis including depression, anxiety, eating disorders, self-harm, psychosis, obsessive compulsive disorder (OCD), developmental disorders and a range of domestic violence, welfare issues and abuse, as noted by Hester *et al.* (2007) and others (Radford *et al.*, 2011). Teenagers fitted into these categorisations and subsequent explanations as to the nature of their well-being were easily validated. These 13–18-year-olds used to present as a fringe of the mainstream population, and the services they required went largely unknown or unseen. The idea that young people got mentally ill was silenced by more pressing physical illness. Yet where we are now heralds a dawn of a new age for the individual and the surrounding macrosystems. As noted by Pavord and Burton (2014), UK CAMHS in 2008 were reviewed and recommendations issued to improve their ability to meet educational, health and social care needs. It was noted that services should become more accessible, responsive, child-centred and relationship-focused with the removal of unhelpful thresholds for referral criteria – an indication that the space between the individual and the macro is ripe for a new emergence.

In this new era the world of safeguarding, risk and diagnosis reflects this uncertainty. It represents the wider implications of a fragmenting multiverse. Young people are no longer a single diagnosis, but rather a complex mix of fuzziness constituting new labels which recognise how their experience of mental health is more dependent on the opinions of others than ever before. In the olden days the physical, genetic, developmental and biologically driven rationalizations would suffice in accounting for why young people felt and behaved the way they did. Yet, at the expense of this certainty the advent of cyber life has all but eradicated psychiatric homogeneity and replaced it with new types of understanding recognised by peers as what it means to be isolated, bedroom-bound, Warcraft-located and all things cyber social. Teenagers today do not have to imagine what it means to be without the physical contact of the macrosystems. They spend over a quarter of their life online. As a result their sense of self is determined by transient friendships maintained over long distances, at immense speeds and incalculable rates. They form a sense of self against a backdrop of emoticons, avatars and pouting selfies at frenzied moments twenty-four hours a day.

The days of riding home for tea and not seeing friends all weekend being long gone has had the effect of making the private more public and the need to present a managed self contextually intense. Teenagers have always been self-conscious, but their experience of mental health is more informed, more diverse and more socially located than at any other time. The idea of professional online referral as proposed by agencies such as Mindful (2013) finds many 11–17-year-olds more adept than the older professionals engaging them. Yet regardless of the accessing of services, being 13 to 18 today means there is no escape from a range of mental health difficulties, including potential victimisation by peers who in turn are susceptible to pressures unconceived by previous generations. If we were to ask the average teenager how they felt about exam pressures, attending school, getting a girlfriend, having spots and the everyday mundane life issues associated with this age group, they would probably shrug and acknowledge that the constant exposure to all things macro in their cyber reality has a poignant impact. Whereas previous generations had to be told they were ill, be professionally diagnosed and seek access to specialist services, young people today are information-savvy and connected in such manners as to rationalise their own experiences. Young people have a pretty good idea of what is happening to them and recognise that like never before the distinction between function and illness is just as much about psychological strategies as it is about pharmacological interventions.

Individual/group task

Referring to your ideas from the first activity in this chapter, discuss how young people are active and engaged in and around those factors identified. Are young people passive in what happens to their mental well-being and access to services, or are they actively controlling many elements, more so than adults recognise?

   Importantly, what might you do with this knowledge and thinking to support CYPs' mental health and well-being?

Conclusion

We have taken you through a journey of child and adolescent mental health in this chapter, introducing a range of debates about the juxtaposition of definitions versus the lives of young people. Those definitions are obviously important, not only in defining what we (often from that adult perspective) mean about something, but crucially in the way they invest power in the user (often healthcare) and in turn impact on interventions. From a historical perspective the enduring influence of medicine has decided what is healthy and unhealthy, leading to an ever-expanding list of diagnoses and conditions (Devitt and Thain, 2011).

   Conversely the lives of young people are more than just diagnoses; they are multifaceted, complex and fluid within the tangible as well as the more intangible technological spheres, all giving rise to the ways in which they navigate their well-being. It is fair to suggest that young people's views of their lives and well-being are probably more akin to Bronfenbrenner's bio-ecological model than those of many professionals, a point on which we would like to end as a precursor to the next chapter on parent partnerships.

Summary points

- Young people's mental health and well-being are complex aspects being located within and influenced by wide social networks.
- Definitions of mental well-being are broad and evolving, reflecting changes in policy and research.
- There is some contest between medical definitions of mental health and the wider approaches to well-being.
- Young people are often perceived as passive both in being mentally unwell and through professionals' responses.
- Changes in young people's networks and access to technology are having profound impacts on the ways in which they navigate their well-being.

Recommended reading

Burton, M., Pavord, E. and Williams, B. (2014) *An Introduction to Child and Adolescent Mental Health*. London: Sage.
Children's Society (2015) *The Good Childhood Report 2015*. London: Children's Society.

References

Ashton, J.R. (2017) Plans, Hopes and Ideas for Mental Health. *British Journal of Psychiatry Bulletin*, **41**(1), pp.3–6.
Belfer, M.L. (2008) Child and Adolescent Mental Disorders: the magnitude of the problem across the globe. *Journal of Child Psychology and Psychiatry*, **49**(3), pp.226–236.
Bone, C., O'Reilly, M., Karim, K. and Vostanis, P. (2015) 'They're not Witches. …' Young Children and their Parents' Perceptions and Experiences of Child and Adolescent Mental Health Services. *Child: Care, Health and Development*, **41**(3), pp.450–458.
Bronfenbrenner, U. (1979) *The Ecology of Human Development*. Cambridge, MA: Harvard University Press.
Bronfenbrenner, U. (1992) Ecological Systems Theory. In R. Vasta (Ed.), *Six Theories of Child Development: Revised formulations and current issues*. London: Jessica Kingsley.
Burton, M. (2014) Infant, Child and Adolescent Development. In M. Burton, E. Pavord and B. Williams, *An Introduction to Child and Adolescent Mental Health*. London: Sage.
Callaghan, J.E.M., Fellin, F.C. and Warner-Gale, F. (2017) A Critical Analysis of Child and Adolescent Mental Health Services Policy in England. *Clinical Child Psychology and Psychiatry*, **22**(1), pp.109–127.
Children's Society (2015) *The Good Childhood Report 2015*. London: Children's Society.
Conrad, P. (1992) Medicalization and Social Control. *Annual Review of Sociology*, **18**, pp.209–232.
Devitt, P. and Thain, J. (2011) *Children and Young People's Nursing Made Incredibly Easy*. London: Lippincott Williams and Wilkins.
Docherty, M. and Thornicroft, G. (2015) Specialist Mental Health Services in England in 2014: Overview of funding, access and levels of care. *International Journal of Mental Health Systems* 9:34. [Online]. http://link.springer.com/article/10.1186/s13033-015-0023-9 (Accessed 11 September 2016).
DoH (2011) *No Health Without Mental Health*. London: DoH.
DoH/NHS England (2015) *Future in Mind: Promoting, protecting and improving our children and young people's mental health and well-being*. London: DoH.
Foresight Mental Capital and Well-being Project (2008) *Final Project Report – Executive summary*. London: Government Office for Science.
Geldard, K. and Geldard, D. (2008) *Counselling Children: A practical introduction*, 3rd edition. London: Sage.
Health and Social Care Act 2012. [Act of Parliament]. London: HMSO.
Hester, M., Pearson, C., Harwin, N. and Abrahams, H. (2007) *Making an Impact: Children and domestic violence*. London: Jessica Kingsley.
Hoagwood, K., Jensen, P.S., Petti, T. and Burns, B.J. (1996) Outcomes of Mental Health Care for Children and Adolescents: a comprehensive conceptual model. *Journal of the American Academy of Child and Adolescent Psychiatry*, **35**(8), pp.1055–1063.
Holyoake, D.-D. (2015) Disservice to Children. *Nursing Standard*, **29**(19), pp.26–27.
House of Commons Health Committee (2014) *Children's and Adolescents' Mental Health and CAMHS. Third Report of Session 2014–15*. London: TSO.
Kendall-Taylor, N. and Mikulak, A. (2009). *Child Mental Health: a review of the scientific discourse*. Washington, DC: FrameWorks Institute.
Kvalsvig, A., O'Connor, M., Redmond, G. and Goldfeld, S. (2014) The Unknown Citizen: Epidemiological challenges in child mental health. *Journal of Epidemiology and Community Health*, **68**(10), pp.1004–1008.
McGorry, P., Bates, T. and Birchwood, M. (2013) Designing Youth Mental Health Services for the 21st Century: Examples from Australia, Ireland and the UK. *British Journal of Psychiatry*, **202**, pp.s30–s35.
Marchant, R. (2003) The Assessment of Children with Complex Needs. In J. Horwath (Ed.), *The Child's World*. London: Jessica Kingsley.
Mental Health Taskforce (2016) A Report from the Independent Mental Health Taskforce to the NHS in England 2016. [Online.] https://www.england.nhs.uk/wp-content/uploads/2016/02/Mental-Health-Taskforce-FYFV-final.pdf (accessed 11 September 2016).

Mindful (2013) [Online]. www.mindful.org (accessed 11 September 2016).

National Institute for Health and Care Excellence (NICE) (2013) *Social and Emotional Wellbeing for Children and Young People*. London: NICE.

NHS England (2015) *Guidance to Support the Development of Local Transformation Plans for Children and Young People's Mental Health and Wellbeing*. London: NHS England.

Pavord, E. and Burton, M. (2014) Interventions with Children and Young People and Families. In M. Burton, E. Pavord and B. Williams, *An Introduction to Child and Adolescent Mental Health*. London: Sage.

Public Health England (PHE) (2015) *Promoting Children and Young People's Emotional Health and Wellbeing: a whole school and college approach*. London: Public Health England.

Radford, L., Corral, S., Beadley, C., Fisher, H., Howat, N. and Collishaw, S. (2011) *Child Abuse and Neglect in the UK Today*. London: NSPCC.

Ravens-Sieberer, U., Herdman, M., Devine, J., Otto, C., Bullinger, M., Rose, M. and Klasen, F. (2014) The European KIDSCREEN Approach to Measure Quality of Life and Well-being in Children: Development, current application, and future advances. *Quality of Life Research*, **23**(3), pp.791–803.

UNICEF UK (2015) *United Nations Convention on the Rights of the Child*. London: UNICEF UK.

Woodhead, M. (2013) Childhood: A developmental approach. In M.J. Kehily (Ed.), *Understanding Childhood: a cross-disciplinary approach*. Bristol: Policy Press/Milton Keynes: The Open University.

World Health Organization (2004) *Promoting Mental Health: Concepts; emerging evidence; practice*. Geneva: WHO.

Section three

Contributing factors to a child's upbringing

6 Formation of partnerships
An ecological paradigm

Ioanna Palaiologou and Trevor Male

Introduction: partnerships and the English context

In England a central government strategy for parental involvement in their children's schooling was first introduced close to the end of the last century through the White Paper 'Excellence in Schools' (DfE, 1997) and embodied in the subsequent Act of Parliament, the School Standards and Framework Act (1998). There were three key aims within this policy initiative: parents were to be provided with information, to be given a voice and to be encouraged to form partnerships with their children's education settings. These partnerships were formalised within a 'Home-School Agreement' which specified the:

1   school's aims and values;
2   school's responsibilities;
3   parental responsibilities; and
4   school's expectations of its pupils.

The emphasis was clearly on the school being the dominant partner in this relationship with parents being required to sign a declaration that they had taken note of the school's aims, values and responsibilities and acknowledged and accepted their responsibilities in relation to the school's expectations of its pupils.

In 2003, the government commissioned a study to investigate the effects of such a strategy and it was found that the formation of effective partnerships can significantly improve children's achievements, their self-concept as learners and increase aspirations (Desforges and Abouchaar, 2003). Since then, working in partnership with parents has become an important running theme in policies and curricular reforms. In 2004, for example, as a part of reforms to ensure working effectively with parents, the government published funding proposals for childcare based on the recognition that parents have by far the biggest influence on children's lives and should be able to spend quality time with their children as part of 'the right work-life balance for them and their children' (HM Treasury, 2004:2). Similarly, the introduction in 2008 of a curriculum framework in England for early childhood, the Early Years Foundation Stage (EYFS), stressed that partnerships with parents/carers were essential to support children's well-being and development. A subsequent government-commissioned report, published in 2011, further emphasised the centrality of partnership to effective student learning, whilst also noting the 'agency of children' to be significant

(Goodall and Vorhaus, 2011:86). This report once again emphasised the difference between parental 'involvement' and 'engagement', as first suggested by Desforges and Abouchaar (2003), with the latter concept embracing more in the way of a proactive relationship with student learning. Perhaps more importantly the report also recognised how outcomes could be improved if children become more engaged in their learning as this was seen to encourage parents to do the same (and vice versa). This appears to be the first recognition in England of the importance of a triangular approach to partnership which not only sought involvement of the school and parents, but also acknowledged the child as an active learner and participant.

At about the same time, the national inspection service, Ofsted, published a report on the relationships between schools and parents based on evidence of visits to 47 schools to evaluate how effectively partnerships had developed. Here they found the Home–School Agreements required by the 1998 Act to be having a low profile by this time and their impact on the day-to-day work between parents and the schools to be very limited (Ofsted, 2011). In the best cases, however, they saw the joint working between the home and the school was leading to much better outcomes for pupils, and where parents had contributed or initiated ideas for strategic improvement these ideas had been taken forward successfully.

Education in England during the early part of this century can thus be judged to have been concerned with how effective collaboration and partnerships with parents could be formed and sustained. Parental engagement was judged to require active collaboration and should be 'proactive rather than reactive, sensitive to the circumstances of all families, recognise the contributions parents can make and aim to empower parents' (Goodall and Vorhaus, 2011:10). Whilst there was some recognition of the need to involve students as active participants in the collaborative structures and processes that were recommended for partnerships, this was still a muted call at this stage.

Individual/group task

Reflective question: before you read on, reflect on your work experience and discuss the relationships between staff in educational settings (managers, teachers, practitioners), children, parents and communities. What forms of communication do they use?

How do you rate their communication?

The evolving model of partnership

The dualistic and exclusive relationship between schools and students as learners can be seen to be being abandoned in terms of national policy initiatives, a pattern that can also be seen on the international stage, with a contemporaneous shift in perspective also being recognised within academic research. In addition to the changes in England previously highlighted, the notion of partnerships in education has been embraced and embedded in curricula and policy documents from around the world. The governments of Australia, New Zealand and Sweden, for example, have all endorsed the importance of home–education connections and the impact for children's well-being and achievements in their preschool curriculum documents (Australian Government Department of Education, Employment and Workplace Relations, 2009; New Zealand Ministry of

Education, 1996; Swedish Government, 2010). Similarly, academic research outcomes stress that parental involvement is essential for a successful learning community and learners' academic achievements (Wolfe, 2014). The conclusion drawn in a meta-review into whether parental involvement interventions increase attainment was that school-led interventions 'are most likely to succeed when they are aimed at young children, and involve parents and staff meeting regularly in an institution, with parental training, on-going support, and co-operative working with teachers' (Gorard and Huat See, 2013:4).

Much of the research focusing on partnerships has often been limited to an examination of the relationships between parents and formal education settings (e.g. Goodall, 2013; Miller *et al.*, 2014). In undertaking an analysis of 378 articles reporting research on partnerships published nationally (Australia) and internationally, Hughes and Mac Naughton (2000) found, for example, that the partnerships between families and schools and other education settings are dominated by the constant othering of parental knowledge by staff. By this they mean the implicit positioning by school-based staff to see people other than themselves as being of lesser importance in the development of student learning and enhanced outcomes. They categorise the 'othering' effect into three themes:

- Parental knowledge is inadequate: [Parents as actual or potential teachers]. Here, parents are seen as ignorant about what and how to teach their children and parent involvement programmes rectify this.
- Parental knowledge is supplementary: [Parents as collaborators]. Here, parents' knowledge of their child allegedly complements staff's professional knowledge, but in reality merely supplements it.
- Parental knowledge is unimportant: [Parents are absent]. Perhaps the simplest and most effective form of 'othering' – parents' voices are absent from much of the literature about parent involvement (242).

These findings seem to reflect those of a much earlier study which suggested that partnership is like the spokes on a wheel where parents were perceived in a variety of alternative ways: as an audience, as direct and active teachers of their children at home, as volunteers within and outside the classroom, serving as unpaid employees or as decision makers (Gordon, 1970). Since then others have examined the parental involvement paradigm and three models depicting parent roles were presented by Swap (1993):

- The Protective Model separates the functions of school and home with parents delegating and holding schools responsible for the education of their children.
- The School-to-Home Transmission Model holds parents accountable for supporting teachers in their efforts to educate children. Supportive activities are outlined by schools and include fundraising, reinforcing school expectations at home, supporting school parties and providing a home environment that nurtures school success.
- The Curriculum Enrichment Model supports the partnership approach to parent involvement, with parents and educators working together.

Since then many studies have examined the development of partnerships that were focused on parenting styles and their relationships with school (Goodall, 2013) and linking parental involvement with children's learning and school success (Goodall and Montgomery, 2014; Miller *et al.*, 2014). This paradigm is characterised as a 'binary relationship with an "other" i.e. "with something else that it is not"' (Hughes and Mac Naughton, 2000:242). In the context of formal educational settings this paradigm of partnership has thus tended to involve one-way communication when parents are provided with suggestions and expectations, are expected to behave in a way that is oriented by the school and to act according to the school's culture and criteria in sameness rather than valuing diversity (Christenson *et al.*, 2009). This way of partnership and indeed family participation is described as a 'top-down approach' (Ruddock *et al.*, 2000) which notably fails to address parental expectations, perceptions and priorities related to their involvement (Souto-Manning and Swick, 2006). Such an approach also fails to recognise educators adhering to the prevailing family involvement paradigm and impedes a full and valid view of the family as a partner.

Consequently, researchers turned their attention to the Empowerment Paradigm of Examining Partnerships, an approach which recognised and amplified the role that could be played by parents, families, children and significant others in terms of student learning and outcomes. Souto-Manning and Swick (2006) developed a six-element empowerment paradigm for parent and family involvement including practices that:

1   focus on family and child strengths;
2   include, validate and engage families;
3   recognise and value multiple forms of involvement;
4   provide lifelong learning for teachers, children and families;
5   build trust through collaboration; and
6   reflect linguistic and cultural appreciation, recognition and responsiveness.

Latterly research thus seems to be concerned with examining the benefits and barriers of effective partnerships in order to identify key characteristics and develop best practices (Christenson *et al.*, 2009; Goodall and Montgomery, 2014). Such research has focused on the examination of the influences that shape relationships between families, school and children and suggested that effective partnerships are actually best achieved through a triangle of relationships based on respect, listening to each other and active cooperation and participation (Thornton and Brunton, 2007). Outcomes from this body of research consistently recognise that effective partnerships include the child (Ruddock *et al.*, 2000; Souto-Manning and Swick, 2006), are consistent and reciprocal (Halgunseth *et al.*, 2009) and responsive to the 'language spoken by the family' (Halgunseth *et al.*, 2009:56). Consequently, for effective partnerships the requirements are shared decision-making, mutual respect, equality, dignity, trust and honesty, commitment by all parties, understanding each other's circumstances and open communication (Madsen, 2009).

This was confirmed in a later study which examined a family-centred practice model in the formation of partnerships in Australia and concluded that effective partnerships require staff in education to 'assist families to be empowered and respected decision makers' (Rouse, 2012:21). Rouse did acknowledge, however, that although empowerment is a key element of family-centred practice, 'not all [...] educators are equally positioned to empower families or, in fact, even demonstrate empowerment in some of the relationships they have with the families of children in their care' (22). Reviews of research and published literature commissioned by the UK government on the relationship between schools and parental involvement, support and family education, and the impacts of this on pupil achievement, had previously recognised similar conclusions, but had indicated a need to recognise a difference between 'parental involvement' and 'parental engagement'. One of the authors of such reviews later concluded that the process of partnership had been understood in a very narrow sense of 'parental involvement with children's schooling' rather than the more useful concept of 'parental engagement with children's learning' (Goodall, 2013:134). Parental involvement, Goodall suggested, is related to school-initiated activities which have as their focus parental interaction with the school rather than with the learning of the child, and is measured by parental presence rather than by student outcome or effect. Such activities may form part of the entire process of parental involvement in children's learning, she argued, but they are only a small section rather than the whole of the concept. The two UK government-commissioned reviews of research had made it clear that the greatest lever for children's achievement is parental *engagement* in their learning and the atmosphere towards learning in the home (Desforges and Abouchaar, 2003; Goodall and Vorhaus, 2011). What we are able to conclude, therefore, is that parental engagement with their children's learning is central when seeking to enhance attainment and achievement at all levels of their development. At all ages what matters are 'the overall attitude towards parenting and children, and the actions that then flow from that attitude, in combination with each other' (Goodall, 2013:137). Parental interest in terms of expectations, encouragement and support is vital, therefore, and this holds good regardless of race, ethnicity or socio-economic status throughout schooling (Catsambis, 2001).

Partnership is a term that since the early 1990s can thus be considered to have become 'imbued with a global sense of virtue' (Fullan and Hargreaves, 1992:63), with our examination of relevant research on the discourse of partnerships suggesting there are three dominant paradigms: firstly, the dualistic view of partnerships between parents/families and school; secondly, the triangular approach to partnerships that includes the school/educational setting, parents/family and children; and thirdly, the empowerment paradigm of partnership.

Individual/group task

Reflect on the following definition of partnership and discuss:

1. What might be effective ways of sharing information among all the stakeholders?
2. What might be effective ways of communicating among all the stakeholders?

We propose as a definition of partnerships those that aim to build a connected network where the nucleus is effective relationships between parents, community, school and students and where all participate in the creation of learning environments that are meaningful, diverse, responsive to the evolving demands of the society and actively engaged in the learning process (Male and Palaiologou, 2016).

Towards the empowerment of parents and families

In partnership paradigms the notion of 'sameness' or 'universality' of partnerships (thinking that all families are the same and should have the same expectations assumes all families or communities expect the same things from education) has been dominant and has failed to recognise difference, which endangers the potential for positive contributions that represent the diversity of relationships that communities and families can bring to the partnership (Keen, 2007; Rouse, 2012). Countering such approaches is central to the empowerment paradigm which offers a welcoming approach to the family, and notably parents, and to the incorporation of their voices in school life such as planning and evaluating their presence within the physical structure of the school (Christenson *et al.*, 2009). The consensus is that this paradigm had been overlooked, with partnerships with parents and family having been primarily managed by the school, which typically ignored the social positioning of the parents and the different socio-economic and educational levels of the families (Levine-Rasky, 2009; Graue and Sherfinski, 2011). Thus researchers added to the empowerment paradigm the notion of cultural capital (Bourdieu, 1986) to examine the different ways families engage with school life and their children's education (Graue and Sherfinski, 2011). Through the concept of cultural capital they sought to explain the formation of partnerships and 'its focus on how structures and institutions play a part in producing inequality in home–school relationships and children's academic success' (Miller *et al.*, 2014:331). The acknowledgement of the sociocultural context and the social positioning of parents thus led researchers to re-examine the roles within the development of partnerships and to recognise that:

> Every time parents and teachers encounter one another in the school setting, their conversations are shaped by their own autobiographical stories and by broader cultural and historical narratives that inform their identities, their values and their sense of place in the world.
>
> *(Lightfoot, 2003:3)*

Building upon this the work of Epstein (1995, 2001) shifted the discourse on partnerships and extended it into the development of partnerships from a critical perspective by describing six types of family/school/community interaction:

- parenting partnerships where the focus is on providing support to families to create home environments to support children as students;
- forms of communication for school to home and home to school;
- volunteering;
- information exchange between home and school so students can be supported in learning at home with homework;
- decision-making partnerships where parents are included; and
- partnerships with the community where resources and services from the community are integrated in the school life to support students' learning and development.

To sum up at this stage, although the concepts of parental engagement and parents' empowerment are illuminative and do illustrate their centrality in the development of student learning and outcomes, this is still only part of the picture, for which further discourse is needed. Key factors such as the environment still need to be factored into the process if partnerships are to be as effective as possible. Hence we considered an ecological paradigm to address some of these issues.

Individual/group task

Reflect on what you have read so far and consider the barriers to effective partnerships. From your experience so far in educational contexts, are there any families that might be at risk of being excluded from the school's outreach activities to parents? Why?

The discourse of partnerships: towards an ecological paradigm

Schools do not exist in a vacuum and have the potential to be shaped by local as well as wider societal influences, including national governments. It also needs to be acknowledged that schools are concerned with complex social phenomena that are multifactorial and multilayered in nature and which go beyond teaching and learning, and that there is a direct relationship of causality with environmental factors that impact on the way partnerships are formed. Relevant and contemporary literature focusing on the development and formation of partnerships indicates that collaboration between school and families should be based on communication, trust, acceptance and shared values and an appreciation of the difference and diversity of families and schools (Male and Palaiologou, 2016).

From our research, explained later in the detailed case study, we propose that the following elements should be recognised in effective partnerships.

Required elements in the formation of partnerships

- Shared values and beliefs so all can engage and participate in the creation of the learning environment. However, we do not propose that families and teachers should hold identical values and expectations, but that they should together set common values and expectations;
- A proximity/nearness meaning of community – parents and students to come physically together as often as possible;
- Willingness;
- Trust;
- Shared responsibility;
- Avoidance of blame culture;
- Avoidance of stereotypic views of people, events, conditions or actions;
- Avoidance of labelling culture;
- Aspirations;
- Resilience as the ability to adapt successfully to situation and circumstance;
- Commitment;
- Altruism;
- Empathy;
- Inclusion;

- Reciprocity;
- Complementarity of needs (cognitive, social, emotional).

As has been demonstrated, however, much of the discussion of partnerships has often been limited to parents and school and ignores how the community forms the values, beliefs and identities of parents and learners that influence the learning process. We argue, therefore, that the discussion on partnerships should start from the premise that families, learners, community and school should all be involved in the creation of learning environments and collaborate in meaningful ways to create educational experiences that will be beneficial to all involved in the process:

> Effective education settings are those which have developed productive and synergistic relationships between learners, families, the team and the community, because the context, the locality and the culture in which learners live are vitally important.
>
> *(Male and Palaiologou, 2012:112)*

The 'equitable dialogue between families and schools' (Miller *et al.*, 2014:341) thus needs to be extended beyond simple home–school connections and be approached from an ecological paradigm. It is important before we explain this to define what is meant by 'ecological paradigm'. Although the term paradigm is widely used in research and is related to the 'set of values and beliefs shared by a scientific society' (Ma, 2016:25), in our work it is used in that sense to describe any number of reciprocal relationships and activities that are shaped by efforts towards common goals whereby all stakeholders are equally engaged to form partnership as an interactive process. Although Bronfenbrenner's (1979, 2005) work on the bio-ecological paradigm (see Chapter 1 for a detailed explanation of his theory) highlights that families are influenced by their environment and this impacts on children's development and learning, we extend this to the impact of systems theory that underpins his theory. Jarvis (1998) stressed that systems exist when there are multilayered elements that are interacting. Through the lenses of systems theory social psychologists approached social phenomena and interacting social groups to consider them as a system. Applying this to partnerships between the school, the families and the community, the nature of the relationships indicates complexity, non-linearity and non-predictability which are influenced by a variety of interrelated and interwoven factors. Systems theory is not concerned with the construction of models that can be applied in all contexts. Instead, the focus is on entities and their complexities and supports the idea that systems are not fragmented (unlike models) and all interwoven factors that are involved in formation of partnerships are interacting in a continual manner. In that sense the specific context of partnerships determines a system of compartmentalised, context-specific relationships between the stakeholders which connects them as a whole and attempts to establish continuity in understanding the rituals and values of this context.

More specifically, in any environment values, beliefs and identities are formed and are inherent within families and children. Schools are also part of the environment and that means either they understand the sociocultural context, expectations and effective interactions with families because they are part of this, or they need to come to such an understanding in order to create a 'shared commitment and responsibility' between school, families, learners and communities (Giovacco-Johnson, 2009:128). In that sense partnerships should be approached from an ecological perspective where 'learning and development of children is essential in forming partnerships and where strengths, perceptions, and priorities can be seen as complementary rather than conflicting' (Giovacco-Johnson, 2009:128). This leads us to conclude that an ethical approach is required:

> that respects values and does not engage in any project that will only benefit the individual, but instead looks after the ecology of the community [for] the creation of learning environments in which the centrality of interactions and relationships among learners, teachers, family and community (i.e. their values, beliefs, culture, religion, customs and economic circumstances) interact with external elements (such as the global economy, climate and social phenomena that additionally influence the life of the community) in order to jointly construct knowledge.
>
> *(Male and Palaiologou, 2015:219)*

Thus we propose that partnerships should be approached from an ecological perspective that represents a way 'to read and corroborate the importance of developing good relationships' (Migliorini *et al.*, 2016:167). The ecological paradigm is concerned with the examination of partnership as a complex social phenomenon while taking into account multiple behaviours, multiple views, non-predictable actions and all key elements for effective relationships that are interrelated, interdependent and interconnected in a non-linear way. When partnerships are developed through the ecological paradigm they become a connected network where the nucleus is effective relationships between parents, community, school and students. It is an approach where all participate in the creation of learning environments that are meaningful, diverse, responsive to the evolving demands of the society and actively engaged in the learning process (Male and Palaiologou, 2016).

We argue that partnership is a complex phenomenon and a process, not an event. As such it requires an in-depth understanding of causality and processual aspects such as knowledge, skills, values and attitudes, and a holistic desire to share responsibilities of home and educational settings and communities which can lead to effective mutual actions that assist the learning environment.

Thus we propose that the study of partnerships requires an ecological ontology which seeks an in-depth investigation of the complexity of partnerships and there is the need for this approach to be:

> extended further to also include the community in order to form effective multi-modal relationships […] partnerships between communities, parents, students and schools need to be approached as a holistic dynamic where relationships are shaped as much by the local culture, values and ethos as well as external influences such as government agendas or policies.
>
> *(Male and Palaiologou, 2016:153)*

Case study: the typology of partnerships

In response to the preceding discussion we undertook research that aimed to approach the formation of partnerships from an ecological perspective and to:

1   explore the views of the relationships between staff in educational settings and children, parents and communities;
2   examine how these relationships are formed;
3   investigate how (if) partnerships are sustained.

This study employed qualitative methodology in twelve educational settings in England where we interviewed all stakeholders (families, children, people from the local community and school staff) and undertook content analysis of press cuttings that focused on the schools. We found that formation of partnerships depends on the conditions in which community, parents, school and students are interacting (social context, structures and organisation) and they are contingent on and depend on the way interactions are accomplished towards a common goal.

Using ecological lenses as explained earlier, data revealed that effective partnerships that are encouraging multimodal, multilayered and multi-factional communication between all stakeholders are the ones that are open to, and interact with, all stakeholders and are resulting in continual evolution rather than reducing them to the properties and values of the school only:

> It is not effective if we tell them (parents) what they must do, it is about understanding what they want as well and telling us [...] otherwise there is no point.
>
> *(Headteacher)*

Interviews with children, parents, community and staff of these settings revealed the influential factors that each stakeholder values when in communication with the educational setting.

Parents valued:

- Acceptance
- Understanding of their goals, cultural values, experiences
- Support.

The community valued:

- Safety
- Outreach activities
- Economic value for the locality
- Reputation.

Children valued:

- Involvement
- Presence of family
- Approachable staff
- Awareness/familiarity of family structures, norms, habits.

Staff valued:

- Willingness
- Cooperation
- Trust
- Communication
- Parental knowledge.

In the light of the interview data we concluded that the influential factors for effective partnerships are based on:

- ongoing communication and not only when there was a crisis or an issue;
- ongoing sharing of information;
- the flow of power and empowerment, meaning that all stakeholders believed that and enhanced the principle that *learning happens at home, in the community and at school*;
- advocacy (the desire to improve the quality of life and promote overall welfare);
- mutual respect between families', educational settings' and community's cultures;
- connectedness and responsiveness to the values and expectations of all stakeholders;
- emphasis on the role of leadership as orchestrator;
- clear commitment to developing partnerships and holistic involvement (of all stakeholders, learners, families, school and community representatives such as local business);
- use of positive communication about students' school performance and productivity;
- avoidance of stereotypes at all levels (family's norms, students' performances and community's norms);
- believing and not doubting the abilities of families and the local community;
- investment of time and funding for outreach activities;
- negotiating situations rather than engaging in conflict.

Finally, we found that there are five strands of partnerships as illustrated in Table 6.1. The first four types include two-way connections and reflect the dualistic approach to partnerships which focuses on school–parents. However, the last one – Dynamic/Ecological – includes multiple ways of establishing connections for which the core element is shared responsibilities between home, educational settings and community reflecting a desire for 'holism' – to identify common goals for the learning environment and joint decisions at all levels.

Conclusions/implications

Having examined partnerships through the ecological lens, defined earlier as a connected network where the nucleus is effective relationships, this led us to conclude that analysis is needed at different levels. The following can become reflective points where the degree to which partnerships are effective and successful can be assessed:

- *Structural:* underlying issues that impact on the structure of the partnership (such as poverty, multi-ethnicities, policy);
- *Contextual:* creation of a diverse environment where shared values and beliefs are negotiated towards the creation of a common culture;
- *Spatial-Organisational:* the physical nearness and how this is achieved to share information and exchange ideas to meet reciprocity and in-depth understanding of complementarity of needs of all stakeholders;
- *Interactional:* examination of individual and collective interactions and behaviours in the localised social context;

Table 6.1   Typology of partnerships

Forms of partnerships	Characteristics	Outcomes	Level of interaction
Malleable	Diffused responsibility Reduced capacity for rational explanations Impulsive behaviour Blame culture Apathy	De-individuation	Anonymous
Isolation	Obedience to authority, antagonism, dominance of opinion/s Ambiguity Anti-inception	Destructive Exclusion	Authoritarian Emphasis of power of the dominant culture – school
Passive	Manipulation Ritualistic Anti-inception – no tolerance for difference Relative deprivation: a gap between what we have done and what we should do Ambiguous situations	De-penetration (deliberately reduce disclosure of information) Destructive	Obedience Bystanders (Stakeholders have bystanders' attitudes; they are likely to participate if they feel they have relevant skills)
Active	Reciprocity Mutualism Emphasis on acceptance Informational exchange from school Reactive	Conformity Perceived quality	Satisfactory Direct private influence
Dynamic-Ecological	Common goals Consolidation Investment Reciprocity Complementarity of needs Strategic Empathy Altruism Proactive	Effective Maintained Identification Consistency Loyalty Developmental	Public influence

- *Leader position power:* focusing on social exchange relationships upon which partnership is dependent;
- *Responsiveness:* a critical consciousness to reflect/challenge/develop/maintain /sustain participation of communities, parents, students and school;
- *Advocacy:* cooperative actions that strive to enrich the lives of children, families, community and staff including challenging injustices and promoting overall welfare.

Consequently, an ecological paradigm of forming and sustaining partnerships should act on the following.

Sources of influence focusing on the human elements such as:

- ensuring the setting has a clear understanding of the needs and expectations of the local community and families;
- undertaking analyses of how the setting and its representatives engage with the community, parents and children when seeking effective relationships.

Nature of influences focusing on the contextual elements such as:

- having clarity of vision and expectations that are shared and based on reciprocity of needs;
- being adaptable with their leadership behaviour according to context.

Summary points

- Education is an important time for all children and equally important for their families. It is pivotal that educational settings are working in harmony and effectively together with the parents and local community.
- Partnerships in education have been the subject of government policies that actively promoted the partnerships with parents and educational settings.
- Most of the literature and published research approach partnerships as dualistic relationships between the parents and the educational settings.
- Influential models of partnerships are:
  - Spokes on a wheel (Gordon, 1970)
  - Three models depicting parent roles (Swap, 1993)
  - A six-element empowerment paradigm for parent and family involvement (Souto-Manning and Swick, 2006)
  - Family-Centred Practice (Rouse, 2012)
  - Six-point model (Goodall, 2013)
  - Six types of involvement in school–family–community partnerships (Epstein, 1995).
- We argue, however, that partnerships should be based on an ecological paradigm and examined as a complex social phenomenon where parents, learners, educational settings and community become a dynamic network.
- This paradigm is an approach that takes into account multiple behaviours, multiple views and non-predictable actions that are interrelated, interdependent and interconnected in a non-linear way.

Recommended reading

Feiler, A. (2010) *Engaging 'Hard To Reach' Parents*. Chichester: Wiley-Blackwell.

Goodall, J. (2015) Ofsted's Judgement of Parental Engagement: a justification of its place in leadership and management. *Management in Education*, 29(4), pp.172–177.

Male, T. and Palaiologou, I. (2016) Working with Community, Parents and Students. In P. Early and T. Greany (Eds.), *School Leadership and Education System Reform*. London: Bloomsbury.

References

Australian Government Department of Education, Employment and Workplace Relations (2009) *The Early Years Learning Framework for Australia: Belonging, being and becoming.* Barton: Commonwealth of Australia.

Bourdieu, P. (1986) The Forms of Capital. In J.G. Richardson (Ed.), *Handbook of Theory and Research for the Sociology of Education.* New York: Greenwood Press.

Bronfenbrenner, U. (1979) *The Ecology of Human Development: Experiments by nature and design.* Cambridge, MA: Harvard University Press.

Bronfenbrenner, U. (Ed.) (2005) *Making Human Beings Human: Bioecological perspectives on human development.* Thousand Oaks, CA: Sage.

Catsambis, S. (2001) Expanding Knowledge of Parental Involvement in Children's Secondary Education: Connections with high school seniors' academic success. *Social Psychology of Education,* 5(2), pp.149–177.

Christenson, S., Palan, R. and Scullin, S. (2009) Family–School Partnerships: An essential component of student achievement. *Principal Leadership,* **9**(9), pp.10–16.

Desforges, C. and Abouchaar, A. (2003) *The Impact of Parental Involvement, Parental Support and Family Education on Pupil Achievement: a literature review.* London: DfES.

DfE (1997) *White Paper: Excellence in schools.* London: Her Majesty's Stationery Office.

Epstein, J. (1995) School, Family, Community Partnerships: Caring for children. *Phi Delta Kappan,* **76**(9), pp.701–712.

Epstein, J. (2001) *School, Family and Community Partnerships: Preparing educators and improving schools.* Boulder, CO: Westview Press.

Fullan, M. and Hargreaves, A. (1992) Teacher Development and Educational Change. In M. Fullan and A. Hargreaves (Eds.), *Teacher Development and Educational Change.* London: Falmer.

Giovacco-Johnson, T. (2009) Portraits of Partnership: The hopes and dreams project. *Early Childhood Education Journal,* **37**(2), pp.127–135.

Goodall, J. (2013) Parental Engagement to Support Children's Learning: a six-point model. *School Leadership & Management,* 33(2), pp.133–150.

Goodall, J. and Montgomery, C. (2014) Parental Involvement to Parental Engagement: a continuum. *Educational Review,* **66**(4), pp.399–410.

Goodall, J. and Vorhaus, J. (2011) *Review of Best Practice in Parental Engagement.* London: DfE.

Gorard, S. and Huat See, B. (2013) *Do Parental Involvement Interventions Increase Attainment? A Review of the Evidence.* London: Nuffield Foundation.

Gordon, I.J. (1970) *Parent Involvement in Compulsory Education.* Urbana: University of Illinois Press.

Graue, M.E. and Sherfinski, M. (2011) The View from the Lighted Schoolhouse: Conceptualizing home–school relations within a class size reduction reform. *American Journal of Education,* **117**(2), pp.267–297.

Halgunseth, L., Peterson, C.A., Stark, D.R. and Moodie, S. (2009) *Family Engagement, Diverse Families, and Early Childhood Education Programs: an integrated review of the literature.* Washington, DC: NAEYC and Pre-K Now.

HM Treasury (2004) *Choice for Parents: the best start for children strategy.* London: HMSO.

Hughes, P. and Mac Naughton, G. (2000) Consensus, Dissensus or Community: the politics of parent involvement in early childhood education. *Contemporary Issues in Early Childhood,* **1**(3), pp.241–258.

Jarvis, R. (1998) *System Effects: Complexity in political and social life.* Chichester, UK: Princeton University Press.

Keen, D. (2007) Parents, Families, and Partnerships: Issues and considerations. *International Journal of Disability, Development and Education,* **54**(3), pp.339–349.

Levine-Rasky, C. (2009) Dynamics of Parent Involvement at a Multicultural School. *British Journal of Sociology of Education,* **30**(3), pp.331–344.

Lightfoot, L.S. (2003) *The Essential Conversation: What parents and teachers can learn from each other.* New York: Random House.

Ma, J. (2016) Making Sense of Research Methodology. In I. Palaiologou, D. Needham and T. Male (Eds.), *Doing Research in Education: Theory and practice.* London: Sage.

Madsen, W.C. (2009) Collaborative Helping: a practice framework for family-centered services. *Family Process,* **48**(1), pp.103–116.

Male, T. and Palaiologou, I. (2012) Learning-Centred Leadership or Pedagogical Leadership? An Alternative Approach to Leadership in Education Contexts. *International Journal of Leadership in Education,* **15**(1), pp.107–118.

Male, T. and Palaiologou, I. (2015) Pedagogical Leadership in the 21st Century: Evidence from the field. *Educational Management Administration and Leadership*, **43**(2), pp.214–231.

Male, T. and Palaiologou, I. (2016) Working with Community, Parents and Students. In P. Early and T. Greany (Eds.), *School Leadership and Education System Reform*. London: Bloomsbury.

Migliorini, L., Rania, N. and Tassara, T. (2016) An Ecological Perspective on Early Years Workforce Competences in Italian ECEC Settings. *Early Years*, **36**(2), pp.165–178.

Miller, K., Hilhendore, A. and Dilworth-Bart, J. (2014) Cultural Capital and Home-School Connections in Early Childhood. *Contemporary Issues in Early Childhood*, **15**(4), pp.329–345.

New Zealand Ministry of Education (1996) *Te whariki: He whariki matauranga mo nga mokopuna o Aotearoa: Early childhood curriculum*. Wellington, New Zealand: Learning Media.

Ofsted (2011) *Schools and Parents*. London: Ofsted.

Rouse, E. (2012) Partnerships in Early Childhood Education and Care: Empowering parents or empowering practitioners. *Global Studies of Childhood*, **2**(1), pp.14–25.

Ruddock, J., Wallace, G. and Day, J. (2000) Students' Voice: What can they tell us as 'partners in change'? In K. Sctoo and V. Trafford (Eds.), *Partnerships: Shaping the future of Education*. London: Middlesex University Press.

Souto-Manning, M. and Swick, K. (2006) Teachers' Beliefs about Parent and Family Involvement: Rethinking our family involvement paradigm. *Early Childhood Education Journal*, **34**(2), pp.187–193.

Swap, S.M. (1993) *Developing Home-School Partnerships: from concepts to practice*. New York: Teachers College Press.

Swedish Government (2010) *Curriculum for the Pre-school Lpfö*. Stockholm: Government of Sweden.

Thornton, L. and Brunton, P. (2007) *Bringing the Reggio Approach to Your Early Years Practice*. Abingdon: Routledge.

Wolfe, V.E. (2014) The Voice of the Parent: Perceptions of the United Kingdom Resilience Programme. *Educational and Child Development*, **31**(4), pp.58–71.

7   Common vigilance
A perspective on the role of the community in safeguarding children

Claire M. Richards and Stuart Gallagher

Introduction

Since the passing of the Children Act 2004 (HM Government, 2004), it has become commonplace to read that *safeguarding is everyone's responsibility*. No distinction is made, though, between 'everyone' *individually* and 'everyone' *collectively*, with the result that efforts to unpick exactly how everyone is able to respond to children's safeguarding and protection needs are frustrated. This chapter asks whether or not 'community' is a useful concept to help organise these efforts and to prevent the slogan from unhelpfully collapsing the issue of responsibility together. It considers Bronfenbrenner's ecological model (Bronfenbrenner, 1979) and bio-ecological model (Bronfenbrenner and Ceci, 1994) to understand how community might animate child protection efforts at a level beyond the scope of distinct families but without encompassing statutory responsibility either. Bourdieu's concept of 'habitus' (Shusterman, 1999) is used to examine the social worlds of children in their respective communities to understand the risk and vulnerabilities of children, on the one hand, and the safeguarding responses by concerned adults in the community on the other.

Recent analysis of serious case reviews (SCRs) and inquiries relating to child sexual exploitation was undertaken to understand how the concept of 'community' informs the discussion of community-level communication regarding common concerns for children's safety and well-being. The chapter proposes that *common vigilance* may serve as a more robust concept than does community in efforts to produce social conditions that secure children's safety from maltreatment. The chapter encourages you to consider your position as a professional who embodies interest in children's safety from harm as well as compliance with statutory procedures and expectations of competence.

Individual/group task

Before you continue to read, please reflect on your own childhood experiences of your local community. How did it feel to live in your community? Was it a safe place and if so, what made it feel safe to you as a child? If it did not feel safe, can you recall why?

Consider what the concept of *community* means to you on a personal level and how you view *community* in a professional context. What differences and similarities emerge?

In the olden days before TVs and social workers

In 1651, Hobbes wrote that the life of man was 'nasty, brutish and short' and this was particularly true of children who died of hunger, neglect, disease, poverty and violence (Cunningham, 2006). Pages of history document diverse experiences of childhoods, some much more idyllic than others. Cunningham writes of childhood in the Middle Ages, 'If you survived your first few hours, days, weeks and months of life, your prospects improved, but perhaps as many as half of all children would fail to live to reach the age of ten' (2006:21). Victorian Britain saw the contrasting childhoods consequent to the Industrial Revolution when the divisions between the wealthy and the poor were stark. There was growing concern for the welfare of children exploited for their labour in factories, which resulted in the earliest legislation for improved protection of their welfare via the Factory Act in 1833. Ferguson (2004) suggests that modern child protection was developed between 1870 and 1914 at a time of governmental transformations in Britain. Indeed he refers to Victorian sentiments and concern over the realities of child maltreatment as 'the public, even in the most deprived neighbourhoods, showed its concern by bringing cases forward' (25) to the magistrates' courts. We know that history reveals evidence of child abuse and that the introduction of legislation and the concept of the welfare of children has made some positive impact in the reduction of fatal child abuse since the Victorian era.

The much-quoted African proverb 'It takes a whole village to raise a child' bears some relevance to the notion that the community (village, town or city) has an informal and perhaps largely undefined role in protecting children and in being vigilant about their welfare. The proverb is given significant mention within Chapter 9 in the context of the politicised concept of 'the big society' and how the notion of community responsiveness may also resonate with safeguarding children. There may be tensions that are related to the suggestion that the community should and does have a role in looking out for the welfare of children. There may be a wealth of knowledge and awareness of children and families in the community not normally accessible or privileged to professionals which could be tapped into as a means of enabling early help and support for vulnerable children. However, the collective community may see this role of 'the protection of children' laid securely at the door of the State and its agents, such as social workers, police, health visitors or early years (EY) practitioners.

Warner (2015) introduces the concept of emotional politics in describing the public outcry in the wake of media attention to a child's death as a consequence of abuse and neglect. The distinction between the community and the official role of the State appears to become blurred as there is a collective shame and guilt as to how and why the child protection systems, both formal and informal, have failed.

There is evidence to suggest that these informal safeguarding responses within the community, provided by families, neighbours and friends, are important and effective (Conley and Berrick, 2010; Holman, 1981; Jack and Gill, 2010). Allnock (2016) poses a challenge in questioning from whose perspective child neglect should be measured and although her question may be pitched to a professional audience, there is merit in advocating the expert view of the public where daily encounters with a child and their family can provide a more persuasive assessment of the child's welfare. Similarly Horwath (2016:77) may be illustrating the potential for the role of the community voice by stating that 'any assessment should start with establishing, from a variety of sources, what life is like for the child'. Of course, as will be considered in the chapter, the recognition of the community, and those who speak out from within about the welfare of a child, is not without its challenges.

B is for Bronfenbrenner and Bourdieu

In Chapter 1, Rozsahegyi provides the theoretical grounding for a critical understanding of Urie Bronfenbrenner's ecological model and more recent bio-ecological model for professional practice and research in children's development. The intention here is to consider this model and its application to the interrelationships of the child within their family and the community in the context of child protection and safeguarding.

Let us begin by seeing whether or not it is possible to establish a common understanding of the meaning of community for the purpose of this chapter and to enable further discussion of its standing to safeguard children. Holman (1981) cites ninety-four known definitions and concludes that none is satisfactory, while Stanley (2010) states that 'Communities are not easily defined and are not always cohesive or caring' (77). For the purpose of this chapter, let us take one as a reference point:

> [Community is a] specific group of people, often living in a defined geographical area, who share common culture, values and norms, [and] are arranged in a certain social structure according to relationships which the community has developed over a period of time. Members of a community gain their social identity by sharing common beliefs, values and norms which have been developed by the community in the past and may be modified in the future. They exhibit some awareness of their identity as a group, and share common needs and a commitment to meeting them.
>
> *(World Health Organization, 1998:5)*

The definition invites a reflection on a community's shared beliefs about children, including how they are expected to be cherished and protected by their families, which is perhaps further augmented by the vigilance of the wider community. The critical issue is where the community intervenes when a child's welfare is at risk, particularly where the family is seen to be failing a child. The sense of connectivity between the child, family and community emerges as an informal safeguarding system.

For many years, children's welfare and well-being were the sole preserve of those with whom they shared their private lives. As the twentieth century unfolded, local government provided social welfare services, including universal services such as education as well as more acute services including the provision of places of safety and corporate parenting. Towards the end of the century, the UK ratified the United Nations Convention on the Rights of the Child (UNCRC) (UNICEF, 1989), thereby agreeing to ensure children receive 'such protection and care as is necessary for his or her well-being' (UNICEF, 1989, article 3.2). The UNCRC formalised the principle that children's best interests were paramount in all matters concerning them and expected that States would take 'all appropriate legislative and administrative measures' to secure children's well-being. These measures were to take into account 'the rights and duties of his or her parents, legal guardians, or other individuals legally responsible for him or her' (article 3.2). Thus, the close relationship of State and individuals (and legal responsibilities pertaining to them) became the model by which children's well-being is secured. Securing each and every child's welfare, then, would be a collaborative accomplishment of a range of people, but in particular families and statutory bodies, as well as normative ideas of well-being.

Shortly afterwards, the Children Act 1989 (HM Government, 1989) detailed this collaboration in terms of parental responsibility (see Part I, Sections 2–3) and the statutory duties of local authorities (see Part III of the Act). The collaborative relationship between State and private family lives here is characterised by *direct* assessment and intervention in matters concerning children's safety: the creation of statutory categories such as *children in need* and *children at risk of harm* became the focus of professional attention.

Some softening of this dualistic view quickly became apparent, when the *Framework for the Assessment of Children in Need and Their Families* (DoH *et al.*, 1990) categorised children's safeguarding needs according to three domains: the child's developmental needs, the family's parenting capacity and the family and environmental factors. The closest this framework came to acknowledging a child's interaction with anything like a local community was in noting factors such as the family's social integration and community resources, intertwined with more concrete environmental factors such as housing, employment and income. Importantly though, the State was acknowledging that children's protection from harm would require attention to dimensions other than the direct, unmediated relationship between families and the State.

Rozsahegyi in Chapter 1 refers to the integrated systems of Bronfenbrenner's bio-ecological model and there is cogency in her use of the term 'distance' between the nested levels. Arguably, the position of the community (mesosystem), as an intermediary in its watchfulness over children (microsystem) and in raising safeguarding concerns with the formal agencies of health, social services or the police (exosystem), is challenging and complex. However, there is some value in accentuating the legitimacy of the community and reducing the 'distance' with the State agents, as a means of ensuring more robust connections in raising early warning signs about a child's welfare next door, or as observed in a local supermarket.

Bronfenbrenner's ecological framework (1979) proposes that any State action in the private life of a child must be understood as *mediated* by different but interrelated social systems. The bio-ecological framework (Bronfenbrenner and Ceci, 1994) acknowledges that, over time, the individual's capacity to engage in State action and shape is similarly mediated, and that this changes in degree and in kind according to the development of the child, from antenatal care through to possible incarceration in a youth offending institution, for example. The bio-ecology of any individual, according to Bronfenbrenner and Ceci (1994), is more varied and layered than any model of State–family co-dependency could allow. It therefore offers the possibility of exploring the extent to which concepts of *community* – existing beyond the individual but never fully comprising the State on its own terms – serve to identify child maltreatment and organise themselves to protect children from harm.

This is a worthwhile enterprise given the UK has acknowledged the limitations of the State–family relationship in securing children's safety. The arrangements of the Children Act 2004 (HM Government, 2004:ss. 10–11) were summarised in the slogan, *Safeguarding is Everyone's Responsibility*. The tightly articulated child-welfare model of State–family (as proposed in the UNCRC and Children Act 1989) was exploded in order to reflect a new children's safeguarding and child protection vision in which all professionals working with children would take responsibility for checking each child's well-being and taking critical action should concerns arise. Guidance continues to be issued under the title of *Working Together to Safeguard Children* (DfE, 2015).

This slogan is perhaps undermined as it collapses together everyone's individual responsibility to take care to note children's well-being and the collective responsibility of a child protection system in which concerns are escalated and de-escalated across formal thresholds of intervention.

Individual/group task

Safeguarding is everyone's responsibility

- What distinguishes my individual responsibility from my professional responsibility?
- How might the private individual work together with the public servant to safeguard the well-being of somebody else's child?
- Is there a danger of assuming that, since everyone else is taking responsibility, I can shirk my own responsibility to safeguard children's well-being?

The French social theorist Pierre Bourdieu offers further insights regarding the intricate nature of power and culture within communities and indeed the wider ecosystems as described by Bronfenbrenner. Bourdieu's concept of *habitus* is one of his most enduring and is popularly cited in the literature. It is best simply described as a system of dispositions, which Laberge (2010) explains are acquired over time by the individual. The notion of disposition (or character) warrants some focus in respect to the role of the citizen within the community, and their *habitus* in the context of the interrelatedness of the child, the family and the State. Wagner and McLaughlin (2015:206) helpfully illuminate this point with reference to the way habitus 'reflects the position of an individual or group in societal structures [and] not only refers to attitudes, beliefs, and concepts of self and the world, but also to individual and collective action'.

The perception of a sense of place or *knowing one's place* is interesting, particularly in relation to the structures of organisational cultures and the status and power taken by, or given to, professionals in the context of their expert position in child welfare (Richards, 2015). The dilemma for the concerned citizen in the community may be experienced in two ways. The first is their perceived *non-expert* position (*habitus*) in intervening in concerns about child abuse and neglect. The decision not to get involved may be based on their reasonable expectation that the State and its agents are *more expert* and therefore will be performing their duty in response to safeguarding a child. The second is that the citizen (neighbour, taxi driver or shopkeeper) may try to intervene by raising their concern about a child but are powerless as they are not heard or taken seriously because of their non-professional position. This response by the State's agents may negatively reinforce the habitus of the individual (and community) and therefore troubles the interconnectedness as described by Rozsahegyi in furthering the distance between the micro-, meso- and exosystems of the child's world.

Individual/group task

In order to further understand Bourdieu's concept of 'habitus' and to further contextualise its relevance to communities and safeguarding children we advise you to read Vitellone (2004).

Community or common vigilance?

We are not aware of any single community, imagined in the everyday meaning of the term, ever being charged with child abuse. We are more familiar, though, with Ofsted condemnations of entire local authority children's services departments (think of Doncaster and Rotherham in the context of child sexual exploitation, recently) and with tabloid scandals exposing shameful parenting and practices of acute neglect and abuse. Powerful discourses of child abuse such as these gloss over the situatedness of people's lives within relationships and places and relationships with places and other people. The way we discuss child abuse often sidesteps common and everyday understandings of what counts as community in a social world. Instead, we are tempted, in the wake of a child abuse tragedy, to see the world in terms of combined local authority failure and parental failure – that family–State co-dependency that was exploded in efforts to remind us that safeguarding is everyone's responsibility. Efforts to determine 'lessons' to learn from child welfare tragedies (DfE, 2015) are made for the purpose of professional learning rather than social recreation, so why have we settled for this way of discussing child abuse and its prevention?

Lessons learnt from SCRs

Implicit in the safeguarding slogan are possibilities for individual negligence, at one end of the scale, and vigilantism, at the other. Viewed through Bronfenbrenner's bio-ecological framework, neither case coordinates community-level mediation of State arrangements and individual development and well-being goals. The DfE's (2016) analysis of 175 SCRs describes some historical instances of the difficulty in aligning individual responsibility for safeguarding children with collective, systems-level responsibility:

> In one final report, it was clear that on at least two occasions someone from the local community alerted children's social care about the young person's behaviour and appearance, making allegations of physical abuse and neglect and concerns about sexualised behaviour but the allegations were not investigated.
>
> *(DfE, 2016:108)*

In this case, the proactivity of members of the local community failed because their concerns carried no value in the eyes of professional assessment. In another example, when professionals did take account of local knowledge and concern, excessive weight was given to the views of the child's mother and the community and professional concerns were overridden:

> In another case a neighbour raised concerns about a young person after he had seen a suicide note. In that case, there was a quick response from children's social care and a safety plan was put in place but that did not involve a visit to the young person as the mother claimed that he was 'attention seeking and didn't want to see a social worker'.
>
> *(DfE, 2016:108, para 5.2.1)*

Let us consider whether or not community really is a sufficiently animating concept in safeguarding practice, given its potential to animate collective responsibility at the level of statutory duty but also its position as negligible evidence in assessment of children's needs. One characteristic of community is something stable, enduring over time. Where such articulations of community pivot on something static and unifying, Bauman (2000) argues that modernity is characterised by fluidity, not hard, static commonality. This suggests that we ought not to assume that community represents only stability, reliability and predictability. Communities are not *necessarily* the outcome of individuals making a long-term commitment to a place or practice, but instead are fluid formations and reformations of mutually attractive possibilities at only ever one point of time. Community, in this sense, is characterised by contingency rather than stable organisation. Where Bronfenbrenner's ecological framework (1979) suggested the consistent, stable mediation of community between an individual child and their wider world, the bio-ecological framework (Bronfenbrenner and Ceci, 1994) indicates the contingency of time – of being in the right place in the right moment – in the child's development and well-being. Here, the combination of *habitus* and the opportunity and threats provided by a child's *bio-ecology* may be a powerful means of developing the safety of children in their social worlds.

To illustrate this distinction, we take two examples from the child protection literature. First, the DfE's recent triennial analysis of 175 SCRs (DfE, 2016) highlights the particular vulnerability of children in families characterised by a 'transient lifestyle':

> Several serious case reviews involved families who appeared to live a very transient lifestyle, with frequent moves and little sense of attachment to any geographical location or community. This has the potential effect of creating an environment in which the child experiences little stability and can, as a result, have few ongoing relationships with potentially caring family members or others.
>
> *(DfE, 2016:87, para. 4.3.2)*

Here, community is synonymous with stability and good-quality, close and ongoing relationships with 'others'. Second, revelations regarding the scale of child sexual exploitation in Rotherham (Jay, 2014), Oxford (OSCB, 2015) and Doncaster (Drew, 2016) have shone a light on the role of community in the protection of vulnerable children. For example, the so-called 'Jay Report' (Jay, 2014:91, para. 11) notes that:

> There was too much reliance by agencies on traditional community leaders such as elected members and imams as being the primary conduit of communication with the Pakistani-heritage community. The Inquiry spoke to several Pakistani-heritage women who felt disenfranchised by this and thought it was a barrier to people coming forward to talk about CSE.

This example indicates that the community was characterised by stable practices of exclusion, established hierarchy and unequal access to power and collaboration with the local authority. In this case, it is this stability of community that has proven to be a substantial barrier to child protection since caring family members and others are not approached as equals. Yet within this community there is an emerging demand for the enfranchisement of women to support the best interests of children, in this case enabling members of the community to speak out about experiences of, and concerns about, the sexual exploitation of children. A community of children's safeguarding is coalescing in the light of the Inquiry's investigations into the scale and prevalence of child abuse. Here, the liquid, fluid formation of a new community of safeguarding practice, rather than the traditional understanding of stable community as a source of caring relationships, is the source of community-level hope for child protection. Children's protection from harm is characterised here by a group's *common vigilance* regarding children's needs, rather than the implicit benefit of an enduring, stable community.

So far, we have seen examples of community-level concerns being both ignored by professional assessment but also used as prompts to investigate. We have also seen how stable aspects of community can act as a barrier to particular members of that community being seen as suffering maltreatment. Yet fluid reformations of that community around children's safeguarding interests suggest that there is hope that this barrier can be overcome. The concept of community itself is charged as both barrier and source of hope. Consequently, it is unlikely to prove a sufficiently useful concept in developing the effective child protection actions that mediate between the State and private families and still coordinate 'everybody's responsibility'. The concept of community itself does not appear to prevent unilateral action being taken with regard to assessments of children's well-being. It may be suggested that factors such as that *common vigilance* may be a more appropriate and helpful concept to promote in the interests of children's well-being than community.

The case for common vigilance in safeguarding children

Jack and Gill (2010) underline the significance of the ecological model in the interconnections between the child, family, community and the formal mechanism of the child protection systems. They lament the fact that despite legislative and organisational developments since the Children Act 2004, there is still a reliance on formal systems of safeguarding to the exclusion of the community. The authors make reference to previous public inquiries on fatal child abuse (as discussed earlier), including the death of Victoria Climbié, mentioning 'only one of the inquiry's reports touching on community-level factors' (86).

Sally Holland's case study (2014) of a Welsh community's informal and formal child safeguarding heralds some interesting features, which she describes as 'enablers'. She examines the features of a safeguarding community and its relationship with community workers that helps to provide for a culture of responsive safeguarding of children. The five enablers identified are *proximity* (that of being a local, raised within and known within the community, which helps to create trust and connectedness between practitioners and local residents), *temporal* (the sense of availability of practitioners within the community, which is indicative of the futility of a restricted office-hours-only service provision), *biographical* (meaning the community's valuing those practitioners and other residents with whom they could identify and relate, perhaps due to some recognition that they too had experiences of troubled family life or hardship, therefore likely increasing understanding and empathy), *style* (the relaxed and easy-going approach of a practitioner helped local residents to feel more at ease and less overlooked in comparison to more formal experiences with professionals) and *scope* (describing the range of knowledge or advice a practitioner may be asked to give in their communications within the community, from 'gas fires to relationship breakdowns' (Holland, 2014:393), which can avoid unnecessary signposting). Holland comments on the contrast to specialist posts within specialist services often involving journeys of travel to imposing unfriendly buildings, which may alienate families and children, further distancing them from help.

This study signifies some valuable lessons in determining the nature and style of local safeguarding services and practitioner dispositions and approachability within a community. There may be a correlation in galvanising community engagement and more specifically community status in recognition of its safeguarding role.

Individual/group task

Consider the benefits and opportunities of the five enablers as described by Holland in the context of EY services. What enablers do you recognise in current EY services and where are the gaps? Make suggestions on how the enablers may be developed.

Conclusion

The chapter has presented a case to highlight and underline the role of the community in safeguarding children within the bio-ecological framework. There is a tacit recognition of the potential strengths and input of the community in raising concerns about a child and adapting informal advocacy to see that the 'right thing is done for the child'. Evidence from previous public inquiries and SCRs has demonstrated the tenacity and courage of members of the community in voicing their concerns. Sometimes, those voices are not heard or taken seriously by the professional experts or the community's own authorities, much to the detriment of the child. It is important that you, as a professional or a developing professional in the field of childhood studies, consider your professional identity and disposition in your safeguarding role and that you are encouraged to identify the enablers as described, which may assist you in being an effective advocate. This advocacy in terms of giving voice to your safeguarding concern is enacted within your multi-professional world and can also be expressed within the world of your own community. The challenge for the practitioner is to be mindful of negotiating their professional role within the regulated professional setting and how they are seen outside their professional context within the community, with whom we share a *common vigilance*.

Summary points

- The concept of community may be difficult to define but there is recognition of the different cultures, values and norms that comprise a community.
- Community is not only characterised by stability but also by fluidity. Due to this contradiction, its usefulness in organising child protection actions is undermined. Instead, the contingent just-in-time formations of groups who share a *common vigilance* may instead prove a more robust concept.
- Children's life experiences in their community will vary and may be determined by factors such as poverty, crime, isolation or in contrast connectivity with others, positive economic factors and community safety.
- Arguably, the community does have an informal role in safeguarding children.
- The safeguarding potential of a community is perhaps linked to the relationships with formal safeguarding agencies and the community voice that is listened to and responded to in raising a concern about a child.

Recommended reading

Barlow, J. with Scott, J. (2010) *Safeguarding in the 21st Century: Where to now?* Totnes: Research in Practice.
Holland, S. (2014) Trust in the Community: Understanding the relationship between formal, semi-formal and informal child safeguarding in a local neighbourhood. *British Journal of Social Work*, **44**(2), pp.384–400.
Reed, M. and Walker, R. (Eds.) (2015) *A Critical Companion to Early Childhood*. London: Sage.

References

Allnock, D. (2016) Child Neglect: The research landscape. In R. Gardner (Ed.), *Tackling Child Neglect: Research, policy and evidence-based practice*. London: Jessica Kingsley.
Bauman, Z. (2000) *Liquid Modernity*. Cambridge: Polity.
Bronfenbrenner, U. (1979) *The Ecology of Human Development: Experiments by nature and design*. Cambridge, MA: Harvard University Press.
Bronfenbrenner, U. and Ceci, S.J. (1994) Nature-Nurture Reconceptualised in Developmental Perspective: a bioecological model. *Psychological Review, 101*(4), pp.568–586.
Conley, A. and Berrick, J.D. (2010) Community-Based Child Abuse Prevention: Outcomes associated with a differential response program in California. *Child Maltreatment, 15*(4), pp.282–292.
Cunningham, H. (2006) *A History of Childhood*. London: BBC Books.
DfE (Department for Education) (2015) *Working Together to Safeguard Children*. London: DfE.
DfE (Department for Education) (2016) *Pathways to Harm, Pathways to Protection: a triennial analysis of Serious Case Reviews 2011 to 2014*. London: DfE.
DoH (Department of Health), Department for Education and Employment and the Home Office (1990) *Framework for the Assessment of Children in Need and their Families*. London: The Stationery Office.
Drew, J. (2016) *Drew Review: An independent review of South Yorkshire's handling of child sexual exploitation 1997-2016*. Sheffield: South Yorkshire Police and Crime Commissioner.
Ferguson, H. (2004) *Protecting Children in Time: Child abuse, child protection and the consequences of modernity*. Basingstoke: Palgrave Macmillan.
HM Government (1989) *The Children Act*. London: The Stationery Office.
HM Government (2004) *The Children Act*. London: The Stationery Office.
Hobbes, T. (1651) The Leviathan. [Online]. http://archive.org/details/hobbessleviathan00hobbuoft (accessed 30 August 2016).
Holland, S. (2014) Trust in the Community: Understanding the relationship between formal, semi-formal and informal child safeguarding in a local neighbourhood. *British Journal of Social Work*, **44**(2), pp.384–400.
Holman, B. (1981) *Kids at the Door: a preventive project on a council estate*. Oxford: Basil Blackwell.
Horwath, J. (2016) Making a Difference to the Child's Lived Experience. In R. Gardner (Ed.), *Tackling Child Neglect: Research, policy and evidence-based practice*. London: Jessica Kingsley.
Jack, G. and Gill, O. (2010) The Role of Communities in Safeguarding Children and Young People. *Child Abuse Review, 19*(2), pp.82–96.
Jay, A. (2014) *Independent Inquiry into Child Sexual Exploitation in Rotherham 1997-2013*. Rotherham: Rotherham Metropolitan Borough Council.
Laberge, Y. (2010) Habitus and Social Capital: From Pierre Bourdieu and beyond. *Sociology, 44*(4), pp.770–777.
OSCB (Oxfordshire Safeguarding Children Board) (2015) *Serious Case Review into Child Sexual Exploitation in Oxfordshire: from the experiences of children A, B, C, D, E, and F. Approved by the OSCB February 26th 2015*. Oxford: OSCB.
Richards, C.M. (2015) Taking a Holistic View: Critically examining complex professional issues. In M. Reed and R. Walker (Eds.), *A Critical Companion to Early Childhood*. London: Sage.
Shusterman, R. (1999) *Bourdieu: A Critical Reader*. Oxford: Blackwell.
Stanley, N. (2010) Engaging Communities and Parents in Safeguarding. *Child Abuse Review, 19*(2), pp.77–81.
UNICEF (1989) *The United Nations Convention on the Rights of the Child*. Paris: UNICEF.
Vitellone, N. (2004) Habitus and Social Suffering: Culture, addiction and the syringe. In L. Adkins and B. Skeggs (Eds.), *Feminism after Bourdieu*. Oxford: Blackwell.
Wagner, B. and McLaughlin, K. (2015) Politicising the Psychology of Social Class: the relevance of Pierre Bourdieu's *habitus* for psychological research. *Theory & Psychology, 25*(2), pp.202–221.
Warner, J. (2015) *The Emotional Politics of Social Work and Child Protection*. Bristol: Policy Press.
World Health Organization (1998) *Health Promotion Glossary*. Geneva: WHO Publications.

8 Child poverty and life chances

Alex Owen

Introduction

As we have seen in Chapter 1, Bronfenbrenner (1979, 1994) understood the process of development for the child as crucially shaped by the environment. According to this theory, the pattern for child development is often determined by the context in which an individual resides. This has great significance as we turn our attention to children who are growing up in a climate of poverty. The actors, cultural atmosphere, world-view and practices experienced by children living in economically deprived contexts combine to form powerful environmental and social processes that can significantly influence the development of the child. According to Bronfenbrenner's bio-ecological model, the child responds to the biological, environmental and interpersonal context by making successive accommodations to the individuals, objects and symbols that they experience. This chapter outlines some of the effects of poverty on childhood and future life chances. Some of the traits of economic deprivation, for example crowded substandard housing, unpredictable and unstructured home lives, or uncertain or unsocial parental working hours, can lead to children developing within an environment characterised by 'chaos' (Evans *et al.*, 2005). This 'chaos' has been shown to impact some of the processes within the various layers of Bronfenbrenner's original ecological model with experiences characterised by unpredictability, stress and lack of control (Bronfenbrenner and Evans, 2000). A healthy environment for childhood development involves 'regularity, consistency, predictability and controllability … The immediate surroundings of low-income [children] are more chaotic, consisting of noisier, more crowded, more frenetic, and less structured and predictable routines of daily living' (Evans *et al.*, 2005:564). These chaotic environments, at each level of the ecological system, can carry with them unfavourable effects for children's development.

Individual/group task

Use the Internet to discover how many children are living in poverty in the UK today. Investigate the impact that poverty can have upon the individual child / the family / local communities / society's attitudes and values.

The impact of poverty: the wider context

In 2015 child poverty was a dominant characteristic of 28 per cent of British children's lives (DWP, 2015). This relative poverty measure takes into account the economic and social situation that the British child is living within (Bennett *et al.*, 2016). It has been shown that poverty has a direct impact upon a child's present-day life experiences, as well as their future life chances. The disparity in holistic development between a child living in poverty and their more affluent peers can begin to emerge as early as 22 months of age (Whitham, 2012). A range of aspects of childhood, including the home learning environment, parental nurturing and parental mental well-being, have been shown to be detrimentally affected within an economically deprived context (Field, 2010). These factors can lead to a disparity in life experience and this difference is often multiplied through the various stages of life, leading to significant variances regarding a child's prospects in the future.

The period of time since the Second World War has seen dramatic changes in society's values, resources, priorities and experiences. These wider attributes have had an impact upon the environment of the 'chronosystem' of many of the children residing within the UK today. One example of change that has taken place involves the period of general economic decline observed in the world markets during the early twenty-first century. This recession was the worst the UK has suffered in recent times and the political decisions made in response to the economic situation have had a direct impact upon the wider experience of many of today's children. Another example of change that has taken place involves the significant increase in parental separation over the last seventy years. The mobilisation of the female workforce and the removal of the dependence of women upon their husbands' provision have also had a direct impact upon the wider experience of 3 million of today's children who live within the context of parental separation.

Both of these factors, combined with a range of other wider historical events, have been shown, in some cases, to lead to the recently increased numbers of children living within a context of poverty. In 2015, 3.9 million children were living in poverty within the UK. This statistic has been rising over recent times, with the number of children living in absolute poverty increasing by 0.5 million since 2010 (DWP, 2015). Research outputs point to the detrimental impact that living within a context of economic deprivation can have on a child. A child living in poverty is less likely to achieve good grades at school (DfE, 2015), is more likely to be undernourished (Miller and Korenman, 1994), is less likely to spend their life in good health and is more likely to have a shorter life expectancy (ONS, 2014). A child living in poverty is more likely to exhibit the inability to take initiatives (Hanson *et al.*, 1997), more likely to suffer from depression (Dornfeld and Kruttschnitt, 1992), will have less opportunity to develop socially and emotionally (Keegan, 2001) and is more likely to experience peer rejection (Patterson *et al.*, 1991).

The 'macrosystem' (which Rozsahegyi describes in Chapter 1) involves this broader socio-economic context and is informed by the political and cultural atmosphere of our time. If this context is defined by poverty, a significant number of aspects are affected, including material capital, future prospects and lifestyles. Therefore, as Field's (2010) work has shown, living within a context of poverty can notably affect a child's present life experience and her/his future life chances. The Child Poverty Act of 2010 sought to reverse this trend, aiming to eradicate child poverty by 2020. This legislation illustrated the strategy to be engaged to address the issue of child poverty, thus seeking to reverse the impact on children and their families by focusing on household income. Child poverty is estimated to cost UK society £29 billion per year and therefore it is a social issue that governments should not ignore (Hirsch, 2008). The New Labour government from 1997 initiated the endeavour to end child poverty by 2020. Labour was replaced by the 2010 Coalition government and the subsequent 2015 Conservative government. The aim to address child poverty is still a goal that all political parties seek to achieve, although the recent Conservative government has moved to using measures supporting household unemployment and educational achievement in relation to child poverty, rather than household income (Lansley and Mack, 2015).

Group task

Read Simon's section 'Example from policy: the Life Chances strategy' in Chapter 11. Discuss the Life Chances strategy in your group. What are the possible positives in relation to this strategy for children and their families living in poverty? How could it be helpful and supportive? What are the possible negatives in relation to this strategy for children and their families living in poverty? How could it fail to be helpful and supportive?

The impact of poverty: the immediate context

The 'microsystems' of the developing child (as Rozsahegyi describes in Chapter 1) involve the immediate settings that they engage with, for instance the home, care-givers and friendship groups. Economic deprivation has been shown to have a significant effect upon the processes that take place within the 'microsystem' of the family (Keegan, 2001). Children are more likely to live within a context of poverty due to the characteristics of the familial 'microsystem' that they belong to. For instance, if a child has a single parent, their mother belongs to an ethnic minority group, the family inhabits rental accommodation or the mother does not have a tertiary-level qualification, then the child is far more likely to experience an economically deprived childhood (Bradshaw and Holmes, 2010).

Research shows that one of the most significant influences on children during their formative years is the quality of their relationships within the home (Tickell, 2011). Parental relationships have a notable impact on the development of the child. Key influences, including family background, parental education and parenting skills, are thus understood to significantly impact a child's holistic development, and poverty is believed to have a substantial effect on the capacity of a parent to offer the support required. The Millennium Cohort Study supports this understanding and emphasises key gauges related to the child's 'microsystems' that are crucial for healthy development (Hansen *et al.*, 2010). Living within an economically deprived environment is shown to affect the familial 'microsystem', causing implications for the home learning environment, child health, child resilience and school readiness. One of the key reasons for this difference is the fact that often economically deprived environments become permeated with an atmosphere of chronic strain and stress as parents struggle to meet the needs of their children (Gupta and Blewett, 2008). This ongoing low-level anxiety caused by the inability to appropriately feed the family, or pay for school trips, or buy new school uniforms, has been shown to increase the likelihood of parental depression. This strain of economic deprivation can negatively impact family relationships and impair the parents' ability to nurture and care for their child. This negative impact on the development of children engaged in economically deprived environments is clearly exhibited (Wandsworth *et al.*,

2008). Additionally, an individual's natural resilience can be eroded over time due to the pressure of living in poverty because of the constant worry experienced (Petterson and Burke Albers, 2003). As Keegan (2001:3) asserts, 'A diminished coping capacity [produced by poverty] creates a sense of powerlessness, which erodes self-esteem and the sense of mastery, control and personal efficacy, making it less likely that individuals will engage in … active problem solving.' Therefore, within the context of the family home, the chronic stress generated by poverty can wear away at parental mental well-being and coping strategies. This can impact parental behaviours and the home learning environment. Negative parental behaviour can be found in all social groups; however, the strain of living in poverty has been shown to add pressure to a family's experience (Barnes and Freude-Lagevardi, 2002).

Not all parents living under the pressure of economic disadvantage suffer from depression, nor do all parents who suffer from depression struggle to effectively parent their child (Jackson, 2000). It has been shown that, in some cases, the family unit is able to adapt to the pressure associated with poverty, and the environment can be stabilised to the benefit of the child's development (Elder and Caspi, 1988). Additionally, the child's personal characteristics can moderate the impact of poverty upon their personal growth. Child temperament and personality have been shown to temper the effect of negative parenting upon child development (McLoyd, 1990). In Chapter 4 Brown and Daly discuss this in relation to child resilience and the role of supportive relationships in negating the influence of adversity, which in this case would involve the negative impact of poverty.

Economic deprivation can also have a significant effect upon the processes that take place within other significant 'microsystems' that the developing child is a part of, including friendship groups and the school environment. Children living in poverty can experience higher rates of peer rejection and higher rates of conflict in their friendships (Kupersmidt *et al.*, 2008). If a child is living in an economically deprived context it may be less likely that s/he can engage in the same activities as her/his peers, potentially leading to isolation and the lack of opportunity to maintain and develop friendships.

The impact of poverty: other contexts

The 'mesosystems' of the developing child (as Rozsahegyi describes in Chapter 1) do not involve the child directly; instead they involve the interconnection of two or more of the developing child's 'microsystems'. Economic deprivation can affect the processes that take place at this level as well, for example by influencing the interactions of the parents with the school environment. One possible instance of this has been shown in regard to mothers from economically deprived situations knowing less about their child's school performance, engaging less with teachers and being less likely to support their child's school achievement. Education has been shown to act as a protective factor against the impact of poverty, and yet poverty itself can act as a barrier to children and their families, preventing them from fully accessing all that the education system has to offer (Keegan, 2001).

Another possible example, in economically deprived situations, involves parents' engagement with external support networks, possibly formed in a place of work or the local Children's Centre, for example. Research supports the notion of the importance of external support networks as a significant resource for parents living in poverty (Attree, 2004). External support can involve formal support interventions, usually offered by statutory or third-sector organisations. One example could be a training course run at a local children's centre that is designed to increase parents' knowledge and skills regarding the role of a parent. These formal mechanisms for support have proved to be successful for some parents and can have an effect upon the prevalence of child maltreatment within economically deprived contexts (Whittaker and Cowley, 2012). The emphasis of these interventions is often to educate with an aim to inform parental behaviours (Edwards and Gillies, 2004).

However, research has shown that not all parents who live within a context of poverty engage with formal support interventions, sometimes due to a distrust of those seen to be in authority (Heinrichs *et al.*, 2005). Single-parent mothers living within an economically deprived environment are the most socially isolated and are the least likely to participate in formal support interventions (Attree, 2004). This isolation can lead to consequences for a parent's ability to cope, thus influencing their parenting behaviours (McKendrick *et al.*, 2003). Therefore, in some cases, a significant group of parents who would possibly benefit from formal mechanisms of support are unlikely to access the professional assistance available to them.

Individual reflective task

Reflect upon why you think some parents from economically deprived environments are least likely to engage with formal services, for example social welfare agencies and health professionals. Who or what has informed parents' opinions and experiences? How could a professional practitioner work to remove some of these barriers to engagement?

External support, often a significant resource for parents living within an economically deprived environment, can also involve informal social support networks. One example could include the friendships built in a parent and toddler group run in a local community hall by volunteers. These informal interventions, usually taking the form of informal social relationships with family members and friends, have been shown to be of significance for parents living in poverty (Owen and Anderson, 2015). Informal networks provide emotional support (when a parent feels cared for and feelings of worthlessness are reduced), informational support (when a parent is provided with guidance and feelings of confusion are minimised) and instrumental support (when a parent is given material assistance and feelings of a lack of control are negated) (Cohen, 2004).

Case study

The Birkenhead Foundation Years Project was founded by the Foundation Years Trust. The aim of the project is to implement the findings of Field's (2010) review in supporting the home environment of young children. Field highlighted the impact of poverty upon a variety of factors, including parental warmth and sensitivity, parental mental health and well-being, and the home learning environment, with a view to a child's current life experience and future life chances. The Birkenhead Foundation Years Project supports a number of community-based interventions that seek to work with families living in poverty.

Research undertaken by Owen and Anderson (2015) found that a group of parents linked with the Birkenhead Foundation Years Project actively chose to attend volunteer-led, community-based groups, instead of more formal interventions. The research found that the primary reason for this was for the informal social support that the parents felt they received. Parents stated that they attended because "'I'm able to talk through difficult situations with my friends", "I like speaking to other people who are going through the same thing as me" and "I can talk to other parents about the challenges I face'" (Owen and Anderson, 2015:9). Further exploration found that the informal social support received by parents in these groups was important to the parents for two reasons:

1. Firstly, the support received maintained parental mental well-being. Parents felt that the friendships they formed within these groups helped with the pressure of parenting. Parents supported this finding with comments such as, "'It gives me an excuse to get out of the house or I'd go stir-crazy", "I attend the toddler group for some sanity", "It's a stress relief knowing you can escape" and "To fill my day. To give purpose to my day'" (Owen and Anderson, 2015:10).
2. Secondly, the support received provided parents with informal peer parenting education. Parents stated that the informal groups helped them to develop their parenting skills in a non-threatening manner. They made comments such as, "'I like to see how the other mums deal with their children, ..." "I attend the group because I value the parenting support I receive" and "I like speaking to other mums who have just been through it – we can share experiences'" (Owen and Anderson, 2015:10).

Research has shown that the majority of parents living in poverty have at least three individuals in their social network that they can rely on for informal social support (Ghate and Hazel, 2002). This understanding challenges the misconception that the majority of economically deprived environments are disjointed socially and emphasises the significance of informal social support for parents. Research supports this understanding and shows the function these external parental relationships play in defending the child against some of the consequences of poverty (Owen and Anderson, 2015). It has been shown that the parents' support relationships can have a primary and secondary influence on the child. The primary influences involve the positive relationships that the members of the support network can have directly with the child to support their development. The secondary influences involve the positive effects that the members of the support network can have on the parent and the parent's child-centred behaviours. These primary and secondary factors have been shown to negate some of the effects of economic deprivation upon the child (Cochran *et al.*, 1990).

Closing group discussion

Consider the value of informal social support networks for parents living in economically deprived environments. Why do you think some parents choose to access this type of support instead of engaging with more formal support interventions? Discuss the primary influences and the secondary influences that the parents' support relationships could have on the child. Can you think of examples of when you have seen either of these factors negate some of the effects of poverty upon the child?

Conclusion

Children do not develop in a vacuum; instead they are crucially shaped by their environment. This chapter has explored some of the aspects of an environment permeated by poverty. We have seen that the actors, culture, world-view and practices experienced by children living in economically deprived contexts can combine to form powerful environmental and social processes that can significantly influence the development of the child. Some of the traits of an economically deprived environment can lead to a situation where children are developing in a context characterised by 'chaos'. These 'chaotic' experiences can affect the processes that take place at the various levels of Bronfenbrenner's ecological model, which has ramifications for the child's present life experience as well as her/his future life chances. From politicians and policy-makers, to teachers and family support workers, to family friends and parents, there is a significant challenge for all those involved in the various environments inhabited by the child living in poverty to provide opportunity, nurture resilience and support child development.

Summary points

- In 2015, 3.9 million children were living in poverty within the UK. The number of children living in absolute poverty has increased by 0.5 million since 2010.
- Some of the traits of an economically deprived environment can lead to a situation where children are developing in a situation characterised by 'chaos'. Chaos has been shown to impact some of the processes within the various layers of Bronfenbrenner's ecological model.
- Living within an economically deprived environment can affect the familial 'microsystem' as home life can become permeated with an atmosphere of chronic strain and stress as parents struggle to meet the needs of their children. This can have implications for the home learning environment, child health, child resilience and school readiness.
- Research supports the notion of the importance of external support networks as a significant resource for parents living in poverty. External support can involve formal support interventions, usually offered by statutory or third-sector organisations. It can also involve informal social support networks, usually taking the form of informal social relationships with family members and friends.

Recommended reading

Bradshaw, J. and Holmes, J. (2010) Child Poverty in the First Five Years of Life. In K. Hansen, H. Joshi and S. Dex (Eds.), *Children of the 21st Century: the first five years.* Bristol: The Policy Press.

Evans, G., Gonnella, C., Lyscha, M., Gentile, L. and Salpekar, N. (2005) The Role of Chaos in Poverty and Children's Socioemotional Adjustment. *Psychological Science,* **16**(7), pp.560–565.

Field, F. (2010) *The Foundation Years: Preventing poor children becoming poor adults. The Report of the Independent Review on Poverty and Life Chances.* London: Cabinet Office.

Ghate, D. and Hazel, N. (2002) *Parenting in Poor Environments: Stress and coping.* London: Jessica Kingsley.

References

Attree, P. (2004) Parenting Support in the Context of Poverty: a meta-synthesis of the qualitative evidence. *Journal of Health and Social Care in the Community,* **13**(4), pp.330–337.

Barnes, J. and Freude-Lagevardi, A. (2002) *From Early Pregnancy to Early Childhood: Early interventions to enhance the mental health of children and families.* London: Mental Health Foundation.

Bennett, K., Mander, S. and Richards, L. (2016) Inclusive Practice for Families. In Z. Brown (Ed.), *Inclusive Education: Perspectives on pedagogy, policy and practice.* Abingdon: Routledge.

Bradshaw, J. and Holmes, J. (2010) Child Poverty in the First Five Years of Life. In K. Hansen, H. Joshi and S. Dex (Eds.), *Children of the 21st Century: the first five years.* Bristol: The Policy Press.

Bronfenbrenner, U. (1979) *The Ecology of Human Development: Experiments by nature and design.* Cambridge, MA: Harvard University Press.

Bronfenbrenner, U. (1994) Ecological Models of Human Development. In T. Husén and T. N. Postlethwaite (Eds.), *International Encyclopedia of Education,* vol. 3, 2nd edition. Oxford: Elsevier.

Bronfenbrenner, U. and Evans, G. (2000) Developmental Science in the 21st Century: Emerging questions, theoretical models, research designs and empirical findings. *Social Development,* **9**(1), pp.115–125.

Cochran, M., Larner, M., Riley, D., Gunnarson, L. and Henderson, C. (1990) *Extending Families: the social networks of parents and their children.* Cambridge: Cambridge University Press.

Cohen, S. (2004) Social Relationships and Health. *American Psychologist,* **59**(8), pp.676–684.

DfE (2015) *Statistical First Release: GCSE and equivalent attainment by pupil characteristics 2013-2014.* London: DfE.

Dornfeld, M. and Kruttschnitt, C. (1992) Do the Stereotypes Fit? Mapping Gender-specific Outcomes and Risk Factors. *Criminology,* **30**(3), pp.397–419.

DWP (2015) *Households below Average Income.* London: DWP.

Edwards, R. and Gillies, V. (2004) Support in Parenting: Values and consensus concerning who to turn to. *Journal of Social Policy,* **33**(4), pp.627–647.

Elder, G. and Caspi, A. (1988) Economic Stress in Lives: Developmental perspectives. *Journal of Social Issues,* **44**(4), pp.25–45.

Evans, G., Gonnella, C., Lyscha, M., Gentile, L. and Salpekar, N. (2005) The Role of Chaos in Poverty and Children's Socioemotional Adjustment. *Psychological Science,* **16**(7), pp.560–565.

Field, F. (2010) *The Foundation Years: Preventing poor children becoming poor adults. The Report of the Independent Review on Poverty and Life Chances.* London: Cabinet Office.

Ghate, D. and Hazel, N. (2002) *Parenting in Poor Environments: Stress and coping.* London: Jessica Kingsley.

Gupta, A. and Blewett, J. (2008) Involving Services Users in Social Work Training on the Reality of Family Poverty: a case study of a collaborative project. *Social Work Education: The International Journal,* **27**(5), pp.459–473.

Hansen, K., Joshi, H. and Dex, S. (Eds.) (2010) *Children of the 21st Century: the first five years.* Bristol: Policy Press.

Hanson, T., McLanahan, S. and Thomson, E. (1997) Economic Resources, Parental Practices, and Children's Well-being. In G. Duncan and J. Brooks-Gunn (Eds.), *Consequences of Growing up Poor.* New York: Russell Sage Foundation.

Heinrichs, N., Bertram, H., Kuschel, A. and Hahlweg, K. (2005) Parent Recruitment and Retention in a Universal Prevention Program for Child Behaviour and Emotional Problems: Barriers to research and program participation. *Prevention Science,* **6**(4), pp.275–286.

Hirsch, D. (2008) *Estimating the Cost of Child Poverty.* York: Joseph Rowntree Foundation.

Jackson, A. (2000) Maternal Self-Efficacy and Children's Influence on Stress and Parenting among Single Black Mothers in Poverty. *Journal of Family Issues,* **21**(1), pp.3–16.

Keegan, M. (2001) The Effects of Poverty on Children's Socioemotional Development: an ecological systems analysis. *Social Work,* **46**(3), pp.256–266.

Kupersmidt, J., Greisler, P., De Rosier, M., Patterson, C. and Davis, P. (2008) Childhood Aggression and Peer Relations in the Context of Family and Neighbourhood Factors. *Child Development,* **66**(2), pp.360–375.

Lansley, S. and Mack, J. (2015) *Breadline Britain: the rise of mass poverty.* London: Oneworld Publications.

McKendrick, J., Cunningham-Burley, S. and Backett-Milburn, K. (2003) *Life in Low Income Families in Scotland.* Edinburgh: Scottish Executive.

McLoyd, V. (1990) The Impact of Economic Hardship on Black Families and Children: Psychological distress, parenting and socioemotional development. *Child Development,* **61**(2), pp.311–346.

Miller, J. and Korenman, S. (1994) Poverty and Children's Nutritional Status in the United States. *American Journal of Epidemiology,* **140**, pp.233–243.

ONS (2014) *Inequality in Healthy Life Expectancy at Birth by National Deciles of Area Deprivation: England, 2009-11.* London: ONS.

Owen, A. and Anderson, B. (2015) Informal Community Support for Parents of Pre-school Children: a comparative study investigating the subjective experience of parents attending community-based toddler groups in different socio-economic situations. *Journal of Early Childhood Research.* [Online]. DOI: 10.1177/1476718X15597022.

Patterson, C., Vaden, N. and Kupersmidt, J. (1991) Family Background, Recent Life Events and Peer Rejection during Childhood. *Journal of Social and Personal Relationships,* **8**(3), pp.347–361.

Petterson, S. and Burke Albers, A. (2003) Effects of Poverty and Maternal Depression on Early Child Development. *Child Development,* **72**(6), pp.1794–1813.

Tickell, C. (2011) *The Early Years: Foundations for life, health and learning. An Independent Report on the Early Years Foundation Stage to Her Majesty's Government.* London: DfE.

Wandsworth, M., Tali, R., Reinhard, C., Wolf, B., Decarlo Santiago, C. and Einhorn, L. (2008) An Indirect Effects Model of the Association between Poverty and Child Functioning: The role of children's poverty-related stress. *Journal of Loss and Trauma: International Perspectives on Stress and Coping,* **13**(2–3), pp.156–185.

Whitham, G. (2012) *Child Poverty in 2012: it shouldn't happen here.* London: Save the Children.

Whittaker, K. and Cowley, S. (2012) An Effective Programme is not Enough: a review of factors associated with poor attendance and engagement with parenting programmes. *Children and Society,* **26**(2), pp.138–149.

9 How big is our society?

Sarah Mander

Introduction

In Chapter 1, Rozsahegyi introduces Bronfenbrenner's bio-ecological model and the relevance of its application to child development. She extrapolates the biological, environmental and interpersonal influences upon children and their interconnectedness with immediate and extended family, childcare and educational settings and local communities. This includes more distanced social contexts such as community, health and social arrangements and national policies. Rozsahegyi's analysis of the PPCT – 'person-process-context-time' (Bronfenbrenner, 1995) – structure brings to mind the African proverb *it takes a village to raise a child*. Discussing early childhood and family service provision which has its grass roots firmly embedded in such *villages* known to us as 'Sure Start locality programmes', Whalley (2013) identifies the current model of integrated service delivery as the contemporary twenty-first-century village, affirming the importance of partnership with the voluntary and community sector to support child and family development. Chapter 7 focuses initially upon the macrosystem of Bronfenbrenner's (1979) ecological model which considers the attitudes and ideologies influencing the cultures in which individuals live. This chapter examines the collaboration of public, private and voluntary organisations to provide services for children and families. Discussions consider transference of health, education and social care services to the voluntary sector which plays an increasingly crucial and valued role as key providers of services for children, young people and families.

The chapter explores the characteristics, values and principles of voluntary organisations, their sense of identity, their independence from public and private sectors and their innovative and entrepreneurial nature. Critical analysis is made of the shifting boundaries between the public, private and voluntary sectors and the associated impact upon communities. The introduction of *the Big Society* policy in 2010 intended to promote civic renewal and rebalance the economy by reducing state-funded provision. The chapter evaluates the effectiveness of the policy in strengthening society and enabling communities to achieve their own ambitions in the current context of economic austerity and reduced public spending. Using Bronfenbrenner's (1979) exosystem and microsystem the voluntary workforce is viewed through the lens of volunteers, including discussion around the necessary skills, knowledge and expertise required to ensure quality service provision by the sector. As an example a best practice case study of partnership working between the private, public and voluntary sectors is included to assist our understanding of the mutual benefits of volunteering for both volunteers and organisations.

Individual/group task

To assist your understanding of the voluntary and community sector, categorise your locality services listed in Table 9.1 into the three different sectors represented by the column headings. Could some services be provided by more than one sector?

Table 9.1   Local services and voluntary and community sectors

Service	Voluntary and community provider	Public provider	Private provider
Primary school			
Scouts			
Church			
Health visitors			
Library			
Childminders			
Mosque			
Children's centre			
Food bank			
Domestic abuse support			

The emergence of the voluntary and community sector as providers of family and community services

The voluntary and community sector is well established as a provider of family and community services and mutual aid welfare support for families and communities is known to have existed as early as the thirteenth century. Today, we are probably more familiar with the notable developments of the nineteenth century when children's charities, including Barnardo's (1870) and the NSPCC (1884), were established in response to the extreme social deprivation and hardship experienced in the UK. The Beveridge Report (1942) identified five 'giant evils' in society, namely squalor, ignorance, want, idleness and disease. Following election in 1945 the Labour government sought to eradicate them by introducing the welfare state. It was intended to assure *cradle to grave* support provided by a National Health Service, welfare benefits and state pensions.

It would be reasonable to conclude that the introduction of the welfare state following the Second World War should have reduced the requirement for voluntary and community services. However, the role of the voluntary and community sector has shifted from being the sole providers of family support services to the supplementary provider, enhancing state provision and more recently replacing some local authority provision entirely (Alcock, 2010). The progressive *contract culture* of the 1990s, where service providers are sourced not only from the state but also from the private and voluntary and community sectors, continues to blur the boundaries between these three sectors to create hybrid models of provision. The theme of hybridity and its impact (Billis, 2010; Billis and Glennerster, 1998) continues to be discussed throughout this chapter, considering whether this enhances or detracts from family service provision.

Individual/group task

List the ways in which voluntary and community providers influenced your childhood. This could include your own or your family's involvement as:

- employees of the voluntary and community sector
- volunteers
- service users
- donors.

Reflect on whether you feel this service could be provided by a different sector – the state or private sector. Justify your conclusions.

Introducing the Big Society

The role of voluntary and community organisations evolved further in 2010 when *the Big Society* policy was introduced by the Conservative Party (see also Chapter 11). This initiative promised to rebalance economy and society by increasing the status and purpose of voluntary and community provision, strengthening society to help people achieve their own ambitions. Assurances were provided that power would be devolved from central government to local communities, giving people the opportunity to take more control over their lives, with responsibilities and decision-making undertaken by individuals within neighbourhoods (Hogg and Baines, 2011; Ishkanian and Szreter, 2012). An example of *the Big Society* in action is the introduction of the National Citizen Service in 2011 (also mentioned by Brown and Daly in Chapter 4), a voluntary personal and social development programme for 15–17-year-olds which has strengthened over time and become a permanent project following the introduction of the National Citizen Bill 2016 (National Citizen Service, 2016). Further illustration of *the Big Society* is evidenced with the creation of Free Schools, which allows parents, teachers, charities and businesses to set up their own educational provision (HMG, 2010a, 2010b, 2011a). Significant concerns have been raised regarding quality assurance and standards in some Free Schools. One of the first to open in 2012, Al-Madinah Free School in Derby, ceased to provide secondary education in 2014 following an Ofsted inspection which placed the school into special measures and described it as 'chaotic, dysfunctional and inadequate'. However, the school has evidenced improved effectiveness and was graded 3, which is 'requires improvement', during re-inspection a year later (DfE, 2013–2016). It should be noted that local authority-run schools can also be placed into special measures, and that the Free School initiative generates continuing debate, particularly given its fluctuating international success in countries such as Sweden and as charter schools in the USA (OECD, 2015). The 2016 requirement for all schools to convert to academy status by 2022 is discussed in Chapter 11.

Social action through increased levels of volunteering is a key function of *the Big Society*. It means people being encouraged to be more involved in their communities through giving time, money and other resources. It has been mooted in discussions about welfare reforms and the associated introduction of universal credit that volunteering may become a mandatory requirement for state benefit recipients: an involuntary requisite which contradicts the action of voluntary engagement. The intention of the UK reforms was for people aged between 18 and 21 to complete a mandatory thirty hours of community work and ten hours of job-hunting each week to qualify for benefits, applicable from day one of claiming, as part of a Community Work Programme initiative (Cameron, 2016). This followed the lead from other countries, including some states in the USA where volunteering or training is a requirement for receiving food stamps (Just Harvest, 2016).

The concept of community empowerment in England was further formalised with the introduction of the Localism Act in 2011 to devolve responsibility to local authorities. New freedoms and flexibilities for local government were extended with increased rights and powers for communities and individuals. Some of the highlights of this Act included improved transparency regarding finance, making governors more accountable, reforms for more democratic, effective planning systems and local decision-making for housing, reducing bureaucracy and also the introduction of directly elected mayors (HMG, 2011b). In Chapter 11, Simon discusses further the impact of the Localism Act upon communities.

How big is our society?

Through introducing the *Big Society* policy, the newly elected Prime Minister David Cameron raised the status of the voluntary and community sector by rebranding it as the first sector of the new economy. Evans (2011) acknowledges that this affords deserved and perhaps overdue value and respect for the voluntary and community sector regarding its achievements and professionalism. However, she also critiques the practical application of the policy and provocatively refers to the voluntary and community sector as *Cinderella* who is regularly clearing up the mess of the other sectors, her *Ugly Sisters*. This suggests that the status afforded to the voluntary and community sector is disingenuous, and that it remains the poor relation to public and private provision. Indeed, *the Big Society* is critiqued by the National Council for Voluntary Organisations (2012) who report that it does not address the needs of the sector, and is too heavily weighted on contracting and meeting state-down objectives, with preference given to larger charities. Recommendation is made to focus on the building of social capital and sustainable opportunities for communities, and to reflect upon what drives the nature of service delivery: Is it a child/family-centred approach or does it primarily aid the state in meeting its statutory obligations?

The final audit of *the Big Society* (Civil Exchange, 2015) describes the current nature and characteristics of community services in the UK. It states that giving time through volunteering is high compared to other countries and in particular social engagement by young people is continuing to increase; volunteering amongst 16–24-year-olds has almost doubled since 2005. Despite an economic recession, individual generosity is high and donating money is increasing. Interestingly, a north/south divide and an urban/rural gap are evidenced. Overall, people in the south feel more empowered, tend to enjoy better services, and are more socially active. Rural and southern areas have more voluntary activity. Charities are plentiful in the south of England which tends to be more prosperous than the disadvantaged, post-industrial north. The south also includes London which represents 40 per cent of the voluntary sector income and may explain these geographical disparities (Civil Exchange, 2015:54). Older people aged 55–74 report most confidence in influencing local decision-making, and formal volunteering amongst black, Asian and minority ethnic (BAME) groups is increasing, from 33 per cent in 2010–11 to 43 per cent in 2012–13 (HMG, 2013).

Individual task

Read the Big Society policy (www.gov.uk/government/uploads/system/uploads/attachment_data/file/78979/building-big-society_0.pdf).

Consider your local community. Reviewing the community empowerment changes promised by the Big Society policy you have been reading about, identify three changes which evidence that local people are in control of their communities.

Tip: you may find it helpful to source local media reports relating to planning, housing, charitable organisations, volunteering centres or political leadership to inform your task.

Sustainability and austerity measures

The elephant in the *Big Society* room was the wider economic decline resulting from almost a decade of worldwide recession. It is no coincidence that a significant consequence of the *Big Society* policy was a substantial saving to the public purse. The policy was established as a mandate for the Conservative Party before the 2010 election and one of its main purposes was to support the Party's promise for economic regeneration. Within our communities we increasingly observe changes in service provision as a result of these efficiency savings. For example, public services such as libraries and mentoring of children in care may more recently have been delivered by a volunteer workforce. The emergence and development of different services such as food banks and credit unions to meet the greater economic needs of communities are also evident and leave us in no doubt that our society is indeed bigger, and holds more responsibilities than before the 2008 recession, albeit as a by-product of economic austerity measures.

Naturally, critique of these shifting boundaries has readily ensued. In discussing the criminal justice voluntary sector, Senior (2011) suggests that the negative effect of contracting to the voluntary organisations is a drift from the original purpose of charity which compromises the values of charity and capacity for innovation. The competition between public, private and voluntary and community sectors is deemed to diminish independence and create principles which are more aligned to for-profit organisations, in effect creating a more business-like ethos. The dependence of voluntary and community organisations upon state funding restricts their ability to be critical of government policy as it is unwise to bite the hand which feeds them. Furthermore, the impact of the worldwide economic recession has resulted in significant budget reductions for the voluntary and community sector which have diminished its power and decreased effectiveness. In particular, the core children's voluntary sector which includes some organisations discussed earlier, such as the NSPCC and Barnardo's, is experiencing a greater proportion of public funding reductions compared to the voluntary sector as a whole: 8.2 per cent and 7.7 per cent, respectively (NCB, 2011, 2012). The outcomes are reduced staffing levels and reductions in the level/range of services, forcing organisations to increase their utilisation of volunteers and to review their fundraising strategies. The public image of charities has been tainted by extreme fundraising tactics. The charities' regulatory body, the Fundraising Standards Board, investigated the menacing nature of street fundraisers, known as *chuggers*, and cold calling by telephone and letter which can exploit vulnerable people (Fundraising Standards Board, 2016). The good reputation and moral values of the voluntary and community sector are threatened by this, affecting donations and further diminishing sustainability. However, it can be argued that aggressive fundraising tactics are the consequence of a more business-like approach to income-generation. It is probable that the root cause of this change in ethos, morals and principles is the combined influence of the blurring of boundaries between the private, public and voluntary and community sectors, austerity measures and changes in political influence. Philanthropic giving is fortunately thriving for some causes, aided by effective communication and the infectious nature of social media which is often endorsed by celebrities. Recent examples include the Teenage Cancer Trust promoted by Stephen Sutton (Teenage Cancer Trust, 2015) and the international ice-bucket challenge which has funded a significant research breakthrough in motor neurone disease (ALS Association, 2016).

Research task

Research social media sites and forums to investigate the influence of social media on fundraising activities. You can read the examples provided earlier or choose your own.
  Examine:

- the role of social media to communicate the fundraising activity. In what way has it enhanced or detracted from the activity?
- to what extent, if any, celebrity involvement is present. If so, how does this influence the fundraising activity?
- the appropriateness for this cause to be funded by charity. Could/should it be funded by the state?
- whether the approach taken is ethical. Justify your conclusion.

Galvanising the community

In our discussions so far we have analysed and evaluated the contribution the voluntary and community sector could make to a child's macrosystem. We have sought to understand how attitudes and ideologies affect cultures through applying policy to practice, and have considered national contexts which determine the ethos and principles of the voluntary and community sector. The chapter will now investigate the role of communities as change agents influencing the exosystem and microsystem (Bronfenbrenner, 1979) and revisit Whalley's (2013) declaration that 'it takes a village to raise a child'.

So, what role does the voluntary and community sector play in raising children? At the heart of services provided for children at the beginning of the twentieth century, such as the NSPCC and Barnardo's, was the requisite to intervene when families found themselves unable to care for their children independently. Children's charities embarked upon the burdensome task of protecting and restoring vulnerable children through provision of basic needs such as food, shelter, clothing and education. Almost a century later, respected research conducted across a range of disciplines informs us that early help, when basic needs are at risk of being unmet, prevents difficulties escalating to crisis level, and is the most effective intervention to aid children's development. Outcomes for children in respect of health, education, economic circumstance, safety and happiness are significantly improved when the right service at the right time is provided (Allen,

2011; Field, 2010; Marmot, 2010; Munro, 2011). Service provision has evolved and a multi-agency approach is now required. It is legislated for in the Children Act 2004 (HMG, 2004) which requires public, private and voluntary and community organisations to collaborate and develop child-centred partnerships. Community engagement, and in particular parental engagement, is considered to be one of the five key threads recommended as best practice to shape service delivery in order to achieve excellence in outcomes for children and their families. *Galvanising the community* is cited as the secret of success; building functional, healthy communities empowers an idea when it is concurrently adopted by a large number of the community (C4EO, 2010a, 2010b). In particular, this is the most encouraging form of intervention to reach the most at-risk children. Involvement of the voluntary and community sector utilising a grass-roots approach has the potential to ensure that *services* are not hard to reach as barriers to engagement such as geographical distance and fluctuation in service provision, lengthy waiting lists and overly bureaucratic referral systems are reduced.

Locality involvement does, however, have its disadvantages. Generic barriers for volunteering include lack of access to childcare, restricted transport, limited availability of suitable clothing and underdeveloped core skills such as literacy, numeracy and IT competency. Volunteers are likely to reside within the community where they are working, and may be privileged to sensitive, familial information about their neighbourhood. The distinction between professional and friend may become unclear; inappropriate and unhelpful hierarchies may emerge. Specialist training and experience may be lacking and may lead to incorrect intervention. This is particularly concerning when vulnerable children and families are service users. Taylor (2007) notes that volunteers may experience vulnerabilities, for example poor health, domestic abuse and disability, which develops their expertise in these fields but which may also cause the responsibilities of volunteering to become onerous and burdensome. There is a long history of organisations demonstrating reluctance to devolve power to volunteers, resulting in imposition of a glass ceiling upon the delegation of tasks available to volunteers. This results in restrictions for the breadth and depth of volunteer involvement as only the more menial and repetitive tasks may be offered. However, if it takes a village to raise a child the best outcomes can be achieved if all *villagers* experience equality of opportunity to utilise their skills and expertise, regardless of employment or volunteer status, or whether it is the public, private or voluntary and community sector which provides the service.

Moving on up: a best practice hybrid model

The golden thread of this chapter which initiates reflection and continuing debate is the blurring of boundaries between the public, private and voluntary and community sectors. There are evidenced reticence and feelings of threat regarding loss of identity and independence for each sector (Baring Foundation *et al.*, 2014). National policy combined with economic influences are a significant driver of reformation and innovation in service design and delivery, producing hybrid models which involve partnerships between the three sectors (Billis, 2010; Billis and Glennerster, 1998). The following best practice model demonstrates the success of hybridity where best outcomes for children and families are evidenced across the ecological system (Bronfenbrenner, 1979).

The context for this anonymous case study example is a Sure Start locality programme in the East Midlands. The programme sought to develop its volunteer activities across seven children's centres within the cluster. Whilst a volunteering programme delivered by a private organisation was already in existence, parent volunteers were not at that time afforded opportunity to participate in higher-level activities but were limited to basic operational tasks (Arnstein, 1969). Building upon earlier research which informs that parental participation in service design and delivery has a positive impact on children's well-being, and specifically upon their educational outcomes (Bennett *et al.*, 2016), the programme strengthened its volunteering programme to maximise parental participation and improve outcomes for their young children. Development based upon this hybrid partnership became feasible due to the commissioning arrangements for the programme; an annual budget of almost £1 million was available and was disseminated through a locality management board. Initial steps involved formulating a parental participation strategy informed by Sure Start Core Purpose and Statutory Guidance (DfE, 2012, 2013). Fundamental drivers for the strategy included the national shift of Sure Start responsibilities from a Core Offer to a Core Purpose in 2011 following the change in government in 2010. The Core Purpose places increased emphasis on the promotion of social mobility, focussing upon supporting parental employment opportunities, building essential skills and confidence to engage in paid employment (DfE, 2012). This aligns with wider welfare reforms implemented by the 2010 Coalition government in response to the economic recession of 2008. The other significant influence was a recent Ofsted inspection which deemed one of the centres 'unsatisfactory', requiring improvements to develop and engage parental involvement at all levels of the programme in preparedness for re-inspection. One area for improvement included ensuring adequate parental representation as equal members on the locality management board. The strategy was an effective mechanism for communicating the requirements and benefits of parental involvement to key stakeholders. Key stakeholders and members of the locality management board included representatives from the local authority including child and adult education services, libraries and housing, health partners such as midwifery, health visitors, school nurses and public health and the voluntary and community sector.

Once a partnership agreement had been secured to progress the strategy, and a budget allocated, discussions regarding how best to implement the project began. This commenced with in-depth consultation amongst existing parent volunteers undertaken in partnership with the private organisation which managed the service, and also with locality partners who specified an interest in the project. The strategy involved the creation of unique, fixed-term children's centre employed positions for existing volunteers. This afforded volunteers the opportunity to progress from volunteering to paid work, and aimed to incorporate a substantial training and development package to enable future social mobility. Parent volunteers were asked what they needed to support their application for these roles; their views contributed significantly to compilation of job descriptions and person specifications. Parents entitled the project *Moving on up* and decided upon terms and conditions which included family-friendly hours, suitable business clothing allowance, travel subsidy, living wage rather than minimum wage, and continuing professional development including regular supervision and accredited study, such as paediatric first aid and safeguarding level-1 training. Prospective candidates were required to submit online applications to the local authority which were subsequently reviewed for interview selection, attend multi-agency interviews where both verbal reasoning and practical tasks were tested, and complete and secure satisfactory DBS checks. Unsuccessful applicants were provided with 1:1 support to aid their development for any future employment applications they may make.

Needless to say, the rigour and attention to detail required for the procedure described resulted in a lengthy process and tended to be highly bureaucratic due to the necessity to secure an employing body – in this case, the local authority – which created and retained legal responsibility for these positions. This included accountability for health and safety requirements: for example all successful applicants completed mandatory IT and Equality and Diversity e-learning, and were entitled to holiday/maternity pay where required. Investment in addition to the allocated budget was greater than originally anticipated because of generosity and *gratis* support from all partners involved in respect of time, expertise, enthusiasm and practical arrangements such as providing facilities for meetings. The multi-agency approach provided enhanced understanding and knowledge which promoted quality in the foundations of the project, although at times conflict of opinion and choice naturally ensued. Speculation occurred regarding the level of support provided to step up into these roles, but this was not sustained because partners were unable to dispute the national and local requirements for the initiative. Moreover, the voice of volunteers stating their starting points was acknowledged and informed the level of support deemed necessary. The hybrid partnership between private, public and voluntary and community organisations sought to extract best practice from each sector, capitalising upon individual strengths and minimising weaknesses. So, with the public sector as the catalyst the budget resource available from the state was utilised successfully by the private sector to develop voluntary and community capacity.

Evidence of impact

Within the contemporary contracting culture for children's services, success is measured across all three sectors, not by what is done but rather by the impact the work has achieved, known as outcomes-based accountability (OBA). Evaluation is made of outcomes which result in positive enhancements for children, young people and their families. The ensuing Ofsted report (2014) for this children's centre cluster described the volunteering programme as outstanding and innovative, delivered through excellent partnership working, and a project which contributed significantly to the sustainability of children's centre activities. *Moving on up* was credited as well thought-through and planned, providing invaluable salaried work experience to assist employment opportunities and evidencing excellent progression routes for volunteers entering employment.

However, it is from parent volunteers that we can gain most insight regarding the success of the project and learn of its impact upon them and their families. Outcomes for the cohort of parents included satisfaction in being provided with an opportunity to give back to their community, helping others whilst also fulfilling their own needs. Individual parents reported that they felt their roles provided them with a renewed sense of identity. Some felt this reduced social isolation and some experienced increased confidence, better mental health, development of their organisational skills and that the role provided a structure and daily routine. Several parents increased knowledge regarding their own children's development and parenting skills were enhanced, resulting in happier and more fulfilled home lives. One parent said 'it gives me something for me' and emphasised the opportunity to use skills they felt might otherwise have been lost. There is evidence of improved social mobility in career opportunities. Following cessation of the fixed-term contracts the first cohort of parents variously progressed to study Accountancy at college, NVQ Level 2 in Communication, Skills and Literacy and Midwifery at university, and secure a role as Teaching Assistant in a primary school. Three parent volunteers became active members of the locality management board and continued to shape future service delivery for the children's centre programme. This *village* has undoubtedly discovered that their society was measurably 'bigger' as a result of this initiative.

Conclusion

The status, value and importance of the voluntary and community sector have been analysed and critiqued throughout this chapter. Current policy drivers to strengthen the sector are deemed to be a successful tool for empowering communities. In particular, the *ownership* of services by the public, private or voluntary and community sector is considered, and we conclude that a hybrid model of providers between these three sectors is feasible. Furthermore, the case study gives evidence that significant success in improved outcomes for children, young people and families is possible through hybridity. The partnerships of integrated services are extremely complex and intricately linked (Whalley, 2013). There remains valid uncertainty regarding the equality of each sector within the hybrid partnership whilst one of the main determinants of equality – funding – is unevenly distributed. It is, however, rather naïve and simplistic for professionals to dismiss new ways of working which are structured in policy, legislation and practice guidance as unsuccessful because of emerging insecurities which are derived from fear of change. Emphasis should rather be placed upon opportunities for innovation which transpire. Bronfenbrenner's ecological model (1979) discusses the inextricable links between the systems and their influences on a child's life. The chapter similarly argues that the public, private and voluntary and community sectors are inextricably linked and suggests that hybridity is an endorsed and viable future for the contemporary twenty-first-century *village* required to successfully raise a child.

Summary points

- Volunteering is a growth area.
- The state is increasingly reliant upon the voluntary and community sector to provide services for children, young people and families.
- Boundaries between the public, private and voluntary sectors are blurred, creating hybrid models which synthesise partnership between the sectors.
- Sustainability of voluntary and community organisations is threatened by public spending cuts.
- The involvement of voluntary and community services has the potential to improve outcomes for children and their families.
- Hybrid models involving private, public and voluntary and community organisations can provide innovative and successful partnerships which have the potential to inform future best practice models.

Recommended reading

Ledwith, M. (2011) *Community Development: a critical approach*, 2nd edition. Cambridge: The Policy Press.

Rochester, C., Paine, A.E., Howlett, S., Zimmeck, M. and Ellis Paine, A. (2012) *Volunteering and Society in the 21st Century*. Basingstoke: Palgrave Macmillan.

The Third Sector Research Centre (TSRC) (2017) [Online]. www.birmingham.ac.uk/generic/tsrc/index.aspx (accessed 30 March 2017).

References

Alcock, P. (2010) A Strategic Unity: Defining the third sector in the UK. *Voluntary Sector Review,* **1**(1), pp.5–24.

Allen, G. (2011) *Early Intervention: the next steps.* London: HMG.

ALS Association (2016) *The Ice Bucket Challenge.* [Online]. www.alsa.org/fight-als/ice-bucket-challenge.html (accessed 31 August 2016).

Arnstein, S. (1969) A Ladder of Citizen Participation. *Journal of the American Planning Association,* **35**(4), pp.216–224.

Baring Foundation, Civil Exchange and DHA Communications (2014) Independence Undervalued: the voluntary sector in 2014. [Online]. www.independencepanel.org.uk/wp-content/uploads/2014/01/Independence-undervaluedfinalPDF-copy.pdf (accessed 22 August 2016).

Bennett, K., Mander, S. and Richards, L. (2016) Inclusive Practice for Families. In Z. Brown (Ed.), *Inclusive Education: Perspectives on pedagogy, policy and practice.* Abingdon: Routledge.

Beveridge, Lord W. (1948) *Voluntary Action.* London: George Allen and Unwin.

Billis, D. (2010) Towards a Theory of Hybrid Organisations. In D. Billis (Ed.), *Hybrid Organisations and the Third Sector: Challenges for practice, theory and policy.* Basingstoke: Palgrave Macmillan.

Billis, D. and Glennerster, H. (1998) Human Services and the Voluntary Sector: towards a theory of comparative advantage. *Journal of Social Policy,* **27**(1), pp.79–99.

Bronfenbrenner, U. (1979) *The Ecology of Human Development: Experiments by nature and design.* Cambridge, MA: Harvard University Press.

Bronfenbrenner, U. (1995) Developmental Ecology through Space and Time: a future perspective. In P. Moen, G.H. Elder Jr. and K. Lüsher (Eds.), *Examining Lives in Context.* Washington, DC: American Psychological Association.

C4EO (2010a) Grasping the Nettle: Early intervention for children, families and communities. [Online]. http://archive.c4eo.org.uk/themes/earlyintervention/default.aspx?themeid=12&accesstypeid=1 (accessed 22 August 2016).

C4EO (2010b) International Experience of Early Intervention for Children, Young People and their Families 2010. [Online]. http://archive.c4eo.org.uk/themes/earlyintervention/files/early_intervention_wave_trust_international_desk_study.pdf (accessed 22 August 2016).

Cameron, D. (2016) Young Unemployed Will Work for Benefits. [Online]. http://news.sky.com/story/pm-young-unemployed-will-work-for-benefits-10371141 (accessed 22 August 2016).

Civil Exchange (2015) Whose Society? The Final Big Society Audit. [Online]. www.civilexchange.org.uk/wp-content/uploads/2015/01/Whose-Society_The-Final-Big-Society-Audit_final.pdf (accessed 22 August 2016).

DfE (2012) *Core Purpose of Sure Start Children's Centre Programme.* London: DfE.

DfE (2013) *Sure Start Children's Centres Statutory Guidance for Local Authorities: Commissioners of local health services and Jobcentre Plus.* London: DfE.

DfE (2013–2016) Al-Madinah Free School Ofsted Report. [Online]. http://reports.ofsted.gov.uk/inspection-reports/find-inspection-report/provider/ELS/138776 (accessed 22 August 2016).

Evans, K. (2011) 'Big Society' in the UK: A policy review. *Children & Society,* **25**(2), pp.164–171.

Field, F. (2010) *The Foundation Years: Preventing poor children becoming poor adults. Report of the Independent Review on Poverty and Life Chances.* London: Cabinet Office.

Fundraising Standards Board (2016) The Standards. [Online]. www.fundraisingregulator.org.uk/ (accessed 22 August 2016).

HMG (2004) *The Children Act 2004.* London: The Stationery Office.

HMG (2010a) *The Academies Act 2010.* London: The Stationery Office.

HMG (2010b) The Big Society Policy. [Online]. www.gov.uk/government/uploads/system/uploads/attachment_data/file/78979/building-big-society_0.pdf (accessed 22 August 2016).

HMG (2011a) *The Education Act 2011.* London: The Stationery Office.

HMG (2011b) *The Localism Act 2011.* London: The Stationery Office.

HMG (2013) *Giving of Time and Money: Findings from the 2012-13 Community Life Survey.* The Cabinet Office. London: The Stationery Office.

Hogg, E. and Baines, S. (2011) Changing Responsibilities and Roles of the Voluntary and Community Sector in the Welfare Mix: a review. *Social Policy & Society,* **10**(3), pp.341–352.

Ishkanian, A. and Szreter, S. (2012) *The Big Society Debate: a new agenda for social welfare?* Cheltenham: Edward Elgar.

Just Harvest (2016) Food Stamps Work Requirements: What you need to know. [Online]. www.justharvest.org/get-help/snap-work-requirements-faqs/ (accessed 22 August 2016).

Marmot, M. (2010) *Fair Society, Healthy Lives: the Marmot Review*. London: The Marmot Review.

Munro, E. (2011) *Munro Review of Child Protection: Final report – a child-centred system*. London: DfE.

National Citizen Service (2016) [Online]. www.ncsyes.co.uk/ (accessed 22 August 2016).

National Council for Voluntary Organisations (2012) Open Public Services: Experiences from the voluntary sector. [Online]. www.ncvo.org.uk/images/documents/policy_and_research/public_services/open_public_services_experiences_from_the_voluntary_sector.pdf (accessed 22 August 2016).

NCB (2011) *The Ripple Effect: the nature and impact of the children and young people's voluntary sector*. London: NCB.

NCB (2012) *Beyond the Cuts: Children's charities adapting to austerity*. London: NCB.

OECD (2015) *Education at a Glance 2015: OECD indicators*. Paris: OECD Publishing.

Senior, P. (2011) The Voluntary and Community Sector: the paradox of becoming centre stage in the Big Society. *British Journal of Community Justice*, **9**(1/2), pp.37–54.

Taylor, M. (2007) Community Participation in the Real World: Opportunities and pitfalls in new governance spaces. *Urban Studies*, **44**(2), pp.297–317.

Teenage Cancer Trust (2015) Stephen Sutton. [Online]. www.teenagecancertrust.org/get-help/young-peoples-stories/stephen-sutton (accessed 22 August 2016).

Whalley, M. (2013) Building Bridges. *Rattler (Sydney)*, **106**, pp.20–23.

Section four

Societal aspirations and expectations on children, young people and families

10 Power, inclusion and diversity

Lynn Richards

This chapter will consider the concepts of power, inclusion and diversity and their potential to impact upon the lives of us all. With a keen focus on the child, the young person and the professional, it will interrogate contested understandings of the three concepts and will draw on Bronfenbrenner's (1979) ecological systems theory in order to demonstrate the contextual nature of developments across the human lifespan. As a way of further theorising the content of the chapter, the work of Thompson (2011) will be used, in particular, his PCS analysis which focuses on the personal, cultural and structural as three levels of oppression within society. Thompson's model is represented visually as three concentric circles, in much the same way as Bronfenbrenner's (1979), and it will be argued that these three levels find strong links with Bronfenbrenner's (1979) micro-, exo-, and macrosystems, so demonstrating the situated and relational contexts of differing lifeworlds. The work of Bronfenbrenner has evolved since 1979 and, in Chapter 1 of this volume, Rozsahegyi has outlined details of his move to the bio-ecological model in which the biological attributes of the child are incorporated into his model of development. For the purposes of this current chapter, it is the environmental and interpersonal factors within the context of lived experience that are focused upon, and so Bronfenbrenner's earlier model is employed here. The reader is encouraged to engage with the content as a way of critically reflecting upon their own attitudes, values and beliefs. Whether as a student or professional, prevailing attitudes, values and beliefs mediate our working with children, young people, their families and other professionals. This necessitates examining ourselves in relation to issues of power, inclusion and diversity and not viewing them as intellectual concepts to be understood only in terms of 'others', or in an abstract way. As an example, in discussing the issue of inclusion within formal education, Frederickson and Cline (2009:70) note: 'Making schools more inclusive may involve staff in a painful process of challenging their own discriminatory practices and attitudes.' As a way of applying Thompson's (2011) theoretical underpinning to relevant issues of the child, young person and professional within society, the chapter is in three sections: concepts of power and how these play themselves out within the lives of young children; concepts of inclusion and how a rights-based approach might usefully offer a way forward in the lives of young people; and concepts of diversity and how the professional is expected to manage issues of difference. While presented in this way, there is an underlying premise that all concepts are interrelated and mention will be made of such overlapping interconnections throughout the chapter.

As already discussed in other chapters, the ecological systems theory provides a conceptual tool to offer explanations as to how, for Bronfenbrenner's (1979) purposes, the human developmental journey is embedded in the wider society and community. His model of interconnected and 'nested structures' (Bronfenbrenner, 1979:3) lays bare the influences of a myriad of variables on the developing person. In similar vein, Thompson's (2011) 'levels of oppression' make visible the differing contexts and ways in which power operates within society. He urges his readers never to stop asking who is exerting power and for whose benefit; as students and/or professionals, the reader is similarly encouraged to consider their own potential to oppress and to what extent their personal and (future) professional power seeks to work towards greater social justice for their clients or whether it might result in reinforcing existing inequalities. For Thompson (2006, 40), oppression is defined as 'Inhuman or degrading treatment of individuals or groups; hardship and injustice brought about by the dominance of one group over another; the negative and demeaning exercise of power', and it is to the issue of power that this chapter now turns.

Individual/group task

Consider for a moment your own potential to oppress. Taking up the challenge of Frederickson and Cline (2009) to engage in the 'painful journey', what might be some of your own practices that you may wish to question or reconsider in the light of thinking about how power is being exerted, and for whose benefit?

Concepts of power and how they play themselves out within the lives of young children

At the personal level, Thompson's (2011) model focuses upon the thoughts, feelings and actions as experienced, and applied, within a relational exchange between people. Framing this within the world of young children, the work of Paley (1992) is insightful: '"Are you my friend?" the little ones ask in nursery school, not knowing. The responses are also questions. If yes, then what? And if I push you away, how does that feel?' (3). Even at this young age, Paley (1992) finds that a 'ruling class will notify others of their acceptability, and the outsiders learn to anticipate the sting of rejection' (3). She paints a harsh picture of life in her kindergarten class where power is already operating to privilege some and disadvantage others; power is expressed here as power 'over', a means to secure one's goal at the expense of others. The widely accepted view of young children as 'innocent' is challenged here and the power of the adult, invested with the authority of the teacher, is overridden, or at least problematised. As a leading proponent on the topic of power, the French philosopher Foucault (1977) argues that socially sanctioned 'truths' provide ways of knowing, thinking and acting that influence how members within that society come to know, think and act; as a result, such ways become the taken-for-granted 'truths', the common-sense and unquestioned rules that govern a society. For Foucault there is no universal 'truth'; it is a product of human interaction that is discursively constructed according to time and place. The situated exchange between people, within the personal level of Thompson's (2011) PCS analysis, is informed by the prevailing wider societal 'truths' so that Paley's (1992) kindergarten children may simply have subsumed their familial norms in ways of operating in relation to others. Teachers may unreflectively collude with such norms, or they may interrogate their own values in order to challenge such ways of operating as in the case of Paley (1992), who works respectfully with her young charges to negotiate the advent of a new rule in the classroom: 'You can't say you can't play.'

Respectful working acknowledges the worth of the youngest within our communities, and in itself this would appear to involve the issue of power, not in the sense of power 'over' but as a way to resist the generally accepted ways of working. Gallagher (2008:396) offers the Foucauldian concept of '[p]ower as ambivalent, both dangerous and full of promise, both a means of control and a means of resistance, [which] is particularly useful for understanding children's participation'. Paley's (1992) text is the journey of her resistance to what she sees as the normative ways of children operating within her classroom. She does not impose her new rule but works to resist the current situation and she does this through dialogue and personal interaction with her pupils.

Individual/group task

Why do you think it is that Paley uses dialogue and personal interaction to introduce this new rule in her kindergarten classroom? Why does she not use the power invested in her as teacher? What might be the strengths and limitations of each method?

Power as resistance, or sabotage, is starkly demonstrated within a study by Ahn (2010) centred on the social power of young children. Working to encourage young middle-class children to use their words rather than less socially sanctioned actions of crying or fighting, middle-class professionals introduce their charges to the 'I feel' format of speaking (Ahn, 2010). Far from producing the equitable ways of interaction that they anticipate, it fosters a means of creating alliances and exclusions within the nursery setting. Oblivious to the underlying current of social power being operated through the medium of emotion, professionals continue to work in the belief they have augmented the equitable nature of the provision. When seen through the lens of Thompson's (2011) PCS analysis, the personal level of human exchange between these young children serves to militate against the intended outcomes of their teachers and presents a sizeable challenge to their authority. At the human interface, young children are ignored, upset and excluded, all under the supervisory eyes of their teachers. In terms of power, the perpetrators of these exclusions are exercising their own power, the power within their sphere of influence, the power of agency. Agentic or agential working breaks away from sanctioned discourses to provide valuable means to effect changes at the personal level, even if these are not witnessed as positive for many of the children within Ahn's (2010) study. At a personal level, negative stereotypes of individuals and groups can be overcome by respectful working and getting to know each other on a personal basis, removed from the prejudice of societal 'truths'. The relatively new 'sociology of childhood' (Mayall, 2002) heralds a way of working that acknowledges, and values, the ability of the child to negotiate within child–adult relations and it is the concept of inclusion, framed within a rights-based approach, that will now be examined in light of Thompson's (2011) cultural level of the PCS analysis.

Concepts of inclusion and how a rights-based approach might usefully offer a way forward in the lives of young people

Foucault's socially sanctioned 'truths' may offer us, via the popular media, a view of young people as intimidating, threatening and feckless; using the cultural level of the PCS analysis has the potential to highlight how such 'truths' might negatively impact on our dealings with young people. The cultural level incorporates the context offered by assumptions and norms of the society or environment in which we are living, inclusive of language and humour. For instance, many of Paley's (1992) children struggled to accept the new rule by the end of their kindergarten year, and yet if the following year group does not encourage the same rule and level of personal negotiation it is difficult to see that any movement towards including everyone in play can be achieved. A whole-school ethos of respecting everyone is required. An initiative that began in the UK in 2006 is the Rights Respecting Schools Award (RRSA), which seeks to embed the principles of the United Nations Convention on the Rights of the Child (UNCRC) (UNICEF, 2012) across schools' curriculum and management. It works to uphold equality, dignity, respect, non-discrimination and participation with children and young people. Such a rights-based approach has the potential to be fully inclusive in terms of a broad definition of inclusion. While historically the notion of inclusive education began with the desire to include learners with special educational needs (SEN), the parameters of inclusion have since widened considerably to encompass the needs of all: 'Inclusion is a deeply rooted political response – moral response – to the movement for social justice' (Nutbrown and Clough, 2006:138). Framed in this way, inclusive education seeks to uphold the human rights of all people in order that they can effectively contribute to society (Stubbs, 2008). However, the current figures for young unemployed people in the UK do not affirm that such an outcome has yet been realised (House of Commons Library, 2017). Whereas 'equal opportunities' were emphasised in past decades, it is the outcomes of education that are now the focus of attention. Using the PCS analysis, it can be seen how the multilayered aspects of the model, reflecting similarly those systems within Bronfenbrenner's (1979) model, are helpful in discerning the many factors at play in the lives of young people. Each level has the potential to either assist or hinder.

The presence of an RRSA school within the neighbourhood – Bronfenbrenner's (1979) exosystem – may assist a young person to be nurtured at a personal level by respectful dialogue and exchange. Within the context of the whole-school ethos, the young person is valued and comes to know the existence of the UNCRC, and in particular Article 12 which enshrines the rights of the child/young person to a say in matters that affect their everyday life. The young person is elected onto the school council so that pupil viewpoints can be articulated, listened to and taken seriously within a rights-based approach. Militating against such an approach, however, is the burgeoning negative societal discourse around young people which can serve to disenfranchise them and sully their character, so resulting in their voices not being valued, and their viewpoints not being included. The Foucauldian concept of power is exercised – it is not a commodity – and it is the effects of participatory working that are important (Gallagher, 2008); thus, while the concept of the democratic school council may be well intended, it is the effects of such intentions that are significant. A study by Cassidy (2012) finds that school councils are regularly left to discuss topics of school uniform, food to buy at break time, and toilet facilities. Such a finding does not indicate a deeply held belief in the abilities of young people to become involved in the running of the school: that is, having a say in matters that affect their everyday life. A school ethos requires not only the instrumentalist implementation of policies and procedures but also the positive attitudes of professionals to ensure the values of acceptance, respect and dignity are upheld (Bennett *et al.*, 2016).

Individual/group task

What are the challenges to teaching staff of the democratic school council and what are the benefits? In terms of democratic working within a rights-based approach, how might the school council afford children and young people the opportunity to acquire skills for later life?

Working in the context of SEN, Frederickson and Cline (2009) have found how small-scale studies based on emotional and behavioural difficulties focus on 'within-child factors' rather than 'teacher factors'. This perseverance of the medical model, as opposed to the social model of disability, puts constraints on the ability of pupils with SEN to have their voices heard in ways that uphold their rights within the UNCRC: 'Secondary schools that genuinely encourage pupil voice (a system where pupils are regularly consulted on whole-school issues that affect them) can promote a more inclusive atmosphere and culture that is embedded within the school community' (Rhoades, 2016:94). However, the attitudinal dispositions of staff and of leadership within all educational institutions are key to inclusive practice. If pupil voice is to be articulated through a school council, it is perhaps interesting to speculate whether the 'challenging' young person – the young person exhibiting challenging behaviour – is put forward as a candidate or indeed to what extent older pupils are permitted to override the voices of those younger members (Wyness, 2009). Frederickson and Cline (2009) highlight the need for teaching staff to be reflexive in their practice: to find time for deep self-questioning in order that they can confront their own prejudices and assumptions about young people. For instance, the taken-for-granted view in the UK is that children – and young people often by dint of media negative portrayal – are not competent (Alderson, 2008). Historically, rights have been linked to competency and a rational mind (Federle, 1994; Quennerstedt and Quennerstedt, 2014), so that viewing children and young people as sufficiently capable to be included in participatory working runs contrary to socially sanctioned 'truths' contained within contemporary discourse. In effect, there is an adultist desire to control childhood so that children behave in accordance with the expectations that we, as adults, have of them: young people are 'low status' (Cassidy, 2012). In addition, young people have somehow to convince adults that what they have to say is of worth. Foucault's notion of power is again evident as the intertwining of 'power/truth/knowledge' becomes visible within what has been termed 'privileged' knowledge and 'subjugated' knowledge (Leese, 2011); the former is that held and valued by those in positions of hierarchical power – in this instance the teachers – and the latter is that held by those in subordinate positions of power – in this instance the young people. To return then to the ostensibly democratic school council, it may be argued that, even within this rights-based context, the ambivalent nature of power (Gallagher, 2008) holds sway; dependent on teacher attitudes, it may be interesting to consider to what extent the school council is a site of pupil resistance or staff control.

Both resistance and control may find a compromise in the concept of 'evolving capacity' (Harcourt and Hagglund, 2013) within the rights agenda; as the child/young person becomes older, it is with guidance and nurturance from caring adults that the capacity to act and think in more competent ways is realised. What is perhaps noteworthy is the extent to which this new-found competency equates to that of adults, since adult competence is valued while child competence is not (Quennerstedt and Quennerstedt, 2014); once more the 'privileged' knowledge of the adult world prevails to sanction the official 'truth'. Moving on to see how evolving capacity can work to effect greater inclusion, the British Youth Council is a youth-led organisation committed to the participation, as active citizens, of all those under the age of 25 years. Its manifesto document for 2015–16 (British Youth Council, n.d:12) declares: 'We believe that we need to tackle educational prejudices ... by creating a curriculum and qualification valued by society and more importantly, by young people.' This is a strong statement conferring on young people the rights to have a say in their education; the UK Youth Parliament chose as its national campaign for 2016 the issue of 'reducing racism and religious discrimination in our communities' (Youth Parliament UK, n.d). In the light of xenophobic instances following the 2016 EU Referendum's 'Brexit' vote, it is salutary to dwell upon this choice by young people. It reflects the more global view of inclusion, already noted earlier, whereby education is a driver to afford everyone the chance to contribute to society (Stubbs, 2008). It reinforces the view that, in order to be perceived as competent, young people require the opportunity to demonstrate such competence (Harcourt and Hagglund, 2013). Lastly it highlights the possibility that we, as adults, might conceive of our children and young people as citizens, exactly the same 'as any other citizen or user of a service' (Rayner, 2003:59).

Individual/group task

How might conceiving of our children and young people as citizens, and as rights-bearers, influence the way in which we, as adults, engage with them?

The world of education has a huge impact upon the life chances of our children and young people and so it is reasonable to suppose that they would wish to have a say in what they learn. Looking to achieve a relevant curriculum has been a declared intention of Youth Parliament UK for some years. In the context of SEN education, the 'interactional analysis' model of Frederickson and Cline (2009) is informative. It is based on the individual characteristics of the learner and the environmental factors; these can be located within the cultural level of Thompson's (2011) PCS analysis. The perceived strengths and weaknesses of the learner will be mediated by the contemporary discourses of childhood or youth, and in this situation, also the discourse of disability. While children and young people struggle generally to be seen as competent, those with SEN may struggle even more for recognition. A rights-based approach, however, seeks to push through the deficit-framing of all children and young people. The drive offered by the UNCRC and its periodic reports to the UK continues to emphasise the need for government action. The fact that it 'continues' to raise such a need is testament to the resistance of government to promulgating such action, and is evidence once again of how power is exercised. Paradoxically, however, while the competency argument in relation to children and young people's rights holds firm, so too does the protectionist discourse (Cassidy, 2012), although it is worth noting that 'rights prohibit those who already have power from exerting it ... they (rights) shift power away from those who have it to those who do not, and equalize relationships' (Federle, 1994:366). Such a view is integral to the Committee on the Rights of the Child which advocates 'respect for the rights of children with disabilities to express their views ... in all decision-making that affect them, including on access to and choice of personal support and education' (CRC, 2016:56). Additional recommendations highlight the need for inclusive education and comprehensive working towards transition to adulthood. This report represents the existence of factors within Bronfenbrenner's (1979) 'macrosystem', where laws, policies and wider global pressures exert their influence on everyday living and can be located in Thompson's final 'structural' level of PCS analysis.

Concepts of diversity and how the professional is expected to manage issues of difference

Structural levels of oppression are to be found within the social, political and economic aspects of a society (Thompson, 2011). They impact, however, on all other levels even though their influence may go unnoticed, unremarked and taken-for-granted by individuals and groups. As an example, and by way of working towards the last section of this chapter with its focus on diversity and the ways in which the professional is expected to manage difference, the study by Pearce (2005) offers useful illustration for the purposes of PCS analysis. As a white teacher, and later researcher, Pearce (2005) catalogues her day-to-day workings within the strictures of the national curriculum in her school where the demographic of children is almost entirely Muslim. On one occasion, she is asked by a pupil: 'Were the Anglo Saxons Muslims, Miss?' (Pearce, 2005:19). Using the PCS analysis model to interrogate this question, at a personal level Pearce (2005) responds respectfully to offer a historical answer but she worries that she is transmitting an essentially white, Eurocentric perspective of culture that excludes her pupils; this is located in the cultural level whereby taken-for-granted assumptions and norms – 'I had become used to the mainly white school I had taught at before' (Pearce, 2005:20) – serve to narrow the viewpoint and to marginalise. For Thompson (2011), the personal level of exchange is necessarily influenced by the cultural level of context, and in turn, this is then set within the broader parameters of the structural social order. In this case, the structural order is represented by the national curriculum and its mechanisms of targets, prescriptive content and assessments. It is the government's Secretary of State for Education who decides what is to be learned, and generally how it is to be learned: an example of how power is exercised within education, but which more democratically might be informed by a rights-based approach to children and young people. The PCS analysis is a conceptual tool to become aware of how discrimination and oppression operate (Thompson, 2011:25) and, as such, awareness can allow us to realise how power is exercised within society. Once aware we can begin to be reflexive in our own ways of working in order to militate against reinforcing inequalities and oppression. For Pearce (2005), the solution began with her personal/agential power to change how she worked in relation to her pupils to offer a more inclusive education: for instance, thinking about the Anglo Saxons as contributing to the UK's diverse composition and as an example of mass migration. The issue of diversity is the final topic of this chapter and will be discussed in relation to the management of difference.

The terminology of difference can be problematic. In past years, the concept of equality has been perceived as 'sameness' (Thompson, 2011:4) so that difference has been negatively framed and professional practices have often demonstrated 'colour blind' strategies (Frankenberg, 1993; Dyer, 1997) in order not to bring attention to issues of racial difference. Current discourse is centred on the terminology of diversity where social variety across groups is recognised as a positive attribute and valued as an asset to be embraced rather than seen as a problem (Thompson, 2011). As such, 'Diversity is often used as shorthand for inclusion, as the "happy point" of intersectionality, a point where lines meet' (Ahmed, 2012:14). Diversity, however, is premised in current discourse on the notion of equality: that is, our differences are equally valued. And yet, socially sanctioned 'truths' offer a less equal landscape wherein values are variously attributed to differences. Social factors based on a range of characteristics, such as race, ethnicity, class, gender, ability, sexuality and age, 'intersect' to offer varied lived experiences which will each be influenced by how such characteristics are valued by the prevailing cultural norms. Diversity, then, can in itself be difficult to promote, despite structural imperatives, via legislation, policies and codes, to do so. The term 'managing diversity' has now found favour and is perhaps indicative of the scale of the task in hand, as for Ahmed (2012:13) '"diversity management" becomes a way of containing conflict or dissent'. In contrast, it may be instructive to focus on the nature of diversity within the natural world, since this chapter is couched within an ecological model. Within nature, diversity is prized as the very aspect which gives strength and continuance to living things; those organisms which fail to adapt and change become obsolete. In the light of changing demographics across the globe and within the UK, population diversity is evident, particularly in terms of racial and ethnic diversity and 'diversity in the policy world still tends to be associated with race. The association is sticky, which means the tendency is reproduced by not being made explicit' (Ahmed, 2012:14). Issues of race continue to offer challenges for professionals, as witnessed by Pearce (2005), where the fear of saying the wrong thing is replaced by doing nothing at all (Gaine, 2005). Awareness of the structural level of oppression, however, allows us to see the bigger picture – to move away from individual character flaws and consider how society operates to privilege some, and not others. Pearce (2005:107) concludes that teachers who have a 'more sociological, or political, view of their role' are able to challenge discriminatory practices more effectively. Ahmed's (2012) stance is more penetrating; she argues that diversity workers – those interested in diversity – are the 'institutional plumbers' (32) seeking out blockages but, because institutional practices become habitual, and so unseen, then the task of those professionals managing difference is one of raising the profile of diversity amid an atmosphere of resistance by the institution: 'While habits save trouble, diversity work creates trouble' (27).

Conclusion

This chapter has explored the use of Thompson's PCS analysis as a tool to consider how power operates, how inclusion might be democratically achieved via a rights-based approach, and how diversity working can offer an ongoing challenge within institutional practices. As a way of bringing the beginning and end of the chapter together, it is perhaps salient to recall Paley (1992) whose 'trouble' was the task of making visible those habitual means of discriminatory exchanges between children that went unnoticed by many, except, of course, those who felt the 'sting of rejection' (3) and their teacher who wanted to create a more inclusive classroom. Paley also employs the notion of habit to lay bare the 'automatic' workings of discrimination and lays down the gauntlet of challenge to us all: 'It is the *habit* of exclusion that grows strong; the identity of those being excluded is not a major obstacle' (117; original emphasis).

Summary points

This chapter has demonstrated that:

- Power is a multifaceted and contested concept which can be exercised by children, young people and adults.
- Inclusion offers a way to afford everyone the chance to contribute to society in a meaningful and purposive manner.
- Diversity is premised on valuing people equally.
- The PCS analysis offers a tool to make visible those ways in which power is operating within society.

References

Ahmed, S. (2012) *On Being Included: Racism and diversity in institutional life.* Durham, NC and London: Duke University Press.

Ahn, J. (2010) 'I'm Not Scared of Anything': Emotion as social power in children's worlds. *Childhood*, **17**(1), pp. 94–112.

Alderson, P. (2008) *Young Children's Rights: Exploring beliefs, principles and practice*, 2nd edition. London: Jessica Kingsley.

Bennett, K., Mander, S. and Richards, L. (2016) Inclusive Practice for Families. In Z. Brown (Ed.), *Inclusive Education: Perspectives on pedagogy, policy and practice.* Abingdon: Routledge.

British Youth Council (n.d.) Our Vision, Mission and Values. [Online]. London. www.byc.org.uk/about-us/our-vision-mission-and-values (accessed 19 July 2016).

Bronfenbrenner, U. (1979) *The Ecology of Human Development: Experiments by nature and design.* Cambridge, MA: Harvard University Press.

Cassidy, C. (2012) Children's Status, Children's Rights and 'Dealing with' Children. *International Journal of Children's Rights*, **20**(1), pp.57–71.

CRC (2016) *Advance Unedited Version. Concluding Observations on the Fifth Periodic Report of the United Kingdom of Great Britain and Northern Ireland.* Geneva: United Nations Committee on the Rights of the Child.

Dyer, R. (1997) *White*. London: Routledge.

Federle, K.H. (1994) Rights Flow Downhill. *The International Journal of Children's Rights*, **2**(4), pp.343–368.

Foucault, M. (1977) Truth and Power. In C. Gordon (Ed.), *Power/Knowledge: Selected interviews and other writings 1972-1977. Michel Foucault.* Brighton, UK: The Harvester Press.

Frankenberg, R. (1993) *White Women, Race Matters: The social construction of whiteness.* London: Routledge.

Frederickson, N. and Cline, T. (2009) *Special Educational Needs, Inclusion and Diversity*, 2nd edition. Maidenhead: Open University Press.

Gaine, C. (2005) *We're All White, Thanks: the persisting myth about 'white' schools.* Stoke-on-Trent: Trentham Books.

Gallagher, M. (2008) Foucault, Power and Participation. *International Journal of Children's Rights*, **16**(3), pp.395–406.

Harcourt, D. and Hagglund, S. (2013) Turning the UNCRC Upside Down: a bottom-up perspective on children's rights. *International Journal of Early Years Education*, **21**(4), pp.286–299.

House of Commons Library (2017) Youth Unemployment Statistics. [Online]. Briefing Paper, Number 5871, 15 March 2017. http://researchbriefings.files.parliament.uk/documents/SN05871/SN05871.pdf (accessed 30 March 2017).

Leese, M. (2011) Foucault: Implications for multiagency working in the changing landscape of children's services. In T. Waller, J. Whitmarsh and K. Clarke (Eds.), *Making Sense of Theory and Practice in Early Childhood: the power of ideas.* Maidenhead: Open University Press/McGraw-Hill Education.

Mayall, B. (2002) *Towards a Sociology of Childhood: Thinking from children's lives*. Maidenhead: Open University Press.

Nutbrown, C. and Clough, P. (2006) *Inclusion in the Early Years*. London: Sage.

Paley, V.G. (1992) *You Can't Say You Can't Play*. Cambridge, MA: Harvard University Press.

Pearce, S. (2005) *You Wouldn't Understand: White teachers in multiethnic classrooms*. Stoke-on-Trent: Trentham Books.

Quennerstedt, A. and Quennerstedt, M. (2014) Researching Children's Rights in Education: Sociology of childhood encountering educational theory. *British Journal of Sociology of Education*, **35**(1), pp.115–132.

Rayner, M. (2003) London Children's Participation in the Office of the Children's Rights Commissioner for London. In C. Hallet and A. Prout (Eds.), *Hearing the Voices of Children: Social policy for a new century*. Abingdon: RoutledgeFalmer.

Rhoades, G. (2016) Inclusive Practice in Secondary Education. In Z. Brown (Ed.), *Inclusive Education: Perspectives on pedagogy, policy and practice*. Abingdon: Routledge.

Stubbs, S. (2008) Inclusive Education: Where there are few resources. [Online]. www.eenet.org.uk/resources/docs/IE%20few%20resources%202008.pdf (accessed 16 July 2015).

Thompson, N. (2006) *Anti-discriminatory Practice*, 4th edition. Basingstoke: Palgrave Macmillan.

Thompson, N. (2011) *Promoting Equality: Working with diversity and difference*, 3rd edition. Basingstoke: Palgrave Macmillan.

UNICEF (2012) Rights under the Convention on the Rights of the Child. [Online]. www.unicef.org/crc/index_30177.html (accessed 21 July 2016).

Wyness, M. (2009) Children Representing Children: Participation and the problem of diversity in UK youth councils. *Childhood*, **16**(4), pp.535–552.

Youth Parliament UK (n.d.) Campaigns. [Online]. London. www.ukyouthparliament.org.uk/campaigns/ (accessed 19 July 2016).

11 Empowering communities
Understanding policy contexts

Catherine A. Simon

Introduction

Concepts of 'community' have long been framed as both the problem with and solution to issues of civil society. This chapter considers historical as well as current political influences, including the way successive governments have mobilised notions of community and civic engagement as an organising tool for social and welfare policy-making. Two particular policy discourses have emerged over time. On the one hand acknowledgement of the power of grass-roots community action for change such as locally organised regeneration projects, and on the other encouragement by the state for participatory action in centrally organised initiatives such as Sport England or the National Citizenship Service for 15–17-year-olds.

Community in political discourse has also become synonymous with the absence or withdrawal of state services central, for example, to New Labour's 'New Public Management' which argued for local solutions to local problems. Community, thus conceived, can offer the promise of social capital linked to social mobility, a safety net in times of need and the civilising, democratising effects of social bonds. Such ideas can be found within the 'Big Society' discourse which was used to frame recent Conservative government social welfare and education policy in 2010–16 under David Cameron. Using the example of the *Big Society* and Cameron's later *Life Chances Strategy*, this chapter explores the concepts of 'community' and its use in government discourse and policy-making with particular reference to what it draws on and adheres to, what it ignores or from what it seeks to disassociate itself.

Individual/group task

Before you read this chapter consider the different communities represented in the events reported in this article. A mutual is an organisation run by its users, e.g. youth mutuals are run by the young people themselves.

First play services mutual gets green light

By Adam Offord (2016): www.cypnow.co.uk/cyp/news/2000612/first-play-services-mutual-gets-green-light

Plans for staff at a London council to run half of its adventure playgrounds through an employee-led mutual have been rubber-stamped in what is thought to be the first move of its kind. Awesome Community Interest Company (CIC) will deliver, operate and manage six of Islington Council's 12 adventure playgrounds from October after being awarded a three-year contract worth £1.8m. A number of youth mutuals – designed to take on the running of local authority youth services – have already been established across the UK, but it is thought that Awesome CIC is the UK's first play services mutual. Council documents state that the aim is to secure an adventure play offer for Islington which is high quality, reaches more and different children and families than the current offer and delivers opportunities for 'excitement, risk and access to nature while being safe in spaces with robust safeguarding arrangements in place'. It has been reported that Islington's six other adventure playgrounds will continue to be run by the Islington Play Association.

Where might these different community interests be in support of or opposition to each other?

Policy and policy-making

The relationships between children, their families, communities and society more generally, the focus of Bronfenbrenner's (1977, 1979) ecological and later bio-ecological systems theory, are governed, to a greater or lesser extent, by policy. It is government policy that decides the minimum age at which a child must enter and leave compulsory schooling, for obtaining a provisional driving licence, purchasing alcohol, voting in local or national elections or the age at which children are assumed to have criminal responsibility. These decisions are informed by social norms and constructs of childhood and adulthood. Indeed, policy does not exist in a vacuum and is influenced by a number of factors: social values and traditions; national and international law, such as the United Nations Convention on the Rights of the Child (United Nations, 1989); notions of social justice; or understandings of globalisation with its attendant perceived risks and dangers.

Policy, therefore, is said to incorporate the 'plans, programs, or more broadly the course of action' that a government, party or politician may wish to take (Dean, 2005:258). It can include deliberate inaction as well as action, as in the case of laissez-faire economics where governments argue for limited state control of, or intervention in, the market. Action and inaction are often held in tension. Social policies that govern the lives of children and families navigate a complex course between promoting social expectations and responsibilities on the one hand, and maintaining personal rights and responsibilities on the other. This brings governments into contested areas.

In the UK, policies relating to child welfare have vacillated between two dominant approaches: that of 'child protection and prevention' on the one hand and 'safeguarding' on the other. Child protection is characterised by a focus on 'alleged predictors of harm' (Kominis and Dudau, 2012:147) which include unemployment, poor parenting and social and economic disadvantage, and on the strategies to alleviate them. Historically these have drawn on the individual specialisms and approaches of key services such as health, social services and the police. Safeguarding, however, suggests a more holistic, joined-up strategy of shared responsibility and multi-agency working. New Labour's *Every Child Matters* (DfES, 2003) took this approach and was characterised by a reconfiguration of government departments, bringing together education and child welfare under one government department, that of the Department for Children, Schools and Families (DCSF), and the creation of a children's workforce which amalgamated all agencies responsible for children and young people under a single vision supported by a Common Core of Skills and Knowledge and a Common Assessment Framework (DfES, 2005).

For governments of most Western, neoliberal democracies, therefore, initiating and implementing social policies concerned with children, families and their communities is highly contentious and complex. It is about finding a balance between promoting free will and choice and 'coercing' or 'nudging' individuals to make the 'right' choice for the common as well as individual good. How far this should be the activity of the state and how far the role of local governance is a key part of this debate.

Localism

As Clarke and Cochrane (2013) argue, there has always been a local element to British politics. At its simplest they suggest that localism is about the decentralisation of political power. The Localism Act of 2011 (HMG, 2011) for example, argued that power had become too concentrated in the corridors of Whitehall. It was in the interests of greater efficiency and democracy that such power was to be disseminated to local authorities and other organisations such as civil society groups, public service professionals and small- to medium-sized enterprises. Such organisations were understood to play a mediating role between the interests of civil society and those of the state. Furthermore, local government was construed as being less bureaucratic than central government agencies. However, if power was to be decentralised then so too was responsibility.

Localism is a way of distinguishing between dominant 'national' and 'global' dimensions of economic, social, and political organisation. It is represented by three different models – the managerial, the representative and the community (Evans *et al.*, 2013). Local authorities traditionally stand for representative models of community where elected councillors serve to act on behalf of their electorate. In contrast, managerial localism is distinguished by a conditional devolution of responsibilities (but not necessarily resources) based on achieving certain goals and objectives. Policy, and therefore power, are still determined at the centre. Community localism, on the other hand, is characterised by rights and the support given to citizens in communities to engage in decisions and actions. It is based on understandings of participatory democracy that operate in sustained ways rather than on the basis of elections every three to four years.

Individual/group task

Think about your responses to the following questions:

- How far should the state intervene in the lives of individuals?
- Should the state be determining what is 'good parenting' or a 'good citizen'?
- Is it right that some policies should be targeted at specific families or communities and not at others?

Community

Community can mean many things to many people. It is a slippery word with many and varied interpretations. The term is variously used for fellowship, joint ownership, a state or organised society, a common identity, or interests, for example legal, scientific, academic, religious or business communities (Yúdice, 2005:51). As such, community often implies a connection such as kinship, faith, cultural heritage or shared values and goals, in other words, something that is deeper than a mere contractual association of individuals such as in the market or the state. Smith (2001) for example uses concepts such as 'place' (locality), 'interest' (non-place forms of community) and 'communion' (a spirit of communion) to identify different, even conflicting, notions of community. These, of course, can include the 'virtual' communities made possible through the Internet and the world wide web. Community, therefore, can refer to the geographical and physical, or groups bound by common interest.

Individual/group task

Make a list of the different communities to which you belong.

- Can you organise these into the different categories suggested previously?
- How easy is this to do?

A tool for policy reform

'Community' has featured strongly as an organising tool in public policy discourse over time, particularly since the late 1960s. The Labour government of the day was faced with a number of interlinked problems including housing, transport and urban renewal, which involved the disruption and upheaval of certain spatial communities (Hoggett, 1997). It is out of this context that two specific political discourses of community have emerged. On the one hand, there is acknowledgement of the positive benefits of grass-roots community action. For example, in the 1970s, priority was given to strategies of conflict, rather than participation, in order to effect local reform (Hoggett, 1997:9). In this respect, some local authorities sought to facilitate new community alliances around identities such as race or gender, as opposed to class. On the other hand, the state also looked to strategies of incorporation, encouraging participatory action in centrally funded initiatives as a means of sustaining administrative stability and subduing 'troublesome elements' (Hoggett, 1997:9), witnessed, for example, during the riots of the 1980s. Community groups therefore became embroiled in the competitive battle for scarce government resources in order to fulfil their aims. This was, inevitably, to have a deleterious effect on any sense of community, exacerbating existing tensions along lines of communities of difference. What was occurring between community groups and providers was also mirrored on a larger scale in that cities and regions were set in competition with one another in a global funding market. In Hoggett's analysis, the problem of community represents either the dysfunctional outcome of social and economic policy (system dysfunction) or dysfunctional families and social networks, social instability and a threat to the existing order (social pathologies).

In order to ameliorate the perceived threats of a Britain in social breakdown, community is represented in much of the policy discourse as an imaginary safety net, or a form of social capital, to be enlisted in the competitive struggle for survival or an essential element of emancipatory politics, a resource of resistance based on identities or a lost ideal of society (Hoggett, 1997).

Models of community

Theoretical models such as Bronfenbrenner's ecological and bio-ecological systems theory serve to throw light on the complex web of interactions with individuals or groups that impact the trajectories of child development at various levels of abstraction (micro-, meso-, exo- or chronosystems) and over time (see Chapter 1). Models of community on the other hand help in the understanding of the connectedness of individuals into social groups or entities and the power contained within such communities to effect or resist change. Frazer (1999) noted the positive values inherent within community, values such as solidarity and trust. There are positive benefits from working together on joint projects that can build self-esteem, self-efficacy and a sense of belonging. Various models of community were drawn upon by key exponents of the Conservative Party notion of a *Big Society* – the antithesis to big government – such as Phillip Blond and Jesse Norman. These included some understandings of organisations of civil society such as the Christian church with its focus on attributes of association such as love, care, fellowship or subsidiarity. The Co-operative movement, established during the nineteenth century, was also held up as an example of communities working together for the good of society. Set against the backdrop of the Industrial Revolution, co-operatives sought to address the welfare issues faced by the working classes in the growing industrial towns of the day. They were exemplified in the work of the Rochdale Society of Equitable Pioneers, established in 1844. The Rochdale Principles, later to be adopted by all members of the co-operative alliance, were based on precepts of democracy and mutual support. Co-operative values are listed as self-help, self-responsibility, democracy, equality, equity and solidarity (Co-operative Group, n.d.).

Other models of community such as communitarianism and community empowerment were also employed in *Big Society* rhetoric to justify the distribution of greater responsibility and accountability to local communities for the services designed and used by them. There was an economic imperative to reduce the cost of public services that was masked by an appeal to the latent powers and skills located within communities to organise services that would best suit their needs.

Etzioni's concept of political communitarianism is of key relevance here: 'Communitarians, [are] people committed to creating a new moral, social, and public order based on restored communities, without puritanism or oppression' (Etzioni, 1995:2).

In essence this promotes a rights and responsibilities approach to community action and democratic engagement, where rights and obligations are embedded within strong social networks. In Western neoliberal societies this is also about the rights of the individual and their ability to exercise choice over the actions that impact them most. In relation to public services this is about individuals making the right choices about the services they use and knowing how to exercise a voice when such services are found wanting. Where this can be deployed in support of government policy, community empowerment is applauded. This was the rationale behind the Free Schools agenda in England under the 2010 and 2015 Conservative governments. An appeal was made to parents and professionals dissatisfied with their local schooling system to set up Free Schools that would meet their particular expectations and presumed need of better schools.

In a similar way, the concept of community empowerment links together ideas of citizenship and the state. Community empowerment can bring about positive change. In the initial discussions about the *Big Society* agenda, the work of Saul Alinsky in Chicago in the 1930s was hailed as an example of what can be achieved. Alinsky used the notion of community empowerment to change conditions for those groups who had become marginalised, 'nonparticipants in the social order' (Pruger and Specht, 1969:125). The poor face barriers which exclude them from accessing or benefiting from certain goods or rewards. These include such benefits as education, social welfare or healthcare which are unevenly distributed in society. By discounting the relevance of such rewards or acquiescing to the status quo, the marginalised also limit their own access to the opportunities available to them. Alinsky's solution was the People's Organisations, the means through which the disadvantaged could exercise power and effect change. For Pruger and Specht (1969:127) there were three apparent goals for People's Organisations:

1. to alter environmental factors such as economic injustice, unequal opportunity, or unemployment
2. to alter men's beliefs about themselves
3. to educate – to understand each other and to manage their own affairs.

It is the exercise of power through democratic means within the organisation that will effect much-needed change. The aim was to unite often disparate groups of people around specific grievances. A key strategy was to identify and train local organisers who would lead the People's Organisations. Success depended on the aims and values of the organisation being shared, at least in part, with the wider community who may support the enterprise with the offer of resources including finance. Conflict resolution was at the heart of the democratic processes thus involved. Examples of community empowerment can be seen in urban renewal projects, particularly in the literature relating to youth and community work.

But it is where communities engage in political activism at odds with government aims that the notion of community empowerment becomes problematic. Of course, *Big Society* rhetoric understandably ignored more negative models of community engagement and action such as those to be found amongst the criminal fraternity or the Mafia. But there was obvious tension at play for government in giving communities a voice in the construction of local social and welfare policy and in trying to pursue wider political ends. The proposals in the 2016 Education White Paper to force academisation on all schools are a case in point. The plan was speedily amended following an outcry from local authorities and Conservative Party members alike (Adams, 2016). In reality, some local communities, organisations and actors were given the mandate to effect change on government lines, whilst others were not. These included institutions of civil society, local and national charities and philanthropies. The Salvation Army, for example, was given responsibility for delivering the government's contract in relation to adult victims of human trafficking. Others, however, who may have had an active role in promoting social and welfare policy aims, were noticeably absent from the government's arsenal. Specific amongst these were trades unions – communities of tax-paying, working citizens who traditionally had sought to change the socio-economic conditions of the employees of British industry. There was also an ambivalent relationship with local authorities, typified by engagement through a managerial model of localism. Local authorities were to be held both responsible and accountable for policies made elsewhere.

Plans to make all schools convert to academy status by 2022 were announced in the budget of 2016 with further detail included in the Education White Paper: *Educational Excellence Everywhere* (DfE, 2016). Even though this would mean no school remaining under local authority control, authorities were still to be held legally accountable for finding every child a school place. However, according to the Local Government Association (LGA, 2016), neither they nor the government would have the powers to force schools to expand to meet the need for more school places should the schools choose not to. Furthermore, such a course of action would potentially make it more difficult for authorities to provide the best education resources for the most vulnerable children for whom they still had responsibility.

Theories of social capital

Prominent amongst more recent social welfare and education policy is the notion of social capital and social mobility. Pierre Bourdieu was amongst a number of authors who theorised notions of social capital. In identifying three principal forms of capital – cultural, social and economic – Bourdieu (2003) considered reasons for the unequal access to these resources based on power and the social divide amongst the classes. Social capital theory is based on an understanding that 'capital' is embedded in social networks, ergo the quality of the network determines the quality of the capital generated. Capital, whether economic, human, cultural or social, represents a surplus gained through a process of interactions and can be invested with the expectation of certain returns. For example parents may invest in education for their children with the expected outcome in the future of their offspring gaining access to financially rewarding occupations. Theories of 'capital' by and large assume that there is a class element at play. What is valued in terms of capital – education, health, skills, knowledge – is generally determined by the dominant class. However, as Lin (1999) argues, such theories point to a more nuanced social structure than the classical worker-capitalist model of Marx. It is the *potential* for the capture of capital surplus and investment, by 'the masses' or ordinary citizen, which distinguishes these later capital theories. In the context of social and welfare policy, this is also what interests policy-makers.

In Lin's (1999) analysis four reasons are given why resources embedded in social networks can enhance the outcome of interaction. First, engagement with certain social networks facilitates the flow of *information.* Having connections with individuals who have been to university will help in setting academic aspirations and understanding of the application processes for a young person. Second, social ties can exert *influence.* Knowing who can 'put in a good word' can facilitate entry into the world of work or access to much-needed resources. Third, social networks add value to an individual in terms of 'social credentials', for example through knowing the right person to write a reference or stand as a character witness. Finally, social relations help reinforce *identity and recognition* and thereby assist in good mental health and entitlement to resources.

Furthermore, Lin (1999) also identifies two prominent discourses in the literature relating to social capital. First is a focus on the individual and their relationships. In a similar way to human capital, social capital here is seen as an investment that can be made by individuals with assumed returns in the form of benefits to the individual alone. It is here that social capital theory links closely with the work of Bronfenbrenner. It is the interactions of the individual at the various levels of the bio-ecological system that impact the development of the child. However, another aspect of social capital is at the level of the group – how groups or communities derive and maintain social capital, as in the cases of Saul Alinsky's People's Organisations or the rhetoric behind Free Schools. Both discourses are evident in policy-making.

Example from policy: the Life Chances strategy

Whereas the notion of a *Big Society* made its appeal more broadly to community groups and organisations, Cameron's *Life Chances* strategy focused on the potential for capital to be accrued by the individual. The *Life Chances* strategy was heralded as 'a comprehensive plan to fight disadvantage and extend opportunity' (Cameron, 2016). The family was identified as holding the potential for social mobility and positive outcomes for children and young people, or, in the new government parlance, 'life chances'. The family therefore was chosen as the instrument for addressing persistent issues of social inequality: 'Families are the best anti-poverty measure ever invented. They are a welfare, education and counselling system all wrapped up into one' (Cameron, 2016).

According to Cameron, previous approaches to social policy had missed the social dimensions of disadvantage and poverty which stifled efforts for social and economic advancement, leaving individuals 'stuck and isolated' (Cameron, 2016). Accordingly, the *Life Chances* strategy was informed by four 'social insights' that emerged from this perspective. These recognised the need to:

- improve family life and the early years;
- develop character and resilience in order to create an education system that is genuinely fit for the twenty-first century;
- build a more level playing field with opportunity for everyone, regardless of their background;
- provide the right support for those with addictions, including to those in crisis (Cameron, 2016).

In other words, the strategy was constructed around the family with education as the principal means whereby children and young people from disadvantaged backgrounds access the potential capital surplus (social, human, cultural and economic) available to all. It was about parents building strong networks with other parents supported by health visitors and parenting classes in the early years; building family financial resilience; assisting parents into work; and tackling issues of truancy amongst the young. Justification was given for a return to a *knowledge-* rather than *skills*-based curriculum with an emphasis on character (persistence, curiosity, honesty, perseverance and service) education, and a national Citizenship Service to show young people 'the power of public service, and not just self-service' (Cameron, 2016) (see Chapter 4 on childhood resilience). The latent power of networks in building social and cultural capital was also acknowledged, together with a commitment to develop those networks through the efficacy of mentoring services. Social housing and health services including promised investment in mental health treatment were also included in the strategy. According to Cameron (2016), the underlying belief was that 'people in poverty are not liabilities to be managed, each person is an asset to be realised and human potential is to be nurtured'.

What is not clear, however, is how the 'family' is perceived here. The terms 'parents' and 'family' were used interchangeably throughout Cameron's *Life Chances* speech. There is little indication as to whether it is individual parents or the nuclear family that is the focus or the wider family of aunts, uncles, cousins and grandparents and their contribution to or impact on the individual child's 'life chances, aspiration and achievement'. Indeed, it is worth considering whether traditional constructs of the family are sufficient for such a strategy, given the more fluid family relations of modern society.

Underpinned by the Welfare Reform and Work Act (HMG, 2016), new measures were put in place to increase employment, including a target of introducing schemes for 3 million new apprenticeships. Under the provisions of the Act, the Child Poverty Act (HMG, 2010) was renamed the *Life Chances Act* and previous targets for eliminating child poverty were removed to be replaced with new measures for improving the life chances of children. Most other duties of the Child Poverty Act were also removed. The Secretary of State for Work and Pensions was given new responsibility to report annually to Parliament on data relating to children in workless households and the educational attainment of children at the end of Key Stage 4.

Government was also to produce data on the *Troubled Families* programme, which was to receive new impetus. Set up during the previous Conservative-led coalition, this programme sought to address the needs of the '120,000 most problematic families' in England by 2015, families that cost the taxpayer an estimated £9bn a year (DCLG, 2014). Troubled families were classed as those with considerable problems and who cause problems to others. The key features of the programme – the family intervention factors – consisted of:

- a dedicated worker, dedicated to a family;
- practical 'hands-on' support;
- a persistent, assertive and challenging approach;
- considering the family as a whole – gathering the intelligence;
- common purpose and agreed action (DCLG, 2014).

The tension between intervention by the state to achieve its strategic goals and the desire to reduce welfare dependency remained, particularly in relation to reducing the cost of welfare to the government purse. It was in this regard that the Act made provision to:

- reduce the benefit cap to £23,000 or £15,410 in Greater London and £20,000 or £13,400 elsewhere;
- freeze certain social security benefits and certain tax credit amounts for four tax years;
- limit the amount of support provided by child tax credit for families who become responsible for a child born on or after 6 April 2017;
- limit the child element of universal credit to a maximum of two children and remove the distinction between the first and subsequent children in the rate of the child element;
- remove the work-related activity component in employment and support allowance and the limited capability for work element in universal benefit;
- change conditionality for responsible carers in universal benefit (conditionality refers to the requirements for claimants to engage in activities – e.g. work-focused interview, work preparation or being available for work – which increase their chances of obtaining paid work, or more or better-paid work) (DCLG, 2014).

This more 'social approach' (Cameron, 2016) therefore drew on understandings of social capital theories and there is clear evidence of Lin's (1999) typology of resources embedded in social networks – information, influence, social credentials and identity and recognition. Set against a backdrop of the *Big Society*, life chances indicate the opportunities available through the power of strategic networking arrangements within a range of communities encountered over the life course of the child or young person.

Group/individual task

Taking the *Life Chances* strategy as an example of policy, apply Bronfenbrenner's framework of context, process, person and time (see Chapter 1).

What assumptions do you make about individuals, families, communities and socio-economic contexts?

Summary points

This chapter demonstrates that:

- Social and welfare policy to do with the child and young person is complex.
- It brings governments into contested areas.
- It draws on a range of theories and theoretical perspectives.
- A range of theoretical models can be applied to illuminate the policy process.

Recommended reading

Cameron, D. (2016) Prime Minister's Speech on Life Chances. 11 January. [Online]. www.gov.uk/government/speeches/prime-ministers-speech-on-life-chances (accessed 2 March 2016).

Hoggett, P. (1997) Contested Communities. In P. Hoggett (Ed.) *Contested Communities: Experiences, struggles, policies*. Bristol: Policy Press.

Lin, N. (1999) Building a Network Theory of Social Capital. *Connections, 22*(1), pp.28–51.

Simon, C.A. and Ward, S. (2010) *Does Every Child Matter?: Understanding New Labour's social reforms*. London: Routledge.

References

Adams, R. (2016) Government Drops Plans to Make All Schools in England Academies. *The Guardian*, 6 May. [Online]. www.theguardian.com/education/2016/may/06/government-backs-down-over-plan-to-make-all-schools-academies (accessed 25 August 2016).

Bourdieu, P. (2003). Forms of Capital. In J.C. Richards (Ed.), *Handbook of Theory and Research for the Sociology of Education*. New York: Greenwood Press.

Bronfenbrenner, U. (1977) Toward an Experimental Ecology of Human Development. *American Psychologist, 32*(7), pp.513–531.

Bronfenbrenner, U. (1979) *The Ecology of Human Development*. London: Harvard University Press.

Cameron, D. (2016) Prime Minister's Speech on Life Chances. 11 January. [Online]. www.gov.uk/government/speeches/prime-ministers-speech-on-life-chances (accessed 2 March 2016).

Clarke, N. and Cochrane, A. (2013) Geographies and Politics of Localism: the localism of the United Kingdom's Coalition Government. *Political Geography, 34*, pp.10–23.

Co-operative Group (n.d.) *Our History.* Manchester: The Co-Operative Group. [Online]. www.co-operative.coop/corporate/aboutus/ourhistory/ (accessed 12 May 2013).

DCLG (2014) *Understanding Troubled Families.* London: DCLG.

Dean, M. (2005) Policy. In T. Bennett, L. Grossberg and M. Morris (Eds.), *New Keywords: a revised vocabulary of culture and society.* Oxford: Blackwell.

DfE (2016) *Educational Excellence Everywhere.* London: DfE. [Online]. www.gov.uk/government/uploads/system/uploads/attachment_data/file/508447/Educational_Excellence_Everywhere.pdf (accessed 11 August 2016).

DfES (2003) *Every Child Matters.* Norwich: TSO. [Online]. http://webarchive.nationalarchives.gov.uk/20130401151715/www.education.gov.uk/publications/eOrderingDownload/CM5860.pdf (accessed 4 February 2014).

DfES (2005) *Common Core of Skills and Knowledge for the Children's Workforce.* Nottingham: DfES Publications.

Etzioni, A. (1995) *The Spirit of Community: Rights, responsibilities and the communitarian agenda.* London: Fontana Press.

Evans, M., Marsha, D. and Stoker, G. (2013) Understanding Localism. *Policy Studies,* **34**(4), pp.401–407.

Frazer, E. (1999) *The Problem of Communitarian Politics: Unity and conflict.* Oxford: Oxford University Press.

HMG (2010) *Child Poverty Act.* London: HMG.

HMG (2011) *The Localism Act, c20.* London: HMG. [Online]. www.legislation.gov.uk/ukpga/2011/20/contents/enacted (accessed 31 August 2012).

HMG (2016) *Welfare Reform and Work Act Explanatory Notes.* London: HMG. [Online]. www.legislation.gov.uk/ukpga/2016/7/pdfs/ukpgaen_20160007_en.pdf (accessed 20 August 2016).

Hoggett, P. (1997) Contested Communities. In P. Hoggett (Ed.) *Contested Communities: Experiences, struggles, policies.* Bristol: Policy Press.

Kominis, G. and Dudau, A.I. (2012) Time for Interactive Control Systems in the Public Sector? The Case of the Every Child Matters Policy Change in England. *Management Accounting Research,* **23**(2), pp.142–155.

LGA (2016) Turning Schools into Academies: Why the LGA opposes forced academisation proposed in Budget 2016.[Online].www.local.gov.uk/turning-schools-into-academies-why-the-lga-opposes-forced-academisation-proposed-in-budget-2016 (accessed 25 August 2016).

Lin, N. (1999) Building a Network Theory of Social Capital. *Connections,* **22**(1), pp.28–51.

Offord, A. (2016) First Play Services Mutual Gets Green Light. *Children and Young People Now.* 25 August. [Online]. www.cypnow.co.uk/cyp/news/2000612/first-play-services-mutual-gets-green-light (accessed 25 August 2016).

Pruger, R. and Specht, H. (1969) Assessing Theoretical Models of Community Organization Practice: Alinsky as a case in point. *Social Service Review,* **43**(2), pp.123–135.

Smith, M.K. (2001) Community. In *The Encyclopedia of Informal Education.* [Online]. www.infed.org/community/community.htm (accessed 31 August 2012).

United Nations (1989) *United Nations Convention on the Rights of the Child* (UNCRC). Geneva: United Nations.

Yúdice, G. (2005) Community. In T. Bennett, L. Grossberg and M. Morris (Eds.), *New Keywords: a revised vocabulary of culture and society.* Oxford: Blackwell.

12 Growing up in the twenty-first century

Gary Beauchamp, Sue Wilkinson, Kieran Hodgkin and Andrew Pickford

Introduction

Earlier chapters have already identified the centrality of social environments, such as the family and educational settings, to Bronfenbrenner's perspective on a child's development. Some of these environments are out of the child's control (such as biological inheritance), some are partially within the child's control, with the potential to influence them more as they grow older, while others become largely within the child's control as an 'active agent' as they grow older (such as interpersonal relationships, both 'in the flesh' and virtual). This complex synergy of influences is situated within 'life spaces' (Bronfenbrenner, 1979:23) which, with devolved government, are becoming increasingly different around the United Kingdom (UK) and, indeed, around the world. Within the UK this is particularly true in 'educational spaces', which increasingly reflect the desire of devolved governments to use education policy to develop a distinct identity and reflect political ideology. The consequence in the UK is that 'in Scotland, Northern Ireland and Wales education is clearly important in the construction of developing and/or re-affirming national identities', with a consequence that England is 'emerging as the outlier' (Beauchamp *et al.*, 2015:164). It could be conjectured that the same may be said of many educational systems around the world, but when it comes to growing up in the twenty-first century, in all educational settings, at all ages, we concur with Luckin (2008:451) that the 'classroom' (whatever form it takes, both indoors and outdoors) comprises 'a set of inter-related resource elements, including people and objects, the interactions between which provide a particular context'.

These interactions, however, are not always with others in the same setting as an added complexity in modern times is the advent of 'virtual' life spaces. The result is that:

> The walls of the classroom and the home have been expanded by social media, the cloud, wikis, podcasts, video-conferencing etc. These are new learning environments and they are local, national and global and populated by whole communities in addition to family, teachers and friends.
>
> *(Digital Education Advisory Group, 2013:4)*

The influence and impact of these various life spaces will provide a focus for this chapter and will be explored and exemplified by three fictionalised, illustrative case studies within different parts of the UK – although they are based on real children encountered in research projects. All of the issues, however, will apply elsewhere within the UK and indeed around the world. The case studies will explore the lived experience of childhood and adolescence across emergent themes (particularly technology, society and community cohesion, the family unit, learning and happiness) in a digital age in all aspects of the children's lives. In order to provide a framework, the case studies will focus on three broad UK age phases, namely preschool (0–4 years), primary/elementary school (5–11 years) and compulsory secondary school (11–16 years).

Individual/group task

Either on your own, or in a group, consider the impact of government policy, both in education and in wider society, on your own childhood wherever you grew up. (You may also want to consider at what age you became aware of this – it could be you just have!)

To contextualise our thoughts it is necessary to briefly examine the 'macrosystems' (Bronfenbrenner, 1995) provided by recent changes in the way various parts of the UK are governed, and what powers are devolved to these systems – see also the discussion of localism in Chapter 11. Despite the concept of a 'United' Kingdom, and until relatively recently, a centralised government, Grosvenor (2005:285) suggests that it was 'not homogenous but is, and always has been, plural, fragmented and differentiated'. The gradual emergence of public interest in devolved powers has led to the formalisation of these fragmented and differentiated systems of government, particularly in education, which increasingly reflect national identity. At the time of writing, England, Wales, Scotland and Northern Ireland all have varying degrees of devolved powers, all including education.

Ongoing changes in these powers and others can be influenced by many factors, not least of which is the cycle of elections to national governments. In England in particular, this can lead to sudden changes in priorities and rhetoric and it is harder to predict the longer-term political direction. In Scotland the rise and consolidation of power by the Scottish National Party (SNP) would suggest a more stable political direction and trust in the Scottish Government seems to be growing as 'In 2015, almost 3 in 4 people (73%) said they trusted the Scottish Government to act in Scotland's best long-term interest compared with 23% who said this of the UK Government' (Scottish Government, 2016:4). By contrast, in Northern Ireland fluctuation in the parties holding power continues, and the legacy of previous sectarian troubles remains in the fact that each Member of the Legislative Assembly, or MLA, 'must designate him or herself as "Unionist", "Nationalist" or "other"' (www.nidirect.gov.uk/articles/overview-government-northern-ireland). Currently, Whysall (2016) suggests that 'the underlying politics of Northern Ireland is such that the institutions remain in some danger – and in the longer term the sands are shifting in unexpected ways'. In Wales there is a more established political direction and, even though the 'vice-like grip of the Labour Party upon Welsh national life' (Jones, 2014:185) has declined since devolution, 'the influence of the Labour Party has prevailed, although now more nuanced by negotiations with other parties to maintain this' (Beauchamp and Jephcote, 2016:114). As well as political history, Wales is also a good example of the impact of industrial and social history as Daugherty and Davies (2011:5) suggest: 'the legacy of industrialization has produced a class structure very different from either England or Scotland … [so] Wales has particular needs that require distinctive policy solutions.'

This variation is important as there are many factors, both human and structural, that will affect the lives of the children in this chapter. Martens *et al.* (2010:10) make a helpful distinction between *policies* (goals and instruments), *politics* (modes and actors involved in decision-making) and *polities* (institutional structures of decision-making), all of which can impact on each other. In this chapter we will be focusing on the impact of policies in some parts of the UK, but we may also need to consider the impact of the 'actors' involved in developing these and the structures they work within. For instance, in educational policy in England the impact of the 'polarizing figure' (Dennis, 2016) of Michael Gove's time in charge of education is still being felt (Finn, 2015).

Case studies

Before we proceed further in the chapter we need to meet our three case study children whose childhood and adolescence in Scotland, England and Wales we will follow. As noted in Chapter 1 of this book, 'Bronfenbrenner never implied (let alone stated outright) that every aspect of the model had to be included within any study' (Tudge *et al.*, 2009:207) and it will be impossible to focus on all aspects of his bio-ecological model in this chapter. Nevertheless, our exploration of the three case studies, which are necessarily stereotyped to model social and cultural 'interactions' (Bronfenbrenner, 1979) in real-life social contexts, will allow the exploration of different biological, environmental and interpersonal relationships and environments. This is necessary as 'social conditions are experienced in increasingly differentiated ways from person to person' (Simmons *et al.*, 2014:8) and the children must 'confront the multiplicity of choices, risks and dangers encountered in post-industrial times unaided by the prefigured scripts of class, gender, religion and culture which characterised earlier generations' (8).

Firstly, we meet *Anna*, who was born in a once-bustling village in the South Wales valleys, on 31 March 2000. The mine which once dominated the community, both physically and in terms of employment, is now decommissioned, the pithead machinery and buildings have been demolished and the grounds landscaped. Nevertheless, the village still retains a strong sense of community (see discussion in Chapter 11) based on kinship and the cultural heritage provided by the mining industry. Unfortunately, all that remains to remind both villagers and passers-by of this industry is a large pit-wheel mounted in the middle of the village, although many generations of some families remain in the village, providing a collective folk-memory of previous times. In contrast, many new families have moved into the village for cheaper housing and easy transport links to the capital city. Anna was born to two university-educated parents; her mother was a primary school teacher and her father worked in management for the local area police force.

Secondly, we meet *Liam* who was born on 1 July 2000 in a three-bedroom flat in an inner-city housing estate in Manchester. Liam's family consisted of his mother, a single mother after divorcing Liam's father a few months after Liam was born, and his two older twin brothers, who are seven years older than Liam. As well as raising her three sons, his mother worked as a cleaner in central Manchester. This meant that Liam spent most of his time with his two brothers. Liam and his brothers played football in the nearby park on a regular basis. From an early age Liam was a keen Manchester United fan and had set his sights on playing for them when he was older.

Finally, we meet *Isobelle*, a privileged child born on 10 August 2000 in a small village in the Highlands of Scotland. She has wealthy and successful parents, also born and bred in Scotland. When she was born, she already had an older brother, Robert, who was three years old. She later gained a little sister, born two years after her. Her parents were highly regarded members of the local community, with her father working as a lawyer and her mother as a consultant paediatrician. Isobelle's family lived in a luxurious five-bedroom detached property set amongst two acres of landscaped gardens.

Individual/group task

Either on your own, or in a group, read the section on 'Theories of social capital' in Chapter 11 and discuss the cultural, social and economic capital of each of the families. Consider potential inequalities and the reasons for them, as well as how these may be addressed as the children grow older.

Preschool (0–4 years)

From the foregoing, it can be seen that an 'accident of birth' results in different social, economic, cultural and personal circumstances. This should be a cause for concern as 'statistics support the British Government's concern over the lack of social mobility in Britain and its relationship with the state/private education divide, a problem unmatched in any other comparable nation' (Connolly, 2013:281). This should not, however, define the child's whole life as Van Leeuwen (2009) suggests that, although concerns about social inequality are important in all societies:

> In a fully open society each individual will achieve as much as his or her talent allows, without being stopped short by 'inherited' inequalities, most notably social background. Societies open to 'talent' are better geared for innovation and economic growth, and we are inclined to think of them as fairer than societies that block the social ascent of their talented members in favour of inherited positions.
>
> *(399)*

As we consider the narratives in what follows, you can begin to consider whether these children live in a 'fully open society'.

Anna's life began happily: she had two parents who doted over her, and despite having little time free from work, they made sure her development was at the heart of everything they did. She was read to every day from an early age, her toys were educationally focused and she went on numerous family trips to stimulate her development. These regular and reciprocal interactions, or proximal processes, provided a relatively stable early environment and Anna's early life was filled with happiness and love. However, Anna noticed as she grew older that there were increasing arguments between her parents, stemming from balancing both work and home life, and her parents' relationship, and hence her own proximal processes, grew increasingly complex as she reached the time she was due to start primary school.

From the start Isobelle's care was largely managed by her nanny, alongside her brother before he started preschool at age four. The nanny came to the house each day to take care of Isobelle and her brother, and later her sister too. Thus, although she saw less of her parents, the context, or microsystem, was provided by her nanny rather than her parents. Hence, this process provided social continuity for Anna, but from a narrow social circle.

By contrast, Liam's early years were spent mainly with his older brothers as his mother worked and we should note the potential impact (highlighted in Chapter 8) of living with a single parent which means Liam is more likely (although by no means certain) to experience an economically deprived childhood (Bradshaw and Holmes, 2010). By the time he was three he would often leave the house with his brothers to go and meet their friends on the estate. Hence, he was socialising with much older children and his dyadic (multi-person) activities provided experience of a range of personal characteristics from these older children; they were very different from those of Anna and Isobelle, who were largely mixing with children their own age or adults. Bronfenbrenner's (1994) idea of 'context' would suggest this allowed Liam to experience a different range of personal experiences in these dyadic interactions, or environments, which along with his other attributes resulted in a unique development as a 'person'. This would also be true of the other children, but their contexts are markedly different and, it could be argued, resulted in unique developmental outcomes for each. It should be remembered, however, that although these micro-time episodes are important for each child, other experiences of (sub-)culture and society changes over (meso- and macro-)time will also affect the development of the children – both positively and negatively (as described in Chapter 8).

Individual/group tasks

Preschool

Either on your own, or in a group, consider the impact of different social and economic backgrounds on the early years of a child. What do you consider to be the impact (if any) of nature and nurture?

It is also worth considering the ideas presented in Chapter 9 on the *Big Society*, with regards to how involved the different families are in their communities in terms of time, money and resources contributed. It may be useful to reflect on how this differs across the case studies and what factors might impact on this (socio-economic status, education, values etc.).

Primary school (5–11 years)

As the children move into a new 'context' in full-time education, they begin to extend their experience of different settings and move from micro- to mesosystems (as described in Chapter 8), which Bronfenbrenner (1994:40) defines as 'the linkages and processes taking place between two or more settings containing the developing person (e.g. the relations between home and school…)'. In addition, we will also see changes in their chronosystems, that is the 'change and consistency over time not only in the characteristics of the person but also in the environment in which that person lives' (Bronfenbrenner, 1994:40).

In common with all our children, in the academic year Liam turned five, he began attending school, in his case Urban Academy. The school had recently converted to an academy after its failing status was identified in successive inspections. Although Liam enjoyed some elements of school, he yearned to get home to go to the park with his brothers. When Liam started school, his brothers were attending secondary school (also a converted academy). However, they spent most of their time 'skiving off' to hang around the local youth centre with their friends. Liam knew this because he shared a small bedroom with one of his older brothers. He didn't mind because he enjoyed talking to his older brother, but did long for the day when he would have a room of his own. This was one of the many aspects of growing up that Liam looked forward to. The real-life social context that Bronfenbrenner claims is central in shaping a child's growth is evident here. Forced to share living space with his brother, Liam craved privacy and independence as he grew up, and this early experience of wanting more personal space than is possible in his home environment could form deep-rooted attitudes towards the environment and surroundings that will influence his choices in adulthood. The other thing he was looking forward to was the local youth centre – thereby extending his mesosystem further. At the time, as part of a social funding project, the youth centre provided young people with the opportunity to get involved in a number of clubs and societies. These opportunities to get involved in community services have the potential to improve outcomes for children, as discussed in detail in Chapter 9. Liam's brothers attended a community football club that ran on Mondays and Wednesdays, but Liam was too young to participate. Whilst his mother was working, Liam was spending these evenings watching his older brothers at the football club. This situation, whereby Liam could not participate but had to observe rather than engage in his own activities, could have an impact as he moves through his 'life course' (Bronfenbrenner, 1995), with the potential to impact (positively and negatively) on his social relations in ways that will not be visible until he has grown up. This is another instance of Bronfenbrenner's real-life social contexts at play, and highlights the importance of a child's surroundings and experiences in shaping their psychological development, even if this is not immediately obvious at the time.

On Liam's tenth birthday, his mother took the day off work and spent the day cooking a Sunday roast. This was one of the main family traditions which provided a stable microsystem for Liam. Every Sunday, without fail they would sit down for a Sunday roast. Liam enjoyed his tenth birthday for several reasons. First, he could join the football club at the local youth centre. Second, his brothers had got him an iPhone, although he wasn't entirely sure where they had got the money for it. His mother also asked the same question as they were only 17, had finished school and didn't have jobs. After a heated discussion, his mother let him keep the phone. At the time, some of Liam's friends at school had iPhones but they had received these as presents from their parents. Now that Liam had an iPhone he was able to create a Facebook account to chat with his friends. Whilst the family had Internet at the house, his mother restricted its use to between 6 and 8 p.m., but this still enabled him to further extend into a new 'virtual' microsystem with its own 'culture or subculture' (Bronfenbrenner, 1994:40). Each of the children would experience this at some point in their development, but this new real-life social context was experienced differently by each, with varying degrees of control and access to differing micro-, meso- and exosystems, both local and international.

Isobelle started in a private fee-paying preschool setting at age four where she was given a head start with core literacy and numeracy skills. Isobelle attended prep school from the age of five in the town closest to her village. For the most part, transport to and from school was managed by the nanny, with the occasional involvement of her parents when possible. Three days a week,

Isobelle attended after-school activities provided by the school. She started to learn the violin and would attend after-school violin lessons at the same time as her brother had trumpet lessons. As Isobelle improved with her violin playing she would practise after school with her peers, in organised group-music sessions. On another day of the week Isobelle would attend swimming lessons, and on another, ballet classes.

All these activities extended and developed her own micro- and mesosystems, but unlike Liam these remained firmly in the 'real' world until she was ten, when she and her older brother were provided with Android smartphones. This made communicating with her friends and peers much easier, and she would spend hours chatting via social media – although this would generally not be allowed until after dinner, and after her homework and chores had been done. Despite this, the development of her mesosystem helped Isobelle build bonds with her friends, and as she grew older the use of social media increased her ability to relate to her peers through shared experience and interaction online. This is an example of a child drawing on their environmental resources to respond to changes in social settings – in accordance with Bronfenbrenner's argument that as a child makes sense of their environment they draw from personal and environmental resources to adapt. Isobelle struggled with some aspects of face-to-face contact with new people due to her sheltered and privileged upbringing, so using the technology available to her (smartphone, social media) she compensated for this by developing her virtual network instead.

Anna's parents finally split up a few days after her fifth birthday, during her first year at school, and her father moved to London for employment. As Anna progressed through primary school, the birth of two siblings to her father and his new wife meant Anna was part of a growing, non-traditional and split family which disrupted her previously relatively stable microsystem. It also had the potential to affect her development as it meant she had to deal with more complex reciprocal interactions. These interactions were further complicated when Anna's mother remarried when Anna was six. By this point, however, Anna was happily engaged in her school life at the local village primary school. Here, she was introduced into the Foundation Phase, the child-centred early curriculum which had replaced KS1 in Wales. She had often heard her parents discussing the merits of this approach to education, with divided opinions causing more arguments. The school Anna attended was heavily influenced by the policy, and Anna would routinely 'play' as a central part of her learning. At this stage, there was very little formal assessment or testing in school – something which would change markedly when she started secondary school. The emotional impact of the family split, however, continued to torment Anna, but at the age of eight she had her first phone and was using it to 'Skype' her dad more than she saw him face-to-face. But, like Liam, she was extending her mesosystem by entering a 'virtual' world.

These systems were further developed as Anna joined the school choir and a football club in a nearby town, where she developed a new circle of friends. Although her family was not particularly affluent, they paid for trips to Germany and Spain with the choir and football club. Anna was aware that two of her best school friends, both of whom lived on a local estate with high levels of unemployment, missed out on the trips as they couldn't afford to go. Anna felt badly for them, but she soon made new friends on the trips. The initial friendship group started to drift apart, notably during the last couple of years of primary school when Anna was placed in the 'coch' (red) group in school with the higher-ability children, and the friends were not. Anna and her friends started to recognise perceived differences in ability, and sadly it seemed to be those children from the estate who were weakest, using conventional measures of achievement.

Task

There is conflicting evidence about the impact of social class on achievement. Research evidence for both sides of the argument and decide which is the stronger.

When Anna was ten, Jacob – her new baby brother – joined the family. Jacob enjoyed the same levels of attention and educational focus that Anna did as she grew up, but a discernible difference was his exposure to the technology of tablets and smartphones. By the time Jacob was 3, the family had numerous tablets, smartphones and laptops, and Anna was often amazed at how Jacob would pick something up so quickly – things she remembered having to learn. Her parents debated the merits of allowing him access to this hardware but felt like they were swimming against the tide by trying to restrict it.

Individual/group task

Primary school

Think about what individual and shared experiences in primary school might impact on a child's development in terms of their self-perception, attitudes towards their environment and relationships, and ability to build friendships and identify with peers. What different issues might arise for Liam, Anna and Isobelle?

Secondary school (11–16 years)

At the age of 11, Isobelle took an entrance exam for a grammar school in Edinburgh, where her brother was already in attendance. As a result, Isobelle moved to Edinburgh to board at the fee-paying mixed-sex school with her brother. This environmental change was significant for Isobelle but she adapted well to life at boarding school. However, this change in 'life space' highlights the potential impact of these 'real-life contexts' in shaping a child's growth, a significant feature of Bronfenbrenner's work. Isobelle easily made the transition from a structured home life where she was restricted in terms of her free time, to being more responsible for her time and how she might spend it. Many of the habits she was used to were carried forward into her teenage years, as her social and educational environment had shaped her preference for routine and structure. She joined the swimming team and the orchestra, started becoming interested in prose recital and worked her way through the relevant examinations.

Isobelle largely kept in touch with friends from prep school via social media and she was now free from her parents' rules regarding when it could be used. Her attitude towards her social environment and the way in which she chose to interact with her friends as a teenager directly related to her experiences earlier in her life. This is an example of Bronfenbrenner's philosophy where it is argued that the child draws from both personal and environmental resources to respond to the social settings of which she or he is a part (Bronfenbrenner and Evans, 2000).

Isobelle's high expectations, fostered throughout her childhood, formed the basis of how she performed in her education and her personal hobbies and activities. Her structured, formal and opportunity-laden upbringing shaped her perceptions of entitlement, success and what is considered to be 'the norm'. This in turn affected her use of social media where it gradually became a showcase for her activities and successes, and this dominated her social interaction with peers during her teenage years. The purpose of social media for Isobelle had shifted from informal communication with friends as part of her microsystem, to serve as more of a repository for achievements and adventures.

The environment in which Isobelle was raised, including her parents' education and professional occupations, and the opportunities available to her as a member of society at a 'higher' level, would indirectly impact on what happened within her immediate environment and how she developed over time. This passage is a pertinent example of Bronfenbrenner's 'macrosystems' in action. Bronfenbrenner (1979) highlighted the significant impact child-rearing had on the development of the child. In addition, biological influences that may have benefitted Isobelle and fostered her development and achievements include genetics and access to high-quality nutrition and health-promoting opportunities.

When Anna made the transition to secondary school, she attended the nearest comprehensive school, which in 2009 had been rated 'Good' by Estyn, the education inspectorate in Wales. Her parents had debated whether or not to send her to a local faith school, but decided that the separation from her friends would not merit the possible improvements in her education. Within a year, under a new inspection regime, her school had been declared 'unsatisfactory' by a school inspection team and following the subsequent re-inspection the school was plunged into 'special measures'. Anna read local media stories about how bad her school was and she and her friends debated in online groups which of her teachers was going to be sacked next. School life was filled with gloom from her teachers and, in addition, she began sitting more and more tests as the government seemed to distance itself from previous more egalitarian policies. Anna was confident in her abilities, but she noticed that many of her friends were ill-equipped to deal with this form of testing.

As Anna went into her GCSE years in school, she began to excel academically. Her two best friends in school were in middle sets and she was in the top sets across the board. She missed them immensely, but they soon began to drift apart. Differences in parental expectations seemed to contribute to her and her friends' outcomes. She would visit one of her friends and her mother would speak disparagingly of her chances in exams and for further success. This saddened her, but it became all the more true throughout this time of her life. When results day came, she had excelled, and her friends had not done as well and seemed destined to leave school.

Liam had also started secondary school. City Comprehensive was an academy in Manchester, the school his brothers attended. Some of Liam's friends from primary school also joined him. However, Liam was also forced to make new friends at his new school. Having shared a bedroom with his brother for five years he had learned that this school was difficult and he began to skip classes to hang out with his friends at the park. His brothers had also bought a PlayStation for the house so Liam would miss classes to play games online with his friends. Increasingly this online world became Liam's virtual 'life space' in which he rearranged his social relations and interactions (Thomas, 1996).

During Liam's teens, his mother spent a lot of her time at work and would argue a lot with his two older brothers. He also noticed that as he grew older the family's Sunday-lunch tradition was not a tradition anymore. His brothers were hardly at the house and his mother was too tired to cook. Sundays now consisted of Liam and his mother sitting on the sofa and ordering a takeaway.

Hence, even the one stable part of his microsystem disappeared. By his fifteenth birthday Liam had lost almost all interest in school. He saw his brothers starting to earn money and buy nice clothes and Liam became more and more interested in his brothers' work. He was not sure where they had got the money for the clothes. He would hear one of his brothers on the phone some nights arranging to meet friends at certain times to make an exchange. Whenever he questioned his brother he would be told to be quiet and go to sleep. By that time Liam had a computer in their room as a result of his brother's income and the 'virtual' world, and the associated proximal processes, further increased in importance at the expense of other interpersonal relationships. He had quit the football club and spent a lot of his time on the computer chatting with his friends. His brother had also invested in a brand-new PlayStation. Liam enjoyed playing new games with his friends, chatting online as they played. He wanted some money to spend on new computer games and one of his brothers had agreed to take his younger brother to 'work' with him when he turned 16. This was something Liam looked forward to with much excitement. More so than any of the other children, by this time, Liam was an 'active agent' in these interpersonal connections – initiating, forming, navigating, changing interfaces – resulting in increased social competence to meet expectations and demands set by changing environments.

Individual/group task

Secondary school

Either on your own or in groups, consider the impact that moving to secondary school had on Liam, Anna and Isobelle. Can you highlight how their development was impacted by environmental, biological and interpersonal factors?

Conclusion

The narratives of all three children have shown how Bronfenbrenner's ecological and bio-ecological models can be used to help understand the conditions and processes affecting children's development. The case studies also exemplify the potential impact of specific 'predictors of children's positive and negative social behaviors' identified by Ashiabi and O'Neal (2015:2), namely: socio-economic status; family and parenting stress; neighbourhood social capital; and parent–child interactions. All of these were affected in some way by the increasing availability and sophistication of technology and the resultant virtual life spaces that children can inhabit – with children becoming active agents in controlling this at relatively early ages as they may know more about the technologies than their parents who might be trying to control them. Bronfenbrenner (1994:40) identifies the 'necessity of going beyond the simple labels of class and culture to identify more specific social and psychological features at the macrosystem level that ultimately affect the particular conditions and processes occurring in the microsystems'. However, given the rapid pace of change in current society in which 'all social forms melt faster than new ones can be cast' (Bauman, 2005:303), it may be that elements of the microsystem facilitated by advances in technology, and children's increasing agency, may now be beginning to affect the conditions in the macrosystems in the lives of children today.

Summary points

This chapter has demonstrated the following:

- The 'virtual life spaces' afforded to a child are growing increasingly significant in terms of the impact on their development, which becomes evident in later life. This has been shown to be due to the marked differences in opportunity, especially educationally, available to these children.
- These changes in 'life spaces' highlight the potential impact of 'real-life contexts' in shaping a child's growth, a significant feature of Bronfenbrenner's work.
- There exists a significant impact of the availability and sophistication of technology on a child's development. The developing child is an 'active agent', and this access to technology facilitates and enhances social competence and the ability to adapt to the surrounding environment.
- Processes affecting a child's development can be framed using Bronfenbrenner's model. This helps to conceptualise the impact of environmental, biological and interpersonal factors on an individual's formative years. The distinction between socio-economic backgrounds and the opportunities available for these individuals has been highlighted.
- Through the use of case studies, the chapter has provided hypothetical evidence of the real-life social context that Bronfenbrenner claims is central in shaping a child's growth.

Recommended reading

Beauchamp, G., Clarke, L., Hulme, M. and Murray, J. (2015) Teacher Education in the United Kingdom Post Devolution: Convergences and divergences. *Oxford Review of Education*, **41**(2), pp.154–170.

Grosvenor, I. (2005) There's no Place Like Home: Education and the making of national identity. In G. McCulloch (Ed.), *The RoutledgeFalmer Reader in History of Education*. Abingdon: Routledge.

Simmons, R., Thompson, R. and Russell, L. (2014) *Education, Work and Social Change*. Basingstoke: Palgrave Macmillan.

Tudge, J.R., Mocrova, I., Hatfield, B.E. and Karnik, R.B. (2009) Uses and Misuses of Bronfenbrenner's Bioecological Theory of Development. *Journal of Family Theory & Review*, **1**(4), pp.198–210.

References

Ashiabi, G.S. and O'Neal, K.K. (2015) Child Social Development in Context: an examination of some propositions in Bronfenbrenner's bioecological theory. *SAGE Open*, **5**(2), pp.1–14.

Bauman, Z. (2005) Education in Liquid Modernity. *Review of Education, Pedagogy, and Cultural Studies*, **27**(4), pp.303–317.

Beauchamp, G., Clarke, L., Hulme, M. and Murray, J. (2015) Teacher Education in the United Kingdom Post Devolution: Convergences and divergences. *Oxford Review of Education*, **41**(2), pp.154–170.

Beauchamp, G. and Jephcote, M. (2016) Teacher Education in Wales: towards an enduring legacy. In G. Beauchamp *et al.* (Eds.), *Teacher Education in Times of Change*. Bristol: Policy Press.

Bradshaw, J. and Holmes, J. (2010) Child Poverty in the First Five Years of Life. In K. Hansen, H. Joshi and S. Dex (Eds.), *Children of the 21st Century: the first five years*. Bristol: The Policy Press.

Bronfenbrenner, U. (1979) *The Ecology of Human Development*. London: Harvard University Press.

Bronfenbrenner, U. (1994) Ecological Models of Human Development. In T. Husén and T. N. Postlethwaite (Eds.), *International Encyclopedia of Education*, vol. 3, 2nd edition. Oxford: Elsevier.

Bronfenbrenner, U. (1995) Developmental Ecology through Space and Time: a future perspective. In P. Moen, G.H. Elder Jr. and K. Lüsher (Eds.), *Examining Lives in Context*. Washington, DC: American Psychological Association.

Bronfenbrenner, U. and Evans, G. (2000) Developmental Science in the 21st Century: Emerging questions, theoretical models, research designs and empirical findings. *Social Development*, **9**(1), pp.115–125.

Connolly, M. (2013) Achieving Social Mobility. *International Journal of Discrimination and the Law*, **13**(4), pp.261–291.

Daugherty, R. and Davies, S.M.B. (2011) Capacity and Quality in Education Research in Wales: a stimulus report for the SFRE – August 2008. *Welsh Journal of Education*, **15**(1), pp.4–23.

Dennis, J. (2016) Review Essay: Michael Gove: the government's reformer in chief? *Pedagogy, Culture & Society*, pp.1–5. [Online]. http://dx.doi.org/10.1080/14681366.2016.1161895

Digital Education Advisory Group (2013) Beyond the Classroom: a new digital education for young Australians in the 21st century. [Online]. https://docs.education.gov.au/system/files/doc/other/deag_final_report.pdf (accessed 15 October 2015).

Finn, M. (2015) *The Gove Legacy: Education in Britain after the Coalition*. Basingstoke: Palgrave.

Grosvenor, I. (2005) There's no Place Like Home: Education and the making of national identity. In G. McCulloch (Ed.), *The RoutledgeFalmer Reader in History of Education*. Abingdon: Routledge.

Jones, J.G. (2014) *The History of Wales*. Cardiff: University of Wales Press.

Luckin, R. (2008) The Learner Centric Ecology of Resources: a framework for using technology to scaffold learning. *Computers and Education*, **50**(2), pp.449–462.

Martens, K., Nagel, A., Windzio, M. and Weymann, A. (Eds.) (2010) *Transformation of Education Policy*. Basingstoke: Palgrave Macmillan.

Scottish Government (2016) *Scottish Social Attitudes 2015: Attitudes to Government, the National Health Service, the economy and standard of living*. Edinburgh: ScotCen Social Research. [Online]. http://natcen.ac.uk/media/1123186/ssa-15-attitudes-to-government-nhs-economy-and-standard-of-living.pdf (accessed 30 March 2017).

Simmons, R., Thompson, R. and Russell, L. (2014) *Education, Work and Social Change*. Basingstoke: Palgrave Macmillan.

Thomas, R.M. (1996) *Comparing Theories of Child Development*. London: Brooks/Cole.

Tudge, J.R., Mocrova, I., Hatfield, B.E. and Karnik, R.B. (2009) Uses and Misuses of Bronfenbrenner's Bioecological Theory of Development. *Journal of Family Theory & Review*, **1**(4), pp.198–210.

Van Leeuwen, M. (2009) Social Inequality and Mobility in History: Introduction. *Continuity and Change*, **24**(3), pp.399–419.

Whysall, A. (2016) The Future of Northern Ireland Politics. [Online]. https://constitution-unit.com/2016/04/06/the-future-of-northern-ireland-politics/ (accessed 15 September 2016).

List of contributors

Gary Beauchamp is Professor of Education and Associate Dean (Research) in the School of Education at Cardiff Metropolitan University. He worked for many years as a primary school teacher before moving into higher education where he has led undergraduate and postgraduate courses in education, as well as supervising Doctoral students. His research interests focus on ICT in education, particularly the use of interactive technologies in learning and teaching. He has published widely in academic journals, as well as writing books, book chapters and research reports. In addition, he has been an Additional Inspector for Estyn, Chair of Governors in two primary schools and has served as external examiner for many universities.

Kay Bennett is a Lecturer in Childhood, Family and Community Studies at the University of Wolverhampton. She has a background in health and her current research interests are early child development and education. She is currently studying for an EdD in Early Childhood Education.

Zeta Brown is a Lecturer in Childhood, Family and Community Studies at the University of Wolverhampton. She is leader of the Childhood, Youth and Families research cluster for the Centre of Developmental and Applied Research in Education. She is an executive member of the British Education Studies Association and the International Society for the Scientific Study of Subjectivity. Her research interests include the practical implementation of inclusion and standards in early childhood and primary education.

Jayne Daly is a Senior Lecturer in Childhood and Family Studies at the University of Wolverhampton. Jayne's previous role was as a Senior Lecturer at Staffordshire University teaching in the areas of Early Childhood and Education. Both of these roles have seen Jayne lead and support teams externally and internally in developing and delivering Foundation Degrees in Early Childhood studies. Jayne is a Senior Fellow of the Higher Education Academy and an experienced external examiner in the field of early education. Jayne has a number of years' practical experience within the field both as an early years practitioner and as a leader. Her current research interests are focused upon childhood resilience, quality early years leadership and reflective practice.

Tracey Edwards is a Lecturer in Childhood, Family and Community Studies at the University of Wolverhampton. She is a course leader of the BA honours in Childhood Studies with Early Years Teacher Status. Her research interests are placement experiences of childhood students and students developing professional identity.

Stuart Gallagher is a Senior Lecturer in the Centre for Children and Families at the University of Worcester. He is course leader for the Foundation Degree 'Collaborative Working with Children, Young People and Families', which is delivered mostly online, and nominated safeguarding officer. He is a member of the British Association for the Study and Prevention of Child Abuse and Neglect (BASPCAN). His research interests include theoretical analysis of learning from serious case reviews.

Kieran Hodgkin is a Lecturer in Education Studies within the School of Education at Cardiff Metropolitan University. Kieran teaches on various modules across the Education Studies programme alongside supervision of part-time and full-time doctoral students. Kieran completed his PhD in July 2014. His research centred on pupils' expectations and experiences of the primary–secondary transition with a specific focus on Physical Education (PE). Kieran is currently exploring the challenges associated with school-based ethnographic fieldwork and significant transitional experiences within the education system.

Dean-David Holyoake has done a lot of social science research and worked at a number of UK universities including the Centre for Lifelong Learning – University of Birmingham, University of Central England, Newman University College, University of Warwick and University of Wolverhampton. He would describe himself as a performance ethnographer and research fabricator (a fabnographer) with a particular interest in exploring mundane culture and seedy interactions. He has written books and professional articles on a variety of issues including Child and Adolescent Mental Health Services, Adolescent In-patient Services, philosophy and custard pies.

Graham Jones is Senior Lecturer in Childhood, Family and Community Studies at the University of Wolverhampton where he is course leader for the Childhood Studies degree programme. He previously qualified as a secondary school teacher and spent fifteen years teaching psychology at a sixth form college. He had various roles during his time teaching in the 16–19 sector including head of department, careers advisor and personal tutor.

Helen Lyndon is a lecturer in Early Childhood, Family and Community Studies at the University of Wolverhampton. She is the country coordinator for the European Early Childhood Education Research Association and her research interests include pedagogic mediation and listening to children.

Trevor Male is Head of Academic Affairs within the London Centre for Leadership in Learning, which is part of the UCL Institute of Education. In addition to this senior leadership role he is also Programme Leader for the MBA Educational Leadership (International). He has worked extensively in education for over forty years including full-time employment in four universities, as an education officer in a local authority and as a teacher. His main area of expertise is in the field of education leadership. He has two published books – *Being an Effective Headteacher* and *Doing Research in Education: Theory and Practice* – and many journal articles and conference papers.

Sarah Mander is a Senior Lecturer in Childhood, Family and Community Studies at the University of Wolverhampton. Sarah also leads the joint award undergraduate programme for Special Needs and Inclusion Studies and Childhood, Family and Community Studies. Her research interests lie in the well-being of children, young people and families and in particular early intervention and prevention within emerging early help service provision.

Alex Owen is Head of Department and Senior Lecturer in Early Childhood at Liverpool Hope University. Her research focuses on the impact of poverty upon young children's current life experience and future life chances. She is a Senior Fellow of the HEA and the Vice Chair of Governors for a local primary school.

Ioanna Palaiologou has worked as a lecturer and researcher in HE for the last twenty years and is now returning to her career as a child psychologist. She is a Chartered Psychologist with the British Psychological Society with a specialism in child development and learning theories. During her time in HE she worked for five universities. Among her main responsibilities was to supervise postgraduate research students and she has mentored early career researchers. Her research interests are focused on ethics in research, child development and implications for pedagogy and the epistemic nature of pedagogy. Her recent books include *Early Years Foundation Stage: Theory and Practice* (2016), *Doing Research in Education: Theory and Practice* (2016) and *Child Observation in Early Childhood* (2016).

Andrew Pickford is a Lecturer in Education Studies in Cardiff School of Education at Cardiff Metropolitan University. He trained as a secondary mathematics teacher at Swansea University in 2004. After leaving schools he has spent time working in policy, performance and projects across the public sector within healthcare, housing and education. From 2009, Andrew worked for the School of Education as project manager for the South East Wales Centre for Teacher Education and Training, a partnership between Cardiff Metropolitan University and the University of South Wales, before taking up his role as Lecturer in 2014.

Michael Reed is a Senior Lecturer at the Centre for Early Childhood, within the Institute of Education at the University of Worcester. He teaches on undergraduate and postgraduate courses exploring practice-based research and leadership. He has co-edited a number of books including *Reflective Practice in the Early Years* (2010), *Quality Improvement and Change in the Early Years* (2012), *Work-Based Research in the Early Years* (2012) and *A Critical Companion to Early Childhood* (2015). His latest writing project explores leadership in early education settings and chapters for a book on pedagogic documentation.

Claire M. Richards is Senior Lecturer within the National Centre for the Study and Prevention of Violence and Abuse (NCSPVA) at the University of Worcester and is Programme Leader for the Masters Degree in Professional Management: Dynamics of Domestic Violence. She has considerable experience of multi-agency partnership working, having been employed within the voluntary and statutory sectors. Her roles have varied in the fields of mental health, substance misuse and domestic abuse. As a non-practising barrister she remains a committed advocate to the rights of children and young people, and researches and writes extensively about aspects of the voice of the child in the context of safeguarding children, professional practice and integrated working. She is engaged with the activities of the Local Safeguarding Children Board and is Chair of the Association for the Study and Prevention of Child Abuse and Neglect for England, Ireland, Northern Ireland, Scotland and Wales (BASPCAN).

Lynn Richards is Course Leader of the Family and Community Studies undergraduate degree programme at the University of Wolverhampton. Her background is in working with children, young people and their families in a variety of provisions: early years settings, play schemes, youth clubs and community projects. She is currently studying for a Professional Doctorate, seeking to gather a storied account of students' sense of belonging at the University. Her research interests include student engagement and the attitudinal dispositions that the workforce brings to bear on the educative process.

Tunde Rozsahegyi is Senior Lecturer and Subject Leader for Special Educational Needs, Disability and Inclusion Studies at the University of Wolverhampton. Previously, she trained and worked as a 'conductor', a specialist educator of children and adults with disabilities through Conductive Education at the Petö Institute in Budapest, Hungary, then played a key role in establishing the National Institute for Conductive Education in Birmingham. Tunde has a strong interest in early pedagogical support for disabled children, their families and professionals; her doctorate examined outlooks on the early development and learning of young children with cerebral palsy.

Catherine A. Simon is Senior Lecturer and Programme Leader for Education Studies at Bath Spa University. She has a specialist interest in English education policy. She has authored and edited a number of books including *Does Every Child Matter?* (2010), *Beyond Every Child Matters* (2017) and *Placements and Work-based Learning in Education Studies* (2017). She has also contributed chapters on education policy to *A Student's Guide to Education Studies* (2008 and 2013). Her research interests encompass schools as organisations, leadership and management. She is currently researching multi-academy trusts and school sponsorship.

John Thain is a Senior Lecturer in Children's Nursing at the University of Wolverhampton. He is involved in a range of activities related to children's nursing as well as education and training on safeguarding children and families. He has been involved in national and international networks and policy development in the field of nursing and safeguarding. His research interests include the impacts of education on families and their children as well as a range of safeguarding topics particularly related to the role of nurses.

Rosie Walker is Assistant Head of the Centre for Children and Families and Foundation Degree Partnership Co-ordinator within the Institute of Education at the University of Worcester. She teaches on undergraduate programmes, particularly in the field of practice-based research. She has co-edited *A Critical Companion to Early Childhood* (2015) and co-authored *Success with Your Early Years Research Project* (2014). Her latest writing project explores the personal and professional effect of the Foundation Degree and a chapter for a book on pedagogic documentation.

Stephen Ward is Emeritus Professor of Education, Bath Spa University, formerly Dean of the School of Education and Subject Leader for Education Studies. A founder member of the British Education Studies Association, he has published on the primary curriculum, primary music teaching and Education Studies. His research interests are education policy and university knowledge.

Sue Wilkinson is a Subject Leader and Lecturer in Education, Psychology, and SEN in the School of Education at Cardiff Metropolitan University. She leads modules in cognition, quantitative research methods and specific learning difficulties, as well as supervising doctoral students. Her PhD in Cognitive Psychology from Cardiff University (2007) used eye-tracking technology to explore how people interact with, and make decisions about, online information. Sue is a Chartered Psychologist and her research interests include neurodiversity, cognitive functions (problem solving, decision making, multitasking) and their impact on teaching and learning, and human–computer interaction.

Index